Ron - Positioning

-[illegible]

MW01622903

Mike - [illegible] - Technical

Tina - Customer Service

Melissa - Bring it all together

Dave S - Aquisition

Dennis H -

Smart Marketing for Engineers

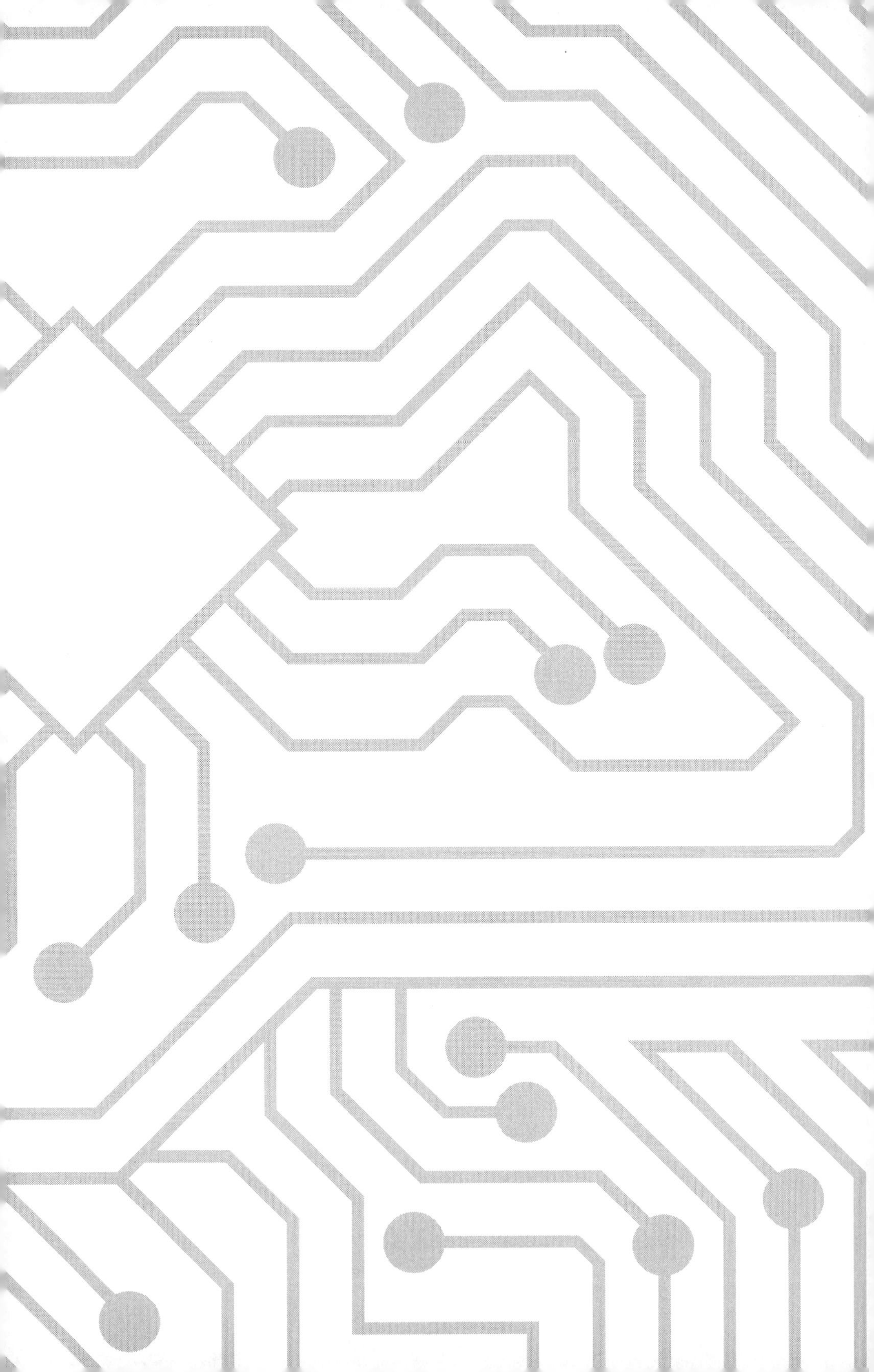

Smart Marketing for ENGINEERS™

An Inbound Marketing Guide to Reaching Technical Audiences

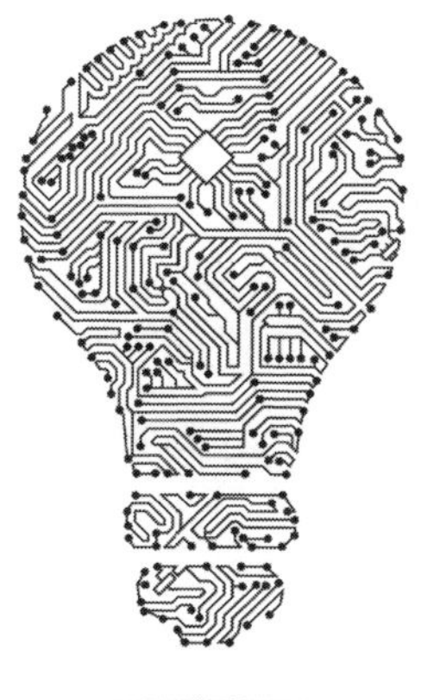

REBECCA GEIER

Rockbench Publishing
Nashville, Tennessee

RockBench Publishing Corp.
6101 Stillmeadow Dr., Nashville, TN 37211
rockbench.com

Printed in the United States of America
Published 2015 | First Printing
Published simultaneously in electronic format

Library of Congress Control Number: 2015953303
978-1-60544-042-2

Visit the web page, trewmarketing.com/smartmarketingforengineers, to see the latest examples, new data, relevant blog posts, and links to informative studies and recommendations to help you with each step.

Connect with Rebecca Geier:
trewmarketing.com | @rgeier

rockbench
PUBLISHING

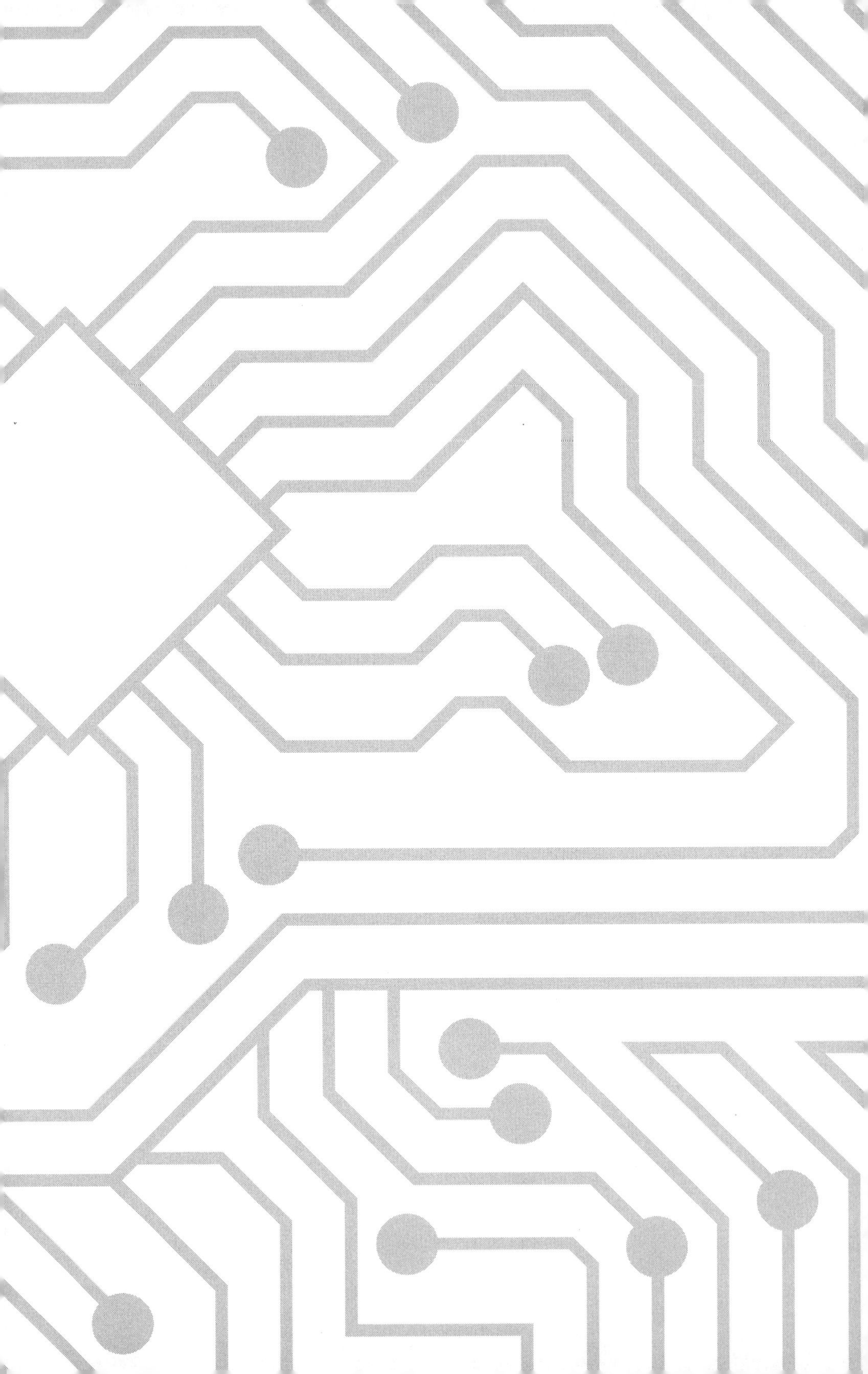

To my dad, Joe Bob, who gave me my work ethic and fun-loving southern spirit. I am so proud and blessed to be your daughter. I love you, Pops!

"After following the inbound playbook outlined in *Smart Marketing for Engineers*, we have seen year-over-year growth on track with our goals for three years in a row! This revenue growth is driven from our traffic volume, lead volume, and the quality of our leads. Silex is proof that executing the techniques Rebecca explains really works."

– **David Smith**
President and CEO, Silex Technology America Inc., and COO, Silex Technology Inc.

"Inbound marketing is ideal for technical audiences because of its data-driven approach. I love that *Smart Marketing for Engineers* provides the first of its kind inbound marketing guide for engineers and scientists complete with research to back it all up."

– **Brian Halligan**
Cofounder and CEO, HubSpot

"Over the last several years, we've invested in our marketing foundation and shifted our investment from a mostly outbound approach with a heavy focus on trade shows to a more inbound approach focused on web and content marketing. As a result, our company has grown over 50 percent, and, today, the majority of our leads come from online sources."

– **Matt Eurich**
President, Wineman Technology

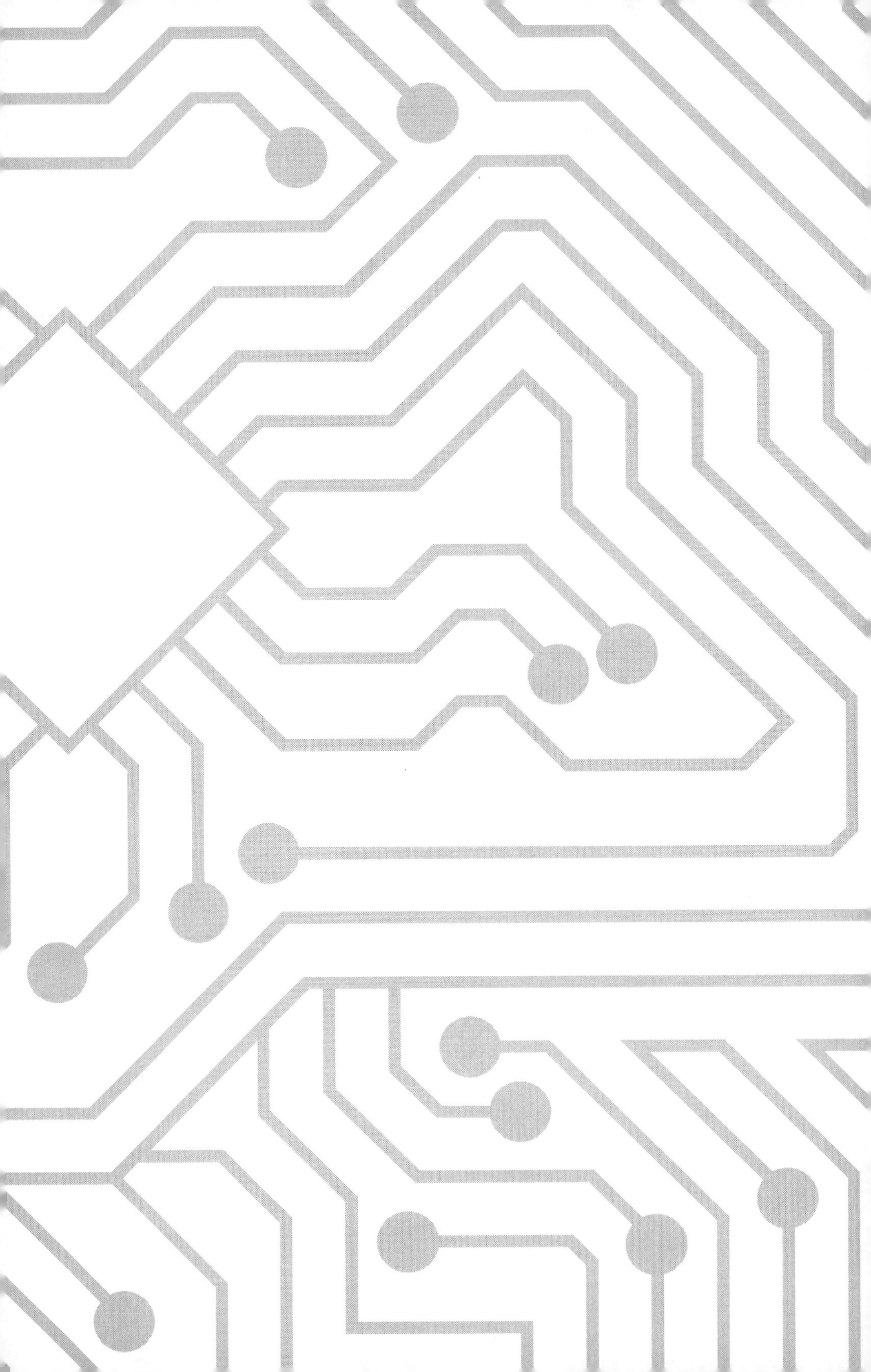

Contents

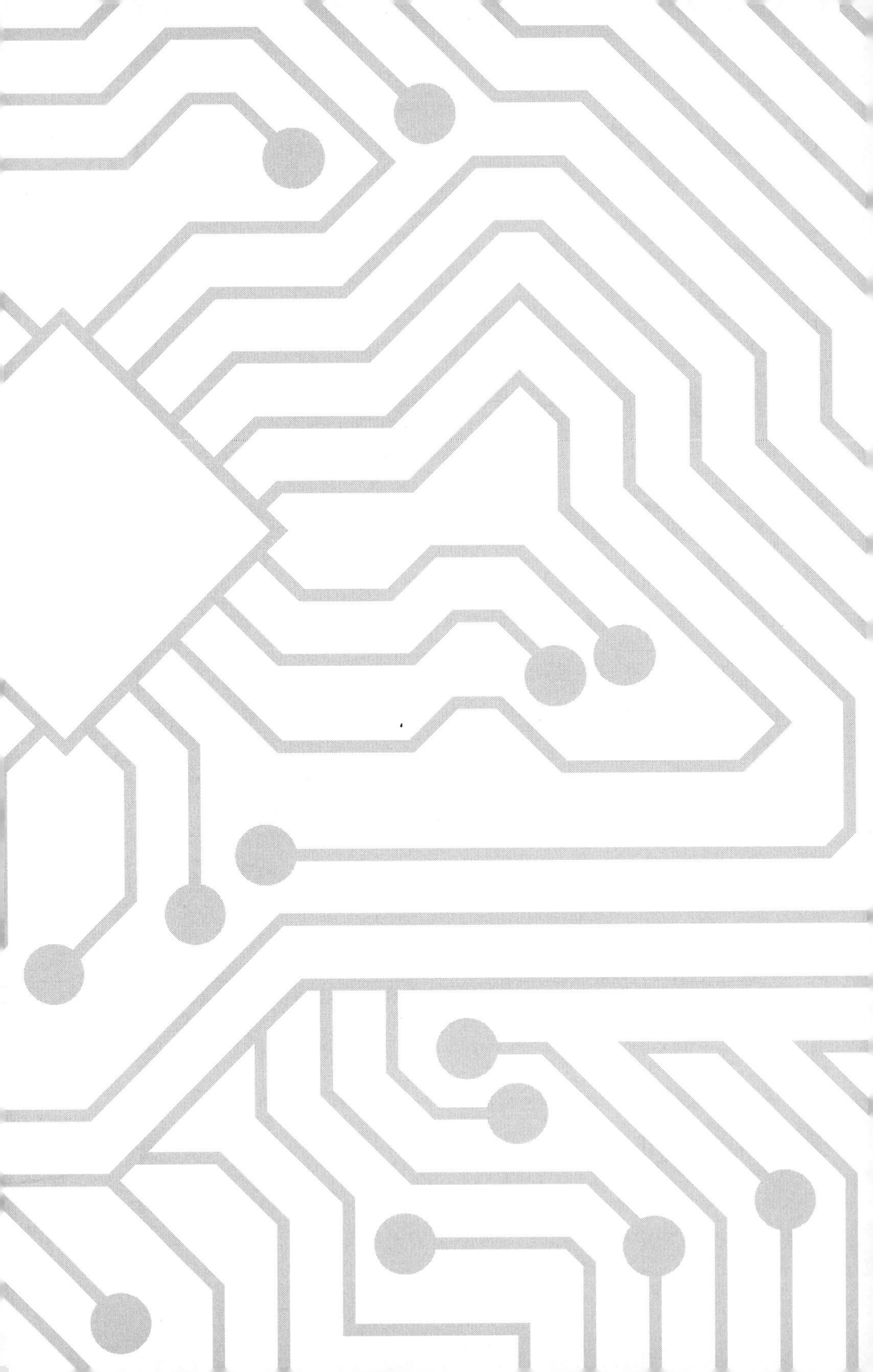

Foreword

Over the last four decades, I have grown my engineering business from a three-man start-up to a billion-dollar multinational organization. I knew that effective marketing was essential to our survival and growth from the start. In the early days of National Instruments (NI), when we were working late hours after our day jobs in my garage creating early product designs and defining our business model, marketing was already on my mind. I handwrote 23 different versions of the press announcement for our first product to address individual audience needs, and I drafted countless personal letters that outlined how we could help with prospects' specific engineering challenges. I am still very engaged in our marketing strategy and messaging today because I know how critical marketing is to the success of a business.

NI has built its brand on making customers successful, and marketing is a big part of that. For us, marketing is about connecting with your audience, educating them, and providing insights on how they can do more, better.

With the explosion of the web, ever-changing search algorithms, community sites, blogs, and social media, there are so many more ways to get information out about your company and your products, but getting noticed is harder than ever. It's not about buying space today; it's about earning it. It's not about blasting out your message to hundreds of prospects; it's about getting them to come to you.

NI was early to the web in 1994 and instantly saw it as a vehicle to help educate engineers and support their success through high-quality content. Before the web, even interactive content that used to be on a CD, like our DAQ Designer tool for product selection, had a remote and disconnected user experience. We had little information about how or how often it was used. With the web, the DAQ Designer user experience was suddenly connected. Engineers could even save their selections, and, in turn, we had useful data about usage and opportunities.

What we did naturally in the 1990s has a name today: inbound marketing, or earning the traffic to your website and building trust and relationships through high-quality technical content. Rebecca Geier spent 14 years of her career at NI helping us navigate this changing marketing landscape and shaping our marketing organization. During the time I worked with Rebecca and the years since, she has proven to be one of the best marketers for engineers who isn't an actual engineer.

From the start, she was a natural at framing content in a way that resonates with technical audiences. In her early years at NI, Rebecca helped create a positioning piece that outlined the performance versus cost of a brand-new, market-changing technology called PXI. She effectively juxtaposed it against incumbent technology and educated the market on its long-term value. It was a cornerstone image of the product launch in the late '90s, and we still use a version of this infographic today. Rebecca was so effective at framing information for engineers and shaping the content NI engineers created that later in her career, we relied on her to develop and train our global leadership and product marketing staff in media and writing communications.

As a leader at NI, she elevated our reputation among global press, local communities, and customers large and small. And once she started TREW Marketing, she really proved herself as a business leader. Named by *The Wall Street Journal* as one of the Top 10 Most Innovative Entrepreneurs in America, Rebecca developed a booming business in the targeted niche of marketing to technical audiences, and her business has steadily grown its revenue and profitability every year since its inception.

Her time at NI, her leadership in her own growing business, and her over 20 years of experience working directly with hundreds of engineering companies have led to this book. In it, Rebecca distills two decades of marketing and business leadership expertise into a unique, comprehensive guide to building modern marketing strategies that fit your business and help you earn the attention of and connect with technical audiences.

When I was starting my business, I taught myself how to do marketing. Years of trial and error led to the success of NI. I see this book as a shortcut to success—something I wish I had been armed with when I was just starting out. *Smart Marketing for Engineers: An Inbound Guide to Reaching Technical Audiences* is filled with research-based, tried-and-true strategies that resonate with engineering and scientific audiences. I encourage engineers and technical business leaders who are looking for a straightforward guide to modern marketing and marketers who are new to targeting technical audiences to read this book and refer back to it as they continue to grow their marketing programs.

– **Dr. James Truchard**
Cofounder, President, and CEO of National Instruments

Introduction

"The optimist: the glass is half full.
The pessimist: the glass is half empty.
The engineer: the glass is twice as big as it needs to be."

– *Anonymous*

The thought of writing a book that engineers and scientists are going to read is daunting. They see things differently. Everything engineers and scientists do, they do critically, and I expect reading this book will be no different.

However, I decided to face this daunting task because I want to help. For the past 20+ years, I have worked side by side with extremely bright, successful engineers and scientists who are at best dumbfounded by marketing and at worst completely disbelieving of it for a few reasons:

- The marketing tactics they've used are expensive and don't work as well anymore.
- They don't know where to invest their limited time and money to get the greatest return.
- They take a DIY approach that fails, leaving them frustrated and even more disbelieving.
- They have unrealistic expectations about ROI or the timeframe needed to achieve results.
- They don't believe marketing works with technical audiences like engineers and scientists.

I have seen firsthand that marketing to technically minded audiences does in fact work, but it has to be as smart as the people it targets. For small engineering and scientific businesses with limited resources or business and sales leaders wearing multiple hats, it's difficult to even know where to start. And you're skeptical that these new ways of marketing you've heard about will even work with your technical audience.

I wrote this book for you.

When I graduated from college, after my first real job at a small company (start-up was not a term then) that made accelerator cards for Macintosh computers like the LC, llsi, and llci, I joined the National Instruments marketing department. I spent the next 14 years learning about the intricacies of marketing to engineers: the importance of accuracy, the spirit of shared information, and the skepticism they have for slogans and slick brands.

Just a year after I started at NI, while I was still reeling with amazement at how quickly I could communicate with branch leaders in Finland and Denmark using an application called email, the engineers in Austin were talking about the World Wide Web. The company made a huge investment early on in the web, and a mind shift across the marketing department and entire company followed. Their financial and mental focus on the web was fortuitous since around the same time, in the mid-'90s, two PhD students at Stanford were testing a search engine at google.stanford.edu (or z.stanford.edu). By 1998, Google was born.

Nearly 20 years later, the entire landscape of marketing has completely transformed. Today the buyer is in charge. For engineers, who are voracious information seekers, it is nirvana. They can search and search and search online—and as research I share in this book shows, they will search much deeper than the average Google user—without ever being interrupted or bothered.

The days of using only a vendor-controlled, outbound approach for which we, as marketers, decide where and when our messages will be heard are over. With buyers in control, the marketer's challenge and opportunity are to get found where and when the buyer is. Some view this as bad news and lost control for marketers, but I don't. I believe marketing has never seen brighter days with the innovation of inbound and content marketing. We have more knowledge, more technology, more measurement, and more control than ever.

Taking advantage of this new marketing landscape doesn't come without challenges. You know you need to change how you're marketing and selling, but you're not sure how to start. You're not convinced the smart engineers and critical scientists you are targeting will respond. And the risk of wasting time and losing money is high.

I wrote this book to remove the mystery and risk and replace them with a step-by-step approach using data and examples to educate and illustrate how you can implement it. To do this, I divided the book into three sections. The first is a critical yet often skipped phase: building your marketing foundation. No matter which type of marketing house you build, if you don't have a strong foundation, it will crumble. Define your position and strategy and make the most important marketing investment of all: redesign your website. The second section takes a deep dive into content: why it's the heart of inbound marketing, how to plan for it, and how to market it to drive results. The third section guides you through taking advantage of all the traffic and leads you're going to get, and how to measure effectively and scale for growth.

I hope this book demystifies modern marketing for the dumbfounded technical business leader. I hope it provides actionable data and insights to help marketers execute in a smarter, more effective way. Maybe it will even inspire the disbelieving to believe again in marketing. Marketing is changing fast, and if the past is any indication of the future, the pace of change is not likely to slow. To help readers navigate this change, I will add new research and recommendations for best practices, tools, and techniques at trewmarketing.com/smartmarketingforengineers.

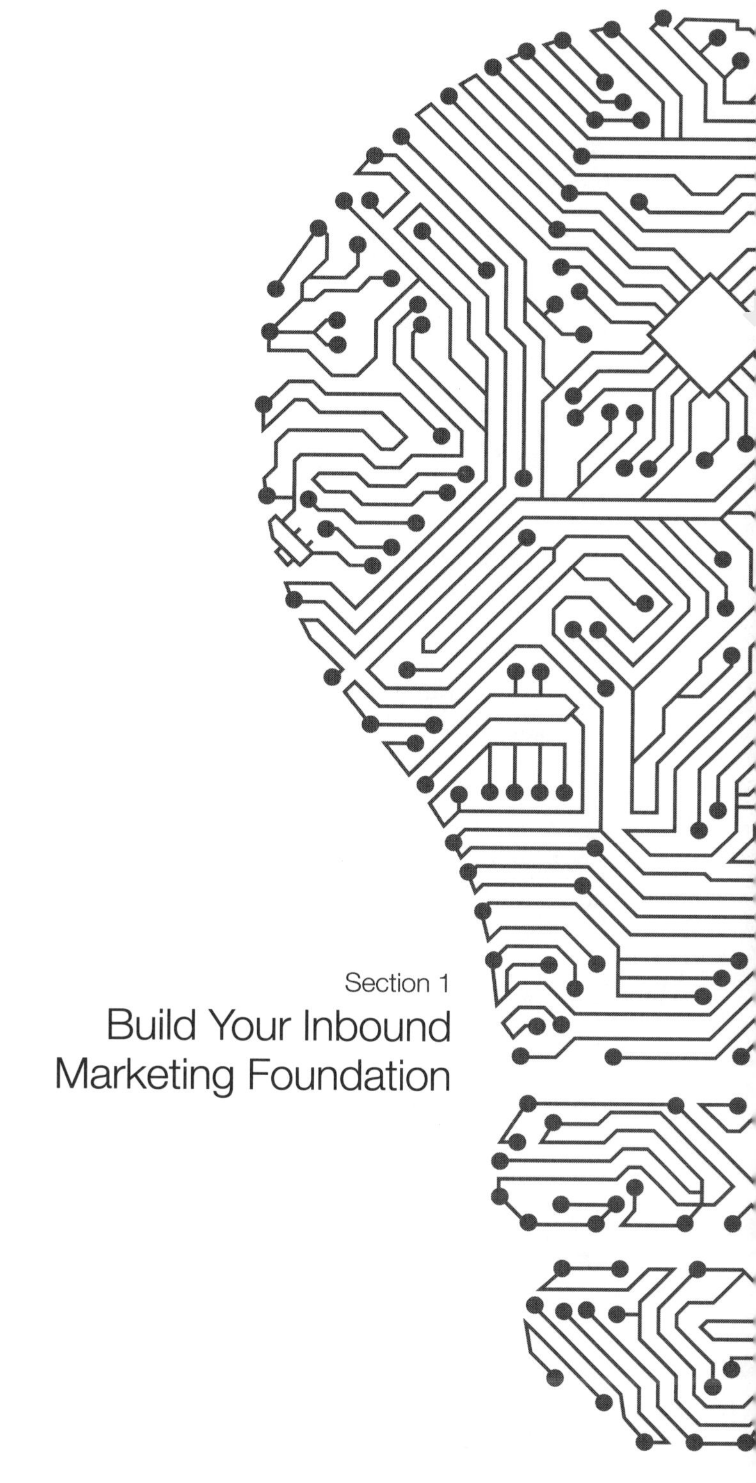

Section 1

Build Your Inbound Marketing Foundation

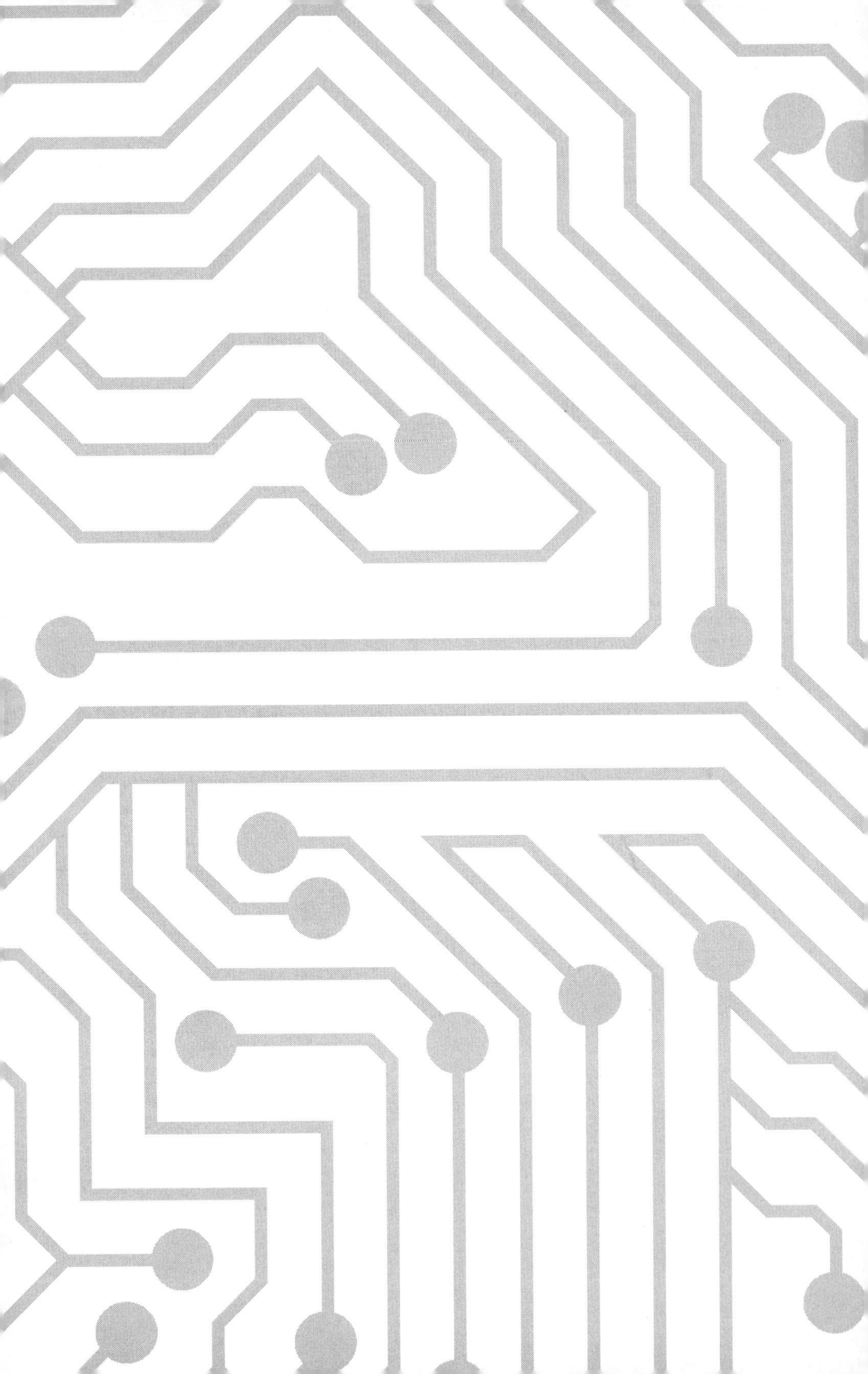

Chapter 1

SAY NO TO GROW

Create a Differentiated Position and Message

"You do not really understand something unless you can explain it to your grandmother."

– *Albert Einstein, Physicist and Nobel Laureate*

In my early 20s, after working at a start-up that made accelerator cards for the early Macintosh models like the LC, llsi, and llci, and after completing a short stint at a national advertising agency marketing Vegas hotels and men's khakis, I landed a job at National Instruments. I found the job in the classifieds and, after multiple interviews, started my 14-year journey learning about working with, and marketing to, engineers and scientists. Sometime in the first year at NI, I remember pinning up on my wall a printout of a slide that was being circulated titled "The Top 10 Traits of an Entrepreneur." One of the traits that stood out to me and was talked about the most was the first one: "Dominate Your Niche." The list came from an article NI CEO and Cofounder Dr. James Truchard (fondly known as Dr. T) read and used as guiding principles in building the company.

NI got its start selling IEEE 488 (a.k.a., General-Purpose Interface Bus, or GPIB) cards that connected scientific instrumentation such as oscilloscopes to Digital Equipment Corporation mainframes, a revolutionary innovation at that point. By the time I joined the company in 1994, nearly 20 years after its founding, NI dominated the GPIB market. With GPIB cards and LabVIEW graphical programming software, a major innovation in the company's second decade, NI had clearly defined its position as a leader in PC-based instrumentation. Today, nearly 40 years later, it dominates this niche. If you ask Dr. T, the early days of dominating the GPIB market—doing one thing better than any other company and expanding out from that core position—was key to the company's stellar financial and brand success.

However, it wasn't easy to stay focused in those early days given the uphill battle to convince scientists and engineers in the '70's to adopt the idea of connecting their instruments to computers. After all, Windows wasn't even out yet—that didn't come until the early '90s. And scientists and engineers aren't the quickest to buy into a new way of doing something. It has to be proven, adopted, and accepted. But the NI engineers stayed laser focused over a 20-year period. They made bold investments for their young company to perfect the GPIB interface, including isolating IP in ASICs that made factors like throughput faster, developing hundreds and then thousands of drivers for every instrument under the sun, and marketing and selling with a vengeance. During this time, Dr. T and the NI leadership team SAID NO to other business opportunities and R&D investments so they could dominate this niche TO GROW.

In my early days at NI, as I took on responsibility for PR, crisis communications, and employee communications beyond my product-focused work, I started a decade-long fascination and study of Southwest Airlines (Southwest), a low-cost carrier headquartered in Dallas, Texas. Although Southwest is not a technology company, and it is the only nontechnical company I talk about in this entire book, I believe it offers an indelible lesson for business and marketing leaders to learn from in how Southwest, like NI, said no to grow. Southwest reported more than $18 billion in revenue in 2014. Even while navigating the last decade's severely recessed economy and an ultracompetitive industry with razor-thin margins, Southwest reported a year-over-year increase in revenue every year except for one. In its 44-year history, the company has had 42 consecutive years of annual profitability, a feat unmatched in the US airline industry.[1]

You'd think an airline this successful would fly a variety of aircraft to take advantage of the many different types of flights airline customers demand. But Southwest flies only one type of aircraft: the Boeing 737. By flying only one type of aircraft fleet (737 has multiple models such as the -700, -800, and 737 MAX), operations are streamlined, pilots have to know how to fly only that one airliner, and crews have to learn the safety procedures for only one fleet. This comes at a cost, however. By flying only 737s, Southwest can fly only the routes the aircraft supports, and these are getting longer and longer daily, given the engineering innovation of models such as the 737 MAX. Many Southwest customers probably wish they could fly every flight on Southwest—the airline's customers love it. But saying no to flying any aircraft other than 737s is exactly what led to Southwest's transformation into one of the most successful US airlines ever.

With this strategy, Southwest has said NO to GROW for going on five decades. This principle is applicable to any business in any industry, whether you're a billion-dollar airline, large engineering firm, or fledgling manufacturing services provider. The thought of turning away business is scary, especially early on when cash is critical to growth. Defining your niche, and then positioning your company with differentiated messaging in this niche, requires careful analysis along with plenty of courage and heart.

---

[1] swamedia.com/channels/Corporate-Fact-Sheet/pages/corporate-fact-sheet

Who Are You?

Quickly take two minutes to write down a couple of sentences that describe the uniqueness of your company—not one of your products or services but your company—and what sets it apart from your competition. Don't overthink it; don't take more than a minute or two to write just two little sentences.

To help you, here are a few examples (more are included at the end of this chapter):

Silex Technology

"You design and develop it, and Silex Technology will connect it to the network. We transform your products into secure, reliable wireless devices and machines that deliver a completely connected, always-on experience for your customers"

Kline Technical Consulting

"KTC brings a unique combination of warrior, academic, and technical expertise to develop and field systems for tracking enemy forces, leading anti-piracy efforts, and developing and implementing large cyber-warfare and advanced security solutions. Its experienced military and engineering specialists work covertly and confidentially to create, develop, and install tools, technologies, and systems frontline warriors need to survive and win."

Avid Solutions

"Avid Solutions offers a unique combination of plant floor experience, IT and operations expertise, and process industry knowledge to solve complex control and information systems challenges in the life sciences, power, paper, and chemical industries."

Now that you have your sentences, let's take a break from thinking about your company and think about other markets. Consider a technical field, like medicine. When medical students complete their residencies, they choose a specialty—psychiatry, internal medicine, pediatrics, etc.—and spend their careers becoming experts in that specialty. If a student becomes a heart surgeon, that's all she does. If one of her patients needs lung surgery, she refers the patient to a lung specialist. If another patient has skin cancer, she refers the patient to an oncologist. The doctor says yes to hearts and no to non-heart-related medical needs, even though she has some training in other areas and could likely make money doing other procedures.

If you discovered you needed heart surgery, which doctor would you rather perform the procedure? Would you prefer a general practitioner of everything from the waist up or one who specializes in the heart? You would choose the heart expert.

Let's look at a less life-threatening scenario. Consider the automotive services industry. Imagine that Austin Mechanics Inc. (AMI) works on any make or model, but German Automotive Specialists (GAS) specializes in only German-made cars. Now, imagine you own a BMW. Which mechanic would you choose? More than likely you'll choose GAS, even if its prices are a little higher than AMI's.

Why? Because GAS mechanics are experts in German engines. You perceive that they have more experience, understand your car better than the generalists at AMI, and offer a higher quality of work. You are willing to pay a more for the expertise you expect to get at GAS.

Say you own a Lexus, and you take it to GAS. The mechanics would likely decline to work on your car and then they'd refer you to a Lexus specialist. Each time GAS mechanics say yes to German autos and no to other makes, they reinforce their expertise and differentiated reputation, and they keep their bays open for the next German car they can fix efficiently with a higher margin.

In both of these cases, the doctor and mechanic said yes to specializing and no to generalizing. This is the key to a differentiated brand position, and it starts with the heart of the company.

Positioning and Differentiation

You may be thinking, "Well, that's easy for the heart surgeon or the German car mechanic, but my company is already established. We already have customers with a wide variety of product and service needs, and we can't change now."

If you want to grow, however, you must start saying no to a generalist approach. You must stop reacting to disparate opportunities and saying yes to a more differentiated position. This is more important than ever in technical markets because engineers and scientists are working on critical applications; they need expert advice and proven solutions instead of general direction. To prove you can be trusted, you must have a clear position and message. Those are not only critical to building trust with your technical target audiences but also key to growing your business.

➔ **Look for data in chapter 8 that shows engineers trust most the content written or published by an engineering expert at a vendor company.**

With that context, let's revisit the two sentences you wrote about your company's position. Reading your description, does your company sound unique or does it sound like other companies similar to yours? Was your description easy to write? Do you like what you wrote? Do you think others inside and outside your company would agree with what you wrote? Does it match what's on your website? If you answered no to even one of these questions, your company positioning needs some attention.

Developing a positioning statement helps you clearly define your company and your audience by articulating customer concerns and the unique solutions your company delivers. The below elements provide a framework for developing your positioning statement:

Who—your potential engineering and scientific customers

Where—their industries or types of organizations

Why—their application pain points

What—your solutions

How—the way you create those solutions

Unlike—the drawbacks of proprietary or competitor solutions

Differentiation—what uniquely sets your company apart from the rest

To begin identifying each element of your positioning statement, think beyond your current customers and projects. Brainstorm the applications for which you want to build products or deliver services with your ideal engineering customers in mind. Consider the following:

- What applications does your team know best?
- What do you and your team love to work on more than anything else?
- What are you better at than any other competitor? (Asked another way: What are your top three strengths in the market, and what are your competitors' top three strengths?)
- What unique market niche can you dominate?

- What do your products or services do that no other competitor's products can touch?
- What are you and your team passionate about and capable of delivering that no other company can to the same level?
- What is the most unique competency you have to offer the market today? In the future?
- What are the two or three most important future opportunities for your company (e.g., market segment, customer type, region, etc.)?

This requires plenty of introspection and sometimes outside research. Query your company stakeholders, including key customers if possible, via a questionnaire or short interviews to learn what others think about your company.

Answers to these questions can serve as great conversation starters for your leadership team to delve into, debate, and ultimately use to create each of your positioning statement elements. Going step-by-step through the positioning process like the one that follows from Silex Technology leads to a definitive statement and elevator pitch that you and all your employees can use to succinctly and clearly describe who your company is, what customer pains you are solving, and how you are uniquely differentiated from competitors to solve those challenges.

Positioning Statement and 30-Word Pitch Example: Silex Technology

Positioning Statement

Who

Technical decision makers who seek a Wi-Fi solution for their product, device, or machine…

Where

…in companies that know reliable wireless connectivity is of paramount concern for product success and customer satisfaction…

Why

…and that need a trusted partner with proven design experience and wireless technology knowledge to develop and deliver a connectivity solution they can trust.

What

You make it—from a medical device to a document imaging product to a video or digital display—and Silex Technology will connect it to the network. With our expertise, we transform your products into reliable wireless devices and machines that deliver a completely connected, always-on experience for your customers.

How

Building on more than 40 years of hardware and software connectivity know-how and IP, custom design experience, and manufacturing capabilities, Silex Technology delivers value to customers with our foundation of technical expertise. As an exclusive Qualcomm Atheros Authorized Design Center, we provide leading wireless technology with support that is unmatched anywhere in the world. Our wireless experts create customized, reliable network connectivity solutions based on your requirements, and support you from design through deployment...

Unlike

...unlike companies providing standardized solutions that don't reach the technical precision required by your devices, or companies with technology that outsource manufacturing or development processes.

Differentiation

With relentless attention to quality, exclusive access to Qualcomm Atheros expertise, in-house manufacturing, and strategic partnerships with leading real-time operating system (RTOS) and semiconductor providers, we are the global leader in reliable connectivity solutions.

We work with companies that need a trusted partner to invest in and understand their business, and who can create a product with reliable Wi-Fi. With Silex Technology, you get a single vendor that provides hardware and software support from design through manufacturing for successful product after successful product. Time and again, we design it, build it, and support it exactly how you need it.

Elevator Pitch

(More examples of these are provided at the end of this chapter.)

You design and develop it, and Silex Technology will connect it to the network. We transform your products into secure, reliable wireless devices and machines that deliver a completely connected, always-on experience for your customers.

After creating a company positioning statement, coming up with two or three sentences that describe your company is easier. When you share this description across your company, your employees and key stakeholders will be able to give a similar elevator pitch that emphasizes the critical differences between your business and the competition.

Before you roll it out, though, consider testing it against the initial set of questions. For instance, does your statement clearly differentiate your company from your competitors? You can also test it from a market probability standpoint. How many competitors are in the space you've defined? If you're competing against only a few, you have a better chance of success, but if you're up against 10 or 15, it's going to be very difficult and clear differentiation is critically important. Revisit what IP you have. How can you own the niche more effectively than others? How high is the barrier to entry?

Testing your position against these questions will strengthen the end product. It doesn't have to be perfect, but it does need to be unique, authentic, and probable for success.

Once you have a good grasp of your company's position, you can commit to it and turn down work that does not fit. In other words, you can confidently SAY NO to distracting business opportunities that do not align with your position. By saying no to the wrong opportunities, you can say yes to the right ones, which allows you to strengthen your position, differentiate, build trust with your skeptical technical audiences who are seeking experts, and grow more efficiently and effectively.[2]

[2] Just because you publicly state your position on your website and in your content doesn't mean that if opportunities arise that are somewhat out of your niche, you can't still decide to pursue them, especially early on. Over time, though, you'll find you don't need, nor will you want, to pursue them.

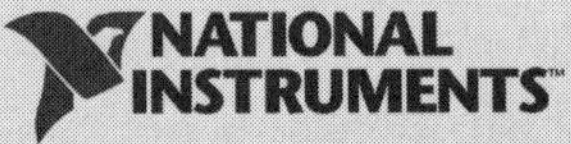

As described at the beginning of this chapter, early in my career at NI, the CEO shared a business motto that guided him and his team as they grew the company: "Dominate your niche." Now that I'm serving as CEO of my own business and leading a marketing team that helps other companies position themselves in their niches, this saying means more to me than ever. It's also reinforced in books such as *Built to Sell,* an Inc. Magazine Best Book for Business Owners. In it, author John Warrillow states:

> **"Don't be afraid to say no to projects. Prove that you're serious about specialization by turning down work that falls outside your area of expertise."**

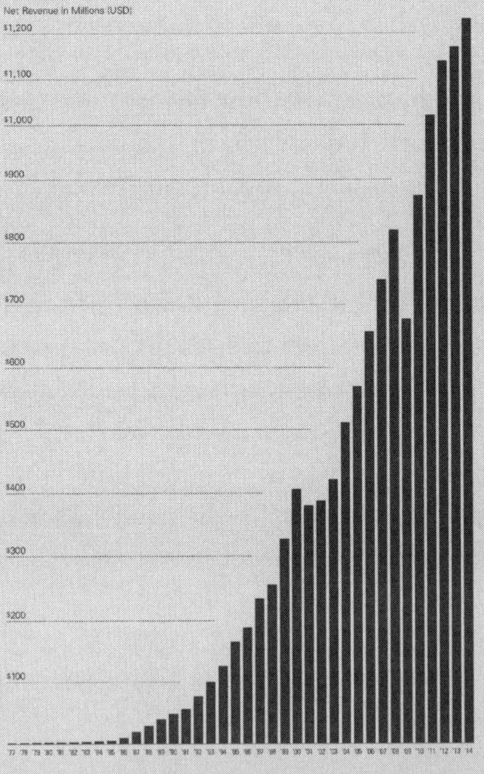

By dominating its niche and staying true to their position, National Instruments has delivered revenue growth every year except two since 1985.

NI started by making one product, a computer-based General-Purpose Interface Bus (GPIB) card that connected Digital Equipment Corporation (DEC) computers to stand-alone scientific instruments. Nearly 40 years later, the company has carefully adhered to this niche, defined as computer-based instrumentation. By dominating one small niche and then another and another, NI has grown into a billion-dollar company that has continually delivered growth with market-leading gross margins. These profits have been reinvested in the company to help it gain market share over much bigger competitors.

Southwest®

Southwest uses only Boeing 737-model jets. By doing this, the airline benefits from the efficiency of total standardization on one platform. Maintenance crews learn how to work on only one type of aircraft. All flight crews need to learn only one set of safety procedures. Pilots fly in one style of cockpit and learn one set of instruments. Every flight has the same passenger capacity.

By flying only one type of plane, Southwest says no to some significant business opportunities. It can't offer longer flight options beyond the capacity of the 737. The airline is limited to acquiring only companies with a similar specialization. However, by saying no to other types of planes, Southwest says yes to its 737 strategy and all the bottom-line benefits that come with it. Because of this focused approach, the company has achieved growth and profitability year after year in the extremely competitive, thin-margin airline passenger market.

Operating Revenue, 1985-2014

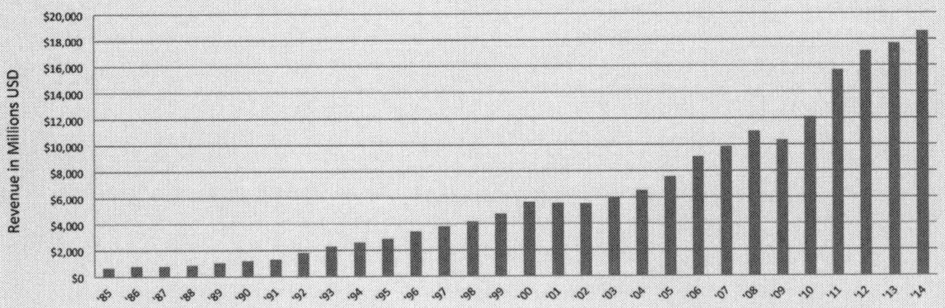

Southwest said no to grow, never veering from its specialization in only flying Boeing 737-model jets. After nearly 50 years in business, it is still delivering growth and profitability.

Additional Example Company Short Pitch Statements

Leading-edge products require equally advanced and refined test systems. Wineman Technology, a proven test system development partner, specializes in developing and deploying exact test technologies and serving clients as an expert resource, advisor, and project manager for complex test challenges.

We are experts in working with small, sensor-based technology. We research and study new inventions and technologies developed in labs across industry, academia, and government and bring those prospects to our small, flexible, and nimble team. We are an innovation factory with the engineering resources and business experience to mature technologies—those with the best market potential—into commercial products.

Marvin Test Solutions is a very agile, vertically integrated aerospace test and measurement company that creates superior test systems for military, aerospace, and manufacturing organizations requiring better test capabilities and excellent customer support.

As the challenge of meeting the world's energy needs becomes increasingly urgent, Rhombus Energy Solutions responds. Our next-generation products, new ways of thinking about complex energy situations, and extensive engineering experience combine to create an innovation engine for energy conversion, storage, management, and monitoring.

Avid Solutions combines firsthand plant floor experience with extensive process industry knowledge to solve complex systems challenges ranging from plant capacity expansion to multi-site, large-scale automation involving several thousand I/O.

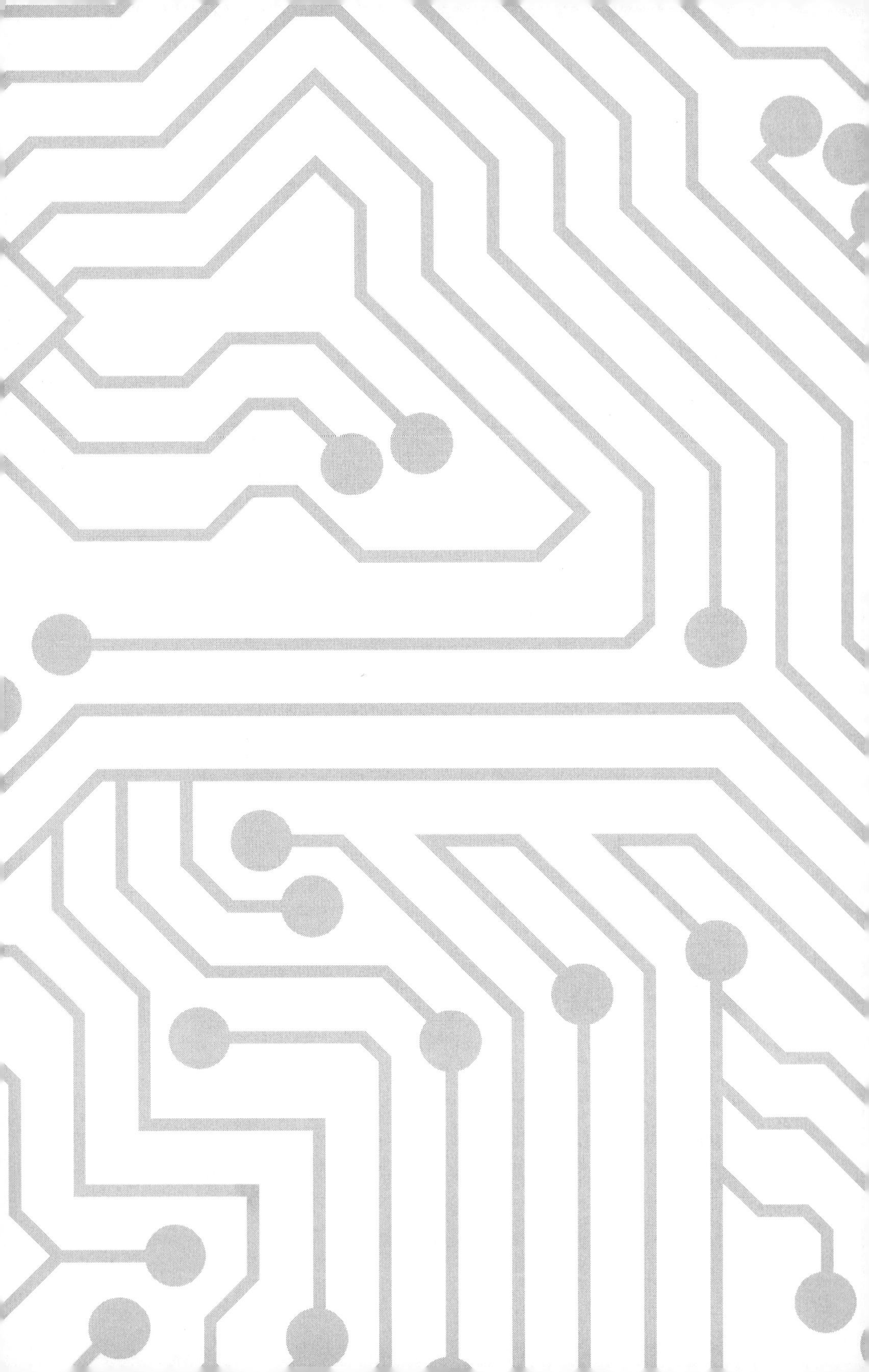

Chapter 2

DEVELOP YOUR MARKETING PLAN

From Goals to Outcomes

"If you want to kill any idea in the world, get a committee working on it."

– Charles Kettering, Founder of Delco

Marketers have a saying: "If you don't know where you're going, any road will take you there." Without planning and a sound strategy, how can you know where you are going or what you need to do to get there?

Many technical business leaders are too busy to stop, focus, debate, and agree on a comprehensive strategic marketing plan. Instead, they rush down a reactive road that leads to mediocre results and higher costs in time, money, stress, and frustration. If you take the time to truly define business and marketing goals, measureable objectives, an execution plan, and an investment strategy, your marketing efforts will more efficiently and effectively deliver the intended ROI.

Define Your Business Goals and Objectives

A sound marketing strategy aligned with your highest-level business goals and objectives helps you create awareness for your company and its products and services, drive website traffic and leads, and generate new sales opportunities that meet your company's target audience profile.

With your goals and objectives in place, you have more insight into what you need to build a marketing strategy, develop an action plan, and define how to measure results. Your business goals are much easier to define if you have created your company positioning statement (chapter 1) that clearly explains your customer pain points and succinctly articulates your company's unique differentiation.

With your positioning statement in place, ask yourself specific questions like these when developing your business goals:

- Do you want to increase revenue and/or profitability in the next year? Two years? Three years? At what rate?
- Do you want to increase your number of customers? By how many and by when?
- Do you want to expand your offerings to new markets? If so, which ones?
- Do you need to reposition your company for change or expansion?
- Are you trying to acquire or be acquired, and, if so, by when?
- Do you need to successfully launch a key product or service?
- Do you need to generate more or higher quality leads?

Are you losing ground to a competitor, and, if so, how will you take back market share?

Just as in chapter 1 when you created your company's positioning statement, you should have a select group of company and functional area leaders around the table during business goal development. Bring this leadership team together and debate these questions and others you come up with until you have majority agreement on the answers. It is critical that you agree on where you want your business to go before you spend a penny on marketing. A word of caution in this process: engineers tend to suffer from prolonged decision making and let "getting it right" kill "getting it done." Have a plan in place to facilitate the discussion in a way that leads to prioritization and agreement while avoiding getting stuck on how to reach perfection.

When developing goals (at the business level or otherwise), write them in the SMART format that ensures accountability. SMART stands for specific, measurable, attainable, realistic, and time-bound and represents business goals such as:

- Increase product line revenue by 30 percent to $2 million in the next 12 months
- Double revenue through distributors in the next two years
- Increase profitability from 25 to 30 percent by the end of the year

Develop at least three and no more than five business goals each year. Assign goal owners who define measurable objectives and action plans to achieve their goals. Two of the many books and websites you can reference to learn more about business goal development and creating accountable internal systems to achieve success are *Get a Grip* by Gino Wickman and Mike Paton and *Traction* by Gino Wickman, both of which describe the Entrepreneurial Operating System (EOS).[1] I've used EOS at my company, and it has had a tremendous impact on the leadership team's ability to set goals and build teams that have clear accountability measures to achieve the goals. And for larger companies, it can be quite useful at the department or business unit level.

[1] eosworldwide.com/eos

Marketing Strategy

In past decades, the marketing funnel was simple: choose from a few proven outbound marketing channels to build awareness at the top, generate leads in the middle, and pass to sales to convert at the bottom. My, what a few years can do! Digital technology and inbound marketing have provided the means for users to search for and learn about anything they want anytime and anywhere.

With so many choices for how to market, and despite being mostly dissatisfied with the results of past marketing efforts, technical business leaders often skip marketing planning and move straight to activity execution. They have marketing deadlines looming and fires to put out: a trade show in three weeks, an ad opportunity that a publication representative just emailed them about, Google ads that are old and need updating, a sales presentation to prepare for a new opportunity next week, and so on. They reluctantly invest valuable time and resources on one-off activities, but the investment does not pay off.

> *Technical business leaders often skip marketing planning and move straight to activity execution.*

You know you don't want to run on this hamster wheel. But in today's information-filled world of easy Internet access and portable, connected devices at our fingertips, what kind of marketing and what message will a skeptical, technical audience of engineers and scientists not only notice but actually respond to?

Ultimately, you want marketing that provides a consistent flow of high-quality leads to help fuel new sales opportunities and drive growth. You want your technical target audiences and customers to be happy to hear from you and not dread it. And you have a limited budget and tight bandwidth.

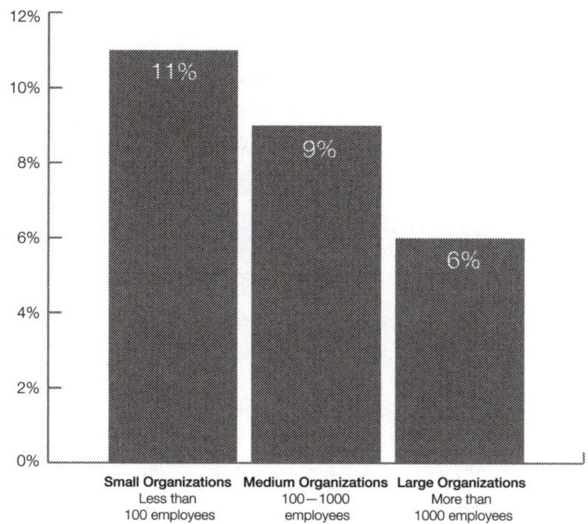

MarketingSherpa B2B Marketing Benchmark Survey

Target an annual marketing budget of 4 to 12 percent of revenue based on company size (as shown in the chart here), margins, past marketing investment, the economy, and revenue forecasts.

The way to achieve all of this is to use a smart marketing approach that builds a marketing strategy and execution plan aligned to your business goals and includes:

- **Audience personas**—titles, types of companies, industries, geographic regions, and pain points placed in priority order (discussed in detail in chapter 3)
- **Marketing SWOT**—strengths, weaknesses, opportunities, and threats in terms of your competitive position, target markets, target audiences, current positioning/messaging, the maturity of your offerings, channel partners, etc.
- **Marketing goals**—up to five SMART goals (using the same approach as above with business goals)
- **Communications SWOT**—strengths, weaknesses, opportunities, and threats that consider your content, website, SEO/keywords, lead quantity and quality, nurturing, etc.
- **Product and/or services SWOT**—strengths, weaknesses, opportunities, and threats that consider the 4 Ps (explained below): product, price, promotion, and place

- **Current lead model**—calculating your current conversion rates along the marketing and sales funnel, from traffic to lead to opportunity (look for a detailed template to calculate your lead funnel metrics in chapter 12)
- **Marketing resources and budget**—the people with a role in marketing, the tools marketing uses (CRM, marketing automation, etc.), and the percent of revenue you will spend on marketing, which may include hard costs such as trade shows or outside agency expenses as well as team member salaries

The 4 Ps:

In 1960, Edmund McCarthy, author of *Basic Marketing: A Marketing Strategy Planning Approach*, introduced the "4 Ps" as four controllable variables a company puts together to satisfy a target market. They are product, price, place, and promotion.

P **Product**—The product aspects of marketing refer to the specifications of the actual goods or services and how they relate to the end user's needs and wants. The scope of a product generally includes supporting elements such as branding, packaging, warranties, guarantees, and technical assistance.

P **Price**—Price refers to the process of setting a price for a product, including discounts. The price may not be monetary but simply what is exchanged for the product or services, e.g., time, energy, or attention. Determining optimal price setting is part of pricing science.

P **Place** (or distribution)—Place defines how the product gets to the customer, for example, point-of-sale placement or retailing. Place can also refer to the channel by which a product or service is sold (e.g., online versus retail), in which geographic region or industry the product or service is sold, to which segment it is sold (young adults, families, business people), and so on. It can also refer to how the environment in which the product or service is sold can affect sales.

P **Promotion**—Promotion includes advertising, sales promotion, publicity, PR, direct marketing, digital marketing, sponsorship, and personal selling and refers to the various methods of promoting the product, brand, or company.

Examples of one-year SMART marketing goals include:

- Grow leads by 10 percent on a flat budget by shifting marketing dollars from outbound to inbound channels
- Increase the number of qualified opportunities passed to sales by 15 percent
- Triple the number of published customer case studies in the top three segments

With your business and marketing goals defined and aligned, and a comprehensive marketing strategy in place, you are now ready to create your marketing execution plan.

Execute Using a Marketing Communications Plan

Now that you've created your marketing goals and have a budget, you are ready to develop your activity plan, also known as a marketing communications plan. The most effective way to approach turning your marketing strategy into an execution plan is by using a campaign structure. You can think of campaigns as buckets of activities focused on a common theme or goal.

With limited time and budget, a campaign approach gives you the big picture before you get into the weeds of which new video you will produce, which white paper you will write and promote, etc. With campaigns, you can create efficiencies with content reuse and increase impact by aligning all media channels while ensuring that focus areas support your overall goals.

When using a campaign structure, the key elements of your marketing communications plan are:

- **Campaigns**—The three to four focus areas that will take the lion's share of marketing resources (see campaign examples below)
- **Content themes**—The key topics around which you will focus your published content (content planning is discussed in chapter 7)
- **Approach**—Prioritized marketing communications channel investment and cornerstone activities (see sidebar "Outbound versus Inbound Marketing")
- **Key events and news**—Big events, such as trade shows or speaking engagements, and news, such as product launches or key partnership announcements
- **Marketing mix of media channels**—Primary communication channels you will invest in for each campaign, such as web, PR, content, video, social media, etc.
- **Marketing automation**—Software platform to enable efficiency and effectiveness of campaign execution, lead nurturing, and reporting
- **Marketing dashboard**—Report that consistently tracks campaign key performance indicators (KPIs) and other activity metrics

Campaigns can run the gamut in scope. They can be anything from a major product launch to building thought leadership in a particular segment to increasing web traffic and leads. Consider these examples of marketing campaigns and their stated goals and KPIs:

- **Campaign—Lead generation and conversion**
  - Description—Through content and partner co-marketing, attract quality leads that convert to opportunities
  - KPI 1—Increase leads by 35 percent to 210 per month
  - KPI 2—Increase lead opportunity conversion from 6 to 8 percent
- **Campaign—Customer loyalty**
  - Description—Target online marketing activities to nurture and grow current customers
  - KPI 1—Produce at least two case studies per quarter
  - KPI 2—Send customer e-newsletter two times per quarter and achieve at least a 35 percent clickthrough rate
- **Campaign—Content marketing**
  - Description—Promote content across the funnel to increase thought leadership and brand awareness
  - KPI 1—Increase web traffic by 20 percent to 7,500 visits per month
  - KPI 2—Produce at least one lead-generating (i.e., gated) piece of content per quarter
- **Campaign—Partner marketing**
  - Description—Develop and implement a channel co-marketing program
  - KPI 1—Publish at least one lead-generating piece of co-branded content per quarter
  - KPI 2—Generate 100 net new leads through co-marketing activities

With each campaign and its corresponding KPIs defined, you then need to determine the best mix of marketing channels to achieve the campaign goals. These channels may include the following inbound channels (I've also included a few of the more common outbound channels for reference):

Marketing Channels

Content	Free or gated content such as white papers, webcasts, case studies, blog posts, video, and new web pages that attract visitors to your website and generate leads through form completion
Web	New or enhanced existing web content, including feature graphics, new web pages, and cross-promotion on other related pages
Search engine optimization	Analysis and continuous implementation of keywords
Email marketing	Lead follow-ups, e-newsletters, and targeted email campaigns
Social media	Amplification of your content and engagement with target audiences on LinkedIn, Twitter, etc.
Comarketing	Cobranded marketing with partners through various channels such as web, PR, email, and events
Public relations	News releases, contributed articles, and media outreach and interviews
Advertising	Online and print industry placements, paid search (e.g., Google AdWords)
Events	Trade shows, conferences, and speaking engagements

As you evaluate which marketing channels to use, avoid the trap of doing what you have always done just because you've always done it. Though your typical approach may be full of viable activities, you have a much better chance of getting the greatest return from your limited dollars and resources by looking at all marketing channels with an open mind. To help you do this, think about where the campaign falls on the funnel. For example, the content marketing campaign above focuses primarily on growing brand awareness and is measured through web visits, so for this campaign, you want to select "top of the funnel" activities, such as blogging, adding new web pages, optimizing your existing content with keywords, and posting on social media. You may also consider not just going to the same trade show at which you've always exhibited but instead trying to secure a speaking engagement to raise your profile.

In contrast, the goal of the lead generation and conversion campaign is to attract quality leads that are closer to becoming an opportunity, so you'll want to use "middle/bottom of the funnel" activities, such as gated content that generates leads, partner co-marketing activities such as co-branded emails, and webinars that target both companies' databases.

➔ **Look for data in chapter 6 that lists content types and tactics used at different stages of the funnel, from attracting traffic to nurturing leads.**

The following two examples in the highly technical embedded space illustrate how the marketing mix can vary by company and campaign. These examples use a product launch as the primary campaign, and each uses a different mix of media channels and activities to successfully launch the product and achieve the desired results.

Silex Technology America Inc.

Silex Technology America Inc. used content and co-marketing activities including web, email, and PR to launch its product with Freescale Semiconductor.

Product Launched

Silex Technology's SX-SDCAN, which adds wireless connectivity to devices based on the Freescale i.MX6 platform

Product Launch Campaign Goals

- Strengthen the Silex brand by building credibility for its embedded Wi-Fi solutions through mentions in Freescale channels

- Generate awareness of Silex's Wi-Fi technologies to prospective i.MX6 customers through traffic from Freescale sources
- Achieve overall campaign traffic and lead conversion objectives

Channel and Activity Mix

Inbound

- Partner co-marketing with Freescale to build awareness and credibility
- White paper serving as premium lead-generating content
- Uniquely designed Freescale landing page on the Silex website
- Lead-nurturing emails to generate opportunities from the white paper
- Co-marketed, online event using a recorded webinar with Silex, Freescale, and Qualcomm Atheros subject-matter experts

Outbound

- Two-page product flyer highlighting the Silex Wi-Fi offering
- News release announcing Silex's new status as a Freescale Proven Partner

Results

- 320 percent monthly lead growth in the first two months of the launch
- Strong, sustained traffic and lead volume post-launch
- Nearly 25 percent traffic lead conversion rate in the first three months of launch
- 46 percent open rate and 17 percent clickthrough rate for lead-nurturing email campaign
- Two placements on the Freescale i.MX6 website

- Three features in the Freescale customer and sales e-newsletters
- 210 news release postings to online sources

Crank Software

Crank Software executed a product launch campaign targeting embedded design engineers using channels along the funnel, from PR and co-marketing with QNX at the top to gated content and an online software evaluation in the middle.

Product Launched

Latest version of the company's flagship software, Storyboard™ Suite

Product Launch Goals

- Increase awareness of Storyboard Suite 3.0 through secured PR coverage in two of the top five priority outlets
- Drive web visits to achieve a 30 percent traffic increase
- Achieve lead goal through software evaluation downloads

Channel and Activity Mix

Inbound

- Search engine optimization
- Video and content marketing
- Launch email and automated direct marketing
- Social media strategy and execution

Outbound

- Media relations strategy and execution
- Search engine advertising
- Partner co-marketing with QNX in the Consumer Electronics Show concept car

Results

- 237 news release postings to online sources
- Two contributed articles in *RTC* and *Embedded Computing Design*
- 38 percent increase in total web traffic following the launch
- 56 percent increase in online leads following the launch
- 85 percent increase in evaluation downloads
- Time-on-site of more than three minutes on launch landing page
- Two hours time-on-site generated solely from Twitter links

As you can see, the campaign product launch goals, marketing channel mix, and results in each example vary, and they should. Every product and campaign is different, and every company's goals and definitions of success will differ. It's not a one-size-fits-all method. And though this book examines an inbound marketing approach, you will still want to complement this majority approach with limited outbound marketing using channels such as PR, search advertising, and events. The more you scrutinize and carefully determine the campaigns, KPIs, and priority channels that will deliver the results you require, the more successful and efficient each campaign will be.

As you work to develop each campaign and KPI, you should track progress on a monthly and quarterly basis. I discuss marketing measurement and the tools and processes you can use to track progress in detail in chapter 12.

Outbound versus Inbound Marketing

With outbound marketing, a.k.a. "push" marketing, you use communication channels external to your company to place your message in front of prospective buyers. Before the digital age, outbound marketing was the only way to do marketing. Pre-Internet, your only choices were to place ads, go to trade shows, mail flyers and postcards from purchased lists, and meet with the media to push your message out to communities where your target audience congregated.

Though you may hear outbound marketing is dead, I don't believe this and I don't think you should, either. This is especially true in technical markets where engineers are making critical decisions that can have an impact on their company's reputation, customers' experience, and even the safety of mankind. For instance, traditional outbound channels such as trade shows are still viable as they give engineers a unique opportunity to meet face-to-face with vendors and subject-matter experts, see product demos, and attend technical sessions. Similarly, with the power of Google and SEO today (which I cover in detail in chapters 4 and 7), securing coverage on technical trade publication websites and blogs can be an excellent way to get found online and drive traffic back to your site. Though outbound marketing is more expensive and harder to measure than inbound marketing channels, the primary benefit in most cases is quick results. For example, you may go to a trade show for three days and leave with a dozen or more qualified opportunities in your pocket. Outbound marketing channels like this give you bursts of results in a short time frame, and if you consistently pay to participate in outbound marketing over time, those bursts can result in a reliable flow of qualified leads to fuel sales opportunities. However, one of the biggest disadvantages to outbound marketing is as soon as you stop paying, the flow of leads slows or stops almost immediately. And the cost per lead for outbound is much higher at above $150 per lead versus sub $100 for inbound.

Inbound marketing, or "pull" marketing, uses online communication channels to draw your customers into your company's website, including web pages, in-depth content, search engine optimization, and social media. In the Marketing to Engineers 2014™ study by TREW Marketing and CFE Media, 87 percent of engineers surveyed said that search engines are their most valued content source when seeking information for their jobs. This was reinforced in the Smart Marketing for Engineers 2015™ study by TREW Marketing and ENGINEERING.com for which 76 percent of engineers surveyed said a keyword search in Google was the method they used often or most often to find work-related content online. Therefore, it is critical that engineers find your content when they are searching online. With a commitment to high-quality content, inbound marketing drives a consistent, long-term flow of traffic and leads at a cost that is much lower than outbound.

Engineers' Most Valued Content Sources

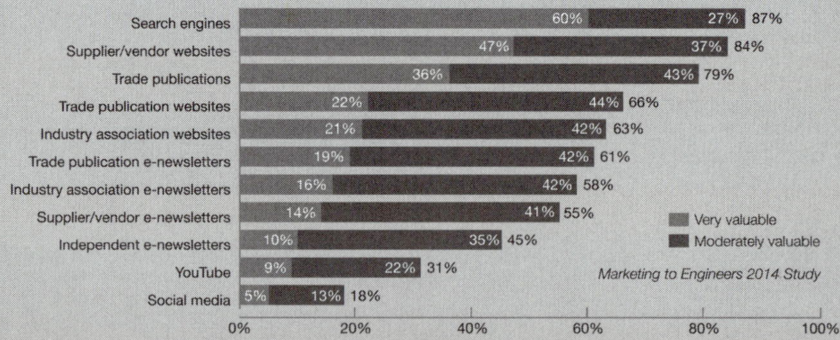

Of the engineers surveyed, 87 percent selected search engines as their most valued content source when seeking information for their job.

The point about high-quality content is critical. The fact is, inbound marketing will fail if you don't consistently publish high-quality optimized content. When you do this correctly, your prospect searches on Google using the keywords he chooses, your content comes up in the results, he reads the search result title and description of that piece of content, and, if he perceives it to match what he's looking for, he clicks on it. He is now on your website and ready to learn more. You have earned his visit to your site through your content, and you now have the opportunity to continue to move this visitor to leads and opportunities through the funnel with continued content offers.

Though a few channels of outbound marketing are still viable for certain companies and industries, your marketing budget should be heavily biased toward inbound marketing and your efforts should focus on producing high-quality content for the long term.

Section 1 of this book examines building your inbound marketing foundation. Then sections 2 and 3 dive into the details of setting up, executing, and measuring your inbound marketing strategy.

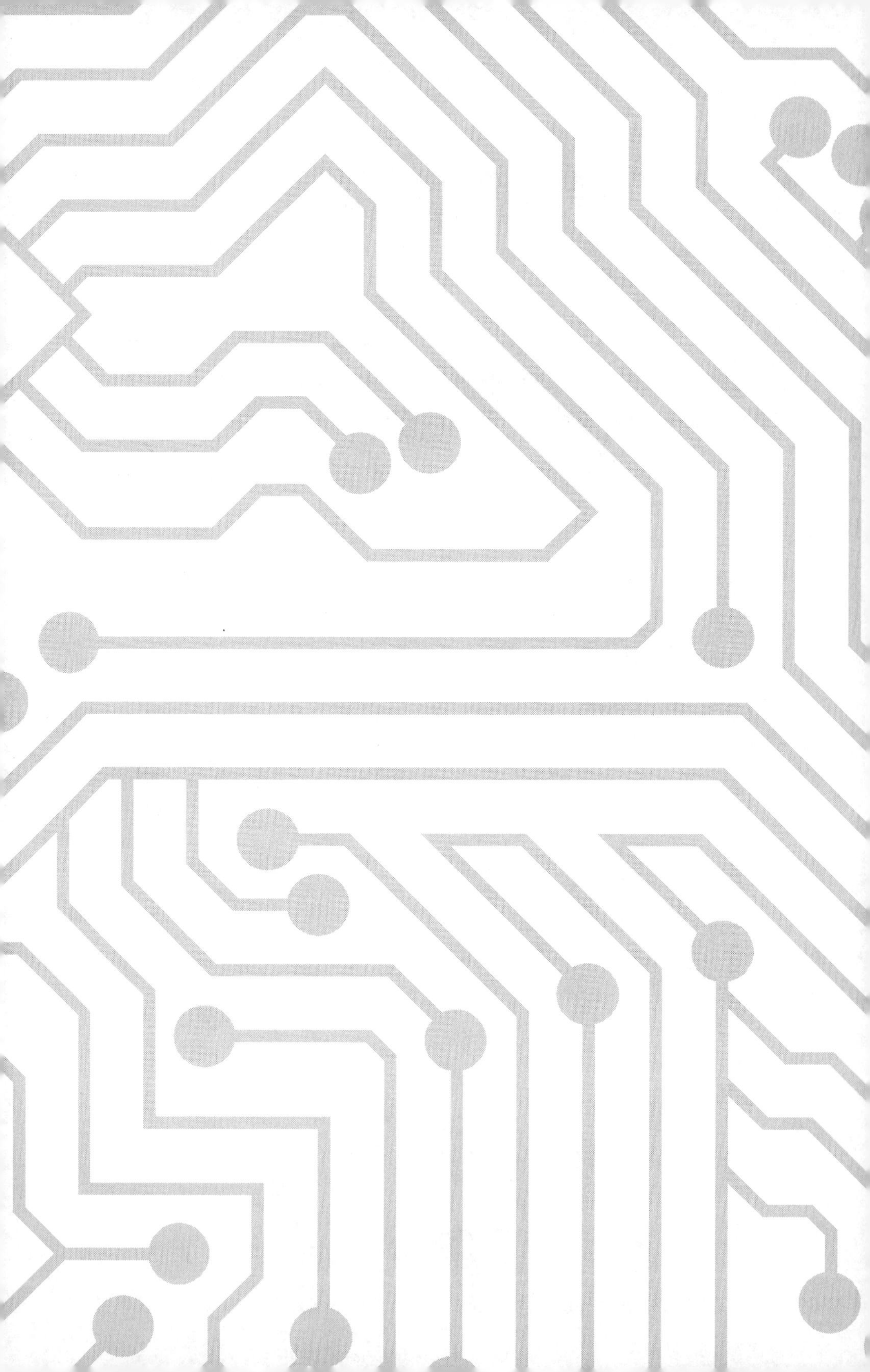

Chapter 3

CREATE TARGET PERSONAS

Define Who, and Who Not, to Target

"Engineers aren't boring people,
we just get excited over boring things."

– Anonymous

You probably know the profile of your most valuable prospects and the sales process your company uses to convert them from leads to opportunities to customers. However, as your company grows, you won't know each prospect's unique situation, and one message won't work for all. You'll need to customize your marketing approach by creating buyer personas.

In small, growing companies, marketers often continue to use the same messaging and approach that worked with the company's initial customer base. What began as a single, focused approach has become a generalized approach. Your client base has evolved and become more diverse, but the way you market to it is still one-dimensional. Likewise, when your company is small, sales can connect with every lead and customize the message to meet each prospect's unique situation. But this approach becomes expensive, inefficient, and broken with growth, and marketing has to take more ownership so sales can focus on the most valuable opportunities.

When you reach this point, you need to move beyond one-size-fits-all marketing by breaking down the large pool of potential customers into audience segments, called buyer personas. Creating personas is a straightforward process and will allow you to customize your messaging and marketing to each group's concerns and needs.

Buyer personas are fictional representations of your ideal customers based on demographic data, online behavior, and your educated speculation about personal histories, motivations, and concerns. For example, you may define one of your personas as VP of Engineering Vince, a business executive who cares most about cost and long-term support. A second persona could be Engineer Elliot, an engineering manager or senior staff engineer who is an expert in your technology area and wants to do a deep dive into the technical capabilities of your product or how you deliver a service. Elliot greatly influences Vince, but Vince makes the final decisions. Vince and Elliot have very different concerns. They want varying types of information about your company and product, and they go to different places to find their information. By walking through the exercise of understanding your customer segments, such as Vince and Elliot, you can put faces, personalities, job descriptions, and key elements of the buying decision to each and better customize your website and marketing efforts, from messaging to content selection. With this approach, you ultimately produce more effective marketing that has a greater impact on your prospects and, in turn, increases your marketing efficiency.

Prioritize Your Personas

The first step in creating your buyer personas is to brainstorm who they could be. Personas consist of both end-user customers and influencers, and you likely need to include both types. To develop a comprehensive list, think of your typical buying process. With whom do you first engage? Who influences that person? Who makes the final decision? Are your personas different across industries, product lines, service types, or company size?

Once you have your full list, identify the ones who have similar needs or roles and consider merging them. From here, prioritize your list of personas by considering their impact on the final purchase decision, their relationship to your company, and the size of the audience persona group. For example, if a key influencer group has only a few members, you may decide it's best for sales to own those relationships and not have marketing prioritize them as a larger group. By the time you're done, you ultimately want to have three to five primary personas because having more becomes too complex to segment, especially when you're just starting.

Once you've finished brainstorming, create your actual personas. To do this, identify the following types of information for each persona. Start by creating three personas and then build from this number to further refine them and generate new ones as needed.

- **Who are they?** Include demographics such as gender, age, location, and education/degree.
- **What is their job?** Include data such as title, company size, industry, career path, and general job responsibilities.
- **What is a day in their life like?** Describe what an average day is like for them, who they work with, how they prefer to communicate, and what decisions they make.
- **What are their primary pain points?** Describe the primary challenges they are trying to overcome that relate to your products and services.
- **What do they value most and what are their goals?** Explain what they value most in making a purchase decision (price, support, etc.) and what they are trying to accomplish in their application.
- **Where do they go for information?** Identify the primary sources they use to gather information in their research and purchase decision processes.

- **What type of information do they prefer?** Consider the style of content they are seeking: content that inspires versus concise guidance versus a very thorough process including all of the research, specs, and small print.
- **What's important to them when selecting a vendor?** List what is most important, such as being a technology leader, having proven experience, being a domain expert, etc.
- **What are their most common objections?** List the reasons you hear most often for why your solutions will not meet their needs.

Meet Ed, Tom, and Victor

The best way to explain personas is to use examples. I'll start with Oil/Gas Engineer Ed. A first step in developing your personas is to select a photo. You don't have to start with a photo, but each persona is not complete without one. You may choose the headshot of an actual customer who represents the prospects you want to target, or you can Google the job title to get ideas. It is important you get the photo right, and you will find the debate that ensues in the search for the perfect photo is enlightening. People often have very distinct images of customer personas. They only wear jeans. They wear designer glasses. They are older. Younger. They look nerdy. Cool. Maybe there is one customer in particular who accurately represents the persona segment. You may want to choose a photo showing the persona at work to give context to the application environment. Keep debating until you find the picture of the person everyone agrees on, and take note of the visual cues throughout the process.

Oil/Gas Engineer Ed

Who is he?

- Male, 20 years of experience in his field
- Master's or PhD-level degree
- Early adopter of new technology; deeply knowledgeable in related technologies and systems
- At the No. 2 or 3 market-leading Fortune 1000 company

What is his job?

- Oil/gas exploration
- Stays abreast of new technologies; serves as internal technology expert/consultant

What is a day in his life like?

- Works on manufacturing/engineering processes
- Regularly evaluates technologies to assess their potential for meeting his needs

What are his primary pain points?

- Top concern is system reliability
- Secondary concern is finding the best, most reliable new technology
- Cost is a concern only in a few corner application areas

What does he value most and what are his goals?

- Reliability
- Specs
- Ease of integrating new technology into his current system

Where does he go for information?

- Trade shows
- Trade journals
- Respected speakers at technical conferences
- Google

What type of information does he prefer?

- Lengthy data sheets
- Testing benchmarks
- Third-party reports from national labs, academic institutions
- Technical content such as white papers and webcasts by credentialed subject-matter experts inside the company

What's important to him in evaluating a vendor/technology?

- Detailed and extensive field and lab testing, third-party testing, reliably proven specs
- Face-to-face meetings, eye contact, high morale

What are his most common objections/concerns?

- Can you pass his business and technology litmus tests?
- Can you do it? Proven? Credible?

What would he be quoted saying?

"I research new technologies that are proven, reliable, and have the potential to give our systems a competitive edge. Company leaders and my engineering peers rely on my technical opinion, so I am analytical and meticulous in my due diligence. I enjoy working with technology and the engineers who create it, especially when I find an innovative new partner who has promising technology and is trustworthy and technically competent. I keep up by reading technical journals and seeing my cohorts in the industry at technical conferences and symposiums."

Looking at Oil/Gas Engineer Ed, you can see he's a well-respected, senior engineer in his energy firm with superior academic and field credentials. He is the go-to guy inside his Fortune 1000 company for opinions on adopting new technologies. When Ed is researching his products, he goes first to the specifications to determine what is required to integrate a new technology in an existing system. In the energy sector, existing systems can live in very remote, rugged areas such as on the ocean floor or in desert terrain, and they are very expensive to maintain, so Ed is thorough in his research.

He reads all the technical information he can and seeks out quality and test/trial data to see proof of real-world performance. He must be convinced that the product is proven and reliable before he ever meets with a technical counterpart at the supplier. He has no room for error in his applications, and his reputation is on the line with each decision he makes.

Ed is well known in his tight-knit community of energy technologists, and he gets most of his information from technical conferences, leading academicians, and peers he trusts.

At the end of the description, a fictional quote summarizes the feelings of the persona. Writing this quote serves to add a voice to personas and helps crystallize what they really care about.

The next example is in the military industry. Unlike Ed in the oil and gas industry, Military Technician Tom is younger with less post-secondary education and only a few years of work in his field. Tom is a hands-on technician who must ensure military systems are working properly for the operator's safety. Because he works in the depot, Tom's time on the Internet is limited, so he mostly seeks out information through his supervisors' recommendations. He must complete annual required training hours and often uses this time to attend trade shows where he can see product demonstrations from experts at supplier companies.

Military Technician Tom

Who is he?

- 20 to 30 years old, mostly male
- Technical certification and/or associate's degree

What is his job?

- Test in the depot or production line
- Will be a supervisor after four years as a technician

What does a day in his life look like?

- Maintains and repairs military systems
- Repairs broken equipment; verifies equipment is mission-ready

What are his pain points?

- Works with complex, difficult-to-operate systems
- Lacks budget to procure best equipment
- Works with dated equipment; short on time and high on frustration

What does he value most and what are his goals?

- Equipment that makes his job easier
- Confidently delivering mission-ready machines

Where does he go for information?

- His supervisors and lead technicians
- Supplier websites and technical support
- Military magazines and newspapers
- Trade shows and conferences

What type of information does he prefer?

- Product manuals and technical documentation
- Certification and training information

What's important to him in evaluating a vendor/technology?

- He doesn't evaluate; he is told what to use
- He may seek services for current systems

What are his most common objections/concerns?

- System is difficult to use
- Unproven company and/or product
- System lacks certain features
- Too different from what he currently knows

What would he be quoted saying?

"I work around military equipment all day, making sure the hardware, software, and mechanical and electrical systems function properly. From repairing broken systems to testing newly added ones, the systems I verify are becoming more and more complex, as is the test equipment I use. I spent two years studying the systems and how to use the equipment to qualify for this technician position. I love being around planes and tanks and having the responsibility of ensuring their proper function. I am new in my military career and don't have much influence today, but once I prove myself, I will move up in rank and responsibility."

"I am starting to form opinions about the vendors whose equipment I work with, and I share those opinions with my superiors as they consider new equipment to procure. I read military journals in the break room at lunch, and will attend my first trade show this year. I'm excited to see all the new technology on the horizon and get a change of scenery from the depot I work in every day."

Manufacturing VP Victor

Our last example is Manufacturing VP Victor. Victor has an undergraduate engineering degree and an MBA. He is a senior business leader who reports to the COO of a multibillion-dollar company with thousands of employees all over the world. His operation is critical to the company's success, and he evaluates and reports on key operational metrics on a weekly basis. He has hundreds of employees and relies on his technical and business managers to run an efficient operation with increasing yields on a flat budget.

He chooses suppliers who can meet his team's demands on price, schedule, and global scale and support. He makes large-scale capital equipment decisions and regularly evaluates optimal locations for geographic expansion. Victor has been in the business a long time and has a peer network he relies on for recommendations. He watches his competitors and the overall industry for trends and proven best practices, and he is sought out as a speaker and expert on global enterprise manufacturing.

Who is he?

- 40 to 50 years old, male
- Mechanical engineering degree and MBA

What is his job?

- Directs global manufacturing operations
- Serves on the leadership team of a multibillion-dollar technology company

What does a day in his life look like?

- Makes large-cap equipment, expansion decisions
- Meets with global teams and community leaders
- Prepares reports for CFO and board of directors on operational metrics and issues

What are his pain points?

- Needs to achieve higher yields with a flat budget
- Has teams spread out on multiple continents
- Faces time zone and language barriers

What does he value most and what are his goals?

- Vendors who move as quickly as he does
- Responsiveness; high-quality, reliable systems and service

Where does he go for information?

- Google
- His manufacturing managers
- Manufacturing and/or business conferences
- Leading industry or supplier websites
- Industry peers

What type of information does he prefer?

- Proven customer success
- ROI comparisons
- Service and support policies
- Company reputation and financial information

What's important to him in evaluating a vendor/technology?

- Proven reliability and support on a global scale
- Volume pricing
- Future-proof solutions

What are his most common objections/concerns?

- Price
- Global support
- Ability to meet rapid timelines

What would he be quoted saying?

"I am an engineer by degree, but I became interested in business early on and went back to school to get my MBA. Today, I lead a global manufacturing team responsible for 24/7/365 operations and solve problems—from technical to operational to financial—on a daily, if not hourly, basis. The C-suite leaders keep a close eye on my department's output, and I report on key metrics weekly."

"Suppliers are critical to my team's success. I work closely with them to secure pricing, support, and delivery commitments on a global scale. With millions of dollars in capital equipment on my books, I have to get the most out of every investment and hold my team accountable to ensure everything is running optimally and reliably. I have to make risk versus reward decisions to meet the growing demands of the business with a flat budget."

"I don't have much time to read up on trends, but my management team members keep me abreast through their research and events they attend, and I try to attend sessions when I'm asked to speak at industry conferences. I am attached to my laptop and mobile devices and am constantly on Google searching for ideas, data, and research."

One last element of persona development to consider adding to your definition is where the persona is on the technology adoption life cycle. This model for high-tech marketing was made famous by Geoffrey Moore in his book, *Crossing the Chasm*. If you haven't read this book, I highly recommend it as an enlightening description of how products and technologies move through the different segments of adoption, and what motivates (or prohibits) customers at each stage of adoption.

Consider where your personas are located on the adoption life cycle (or, said another way, how willing they are to take risks with new technologies). For instance, Victor is willing to take the most risk. He's experienced and in a position of authority to weigh financial and operational risk while striving to stay competitive and efficient. He would be the farthest to the left in the adoption life cycle, toward

The Technology Adoption Life Cycle

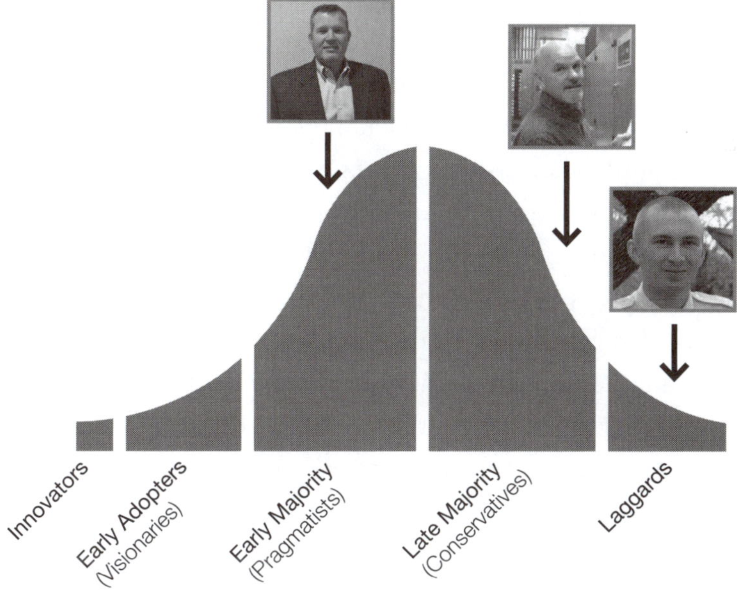

A step in defining personas can include placing them on the technology adoption life cycle from risk-taking early adopters to risk-averse laggards.

the early majority. Next is Ed, who is meticulous in his evaluation of new technologies. He wants to know they're proven but also needs to stay competitive. His company's leaders are relying on him to find new technologies to adopt before competitors do. Less of a risk taker than Victor, Ed falls between the early and late majority at the top of the bell curve of the adoption life cycle. Last is Tom, who is early in his career and working on mission-critical systems that require fully adopted, reliable operation. As the most risk-averse of the group, he falls toward the end of the late majority toward laggard.

As you can see through this complete exercise, customer personas can vary widely with differences in educational levels, pain points, care-abouts, preferred information sources, and risk level. By defining these and other elements and finding the right persona photo, you are ready to prioritize your audiences, segment your messaging, plan your content development, and decide on the optimal marketing approach to reach each group.

Another benefit of clearly defining your buyer personas is aligning your organization, from the CEO and sales to engineering and support. Many organizations feel a lack of clarity in identifying their customer audiences, and employees often do not fully understand how their actions directly impact potential customers. Even engineering teams are at times charged with creating a new product, but no one is exactly sure whom the product is targeted. Unfortunately, this misalignment can translate into wasted time and resources. For marketing, this reality sets in when you or your team members are reworking content multiple times, debating what your next white paper should focus on, or trying to reconcile conflicting opinions that slow down initial, clearly defined objectives.

Using informed data, outside research when needed, and your collective experience to create your personas, and then ensuring leaders in your organization agree and understand them, can result in significant efficiency gains and employee confidence. When these fictional characters start to become part of your regular language and references to Engineer Ed or Technician Tom lead to heads nodding in agreement and understanding, you will experience the power of personas!

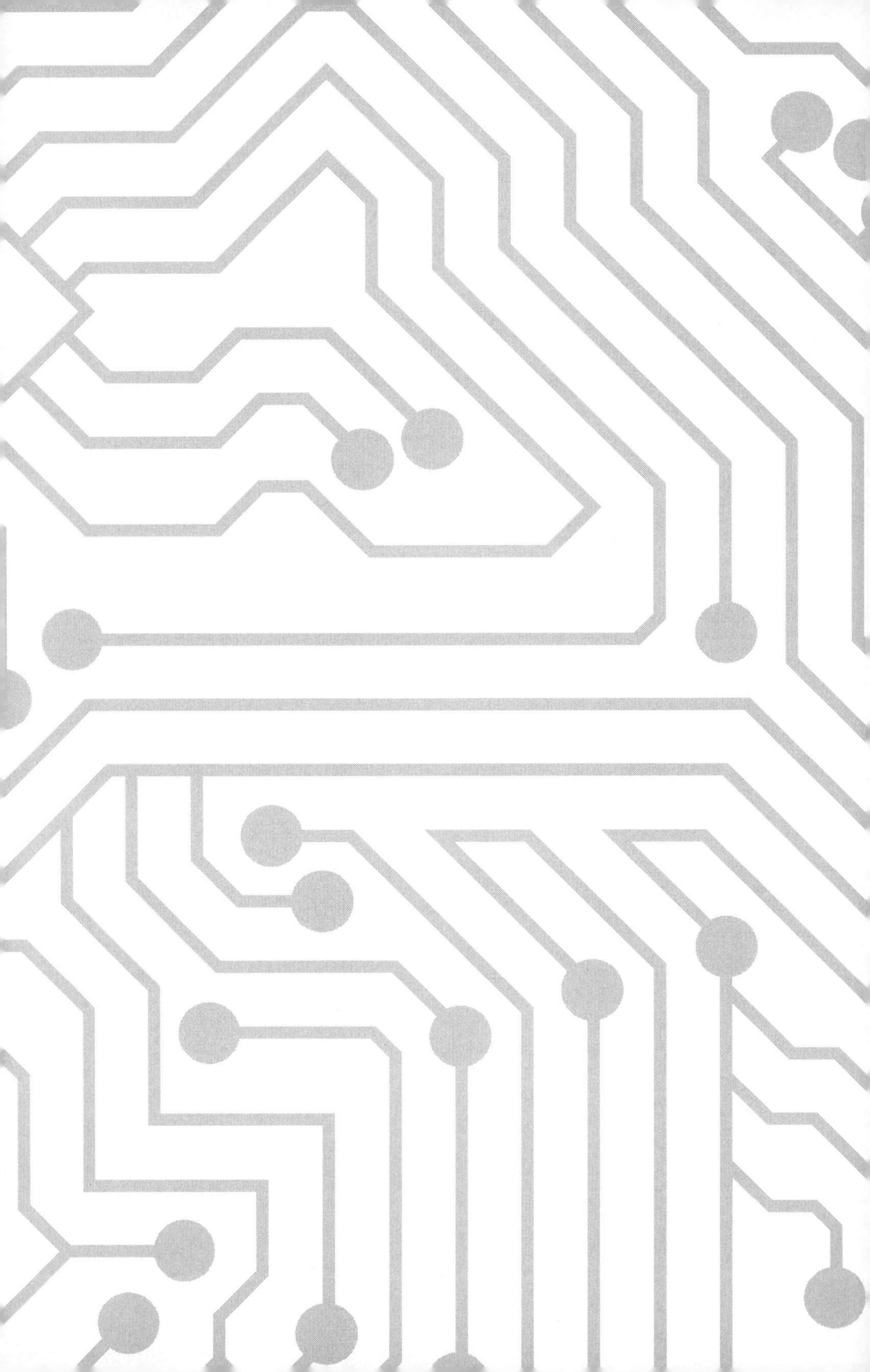

Chapter 4

SELECT YOUR KEYWORDS

Use a Long-Tail Approach to Get Found

"The fewer moving parts, the better."

– Christian Cantrell, Science Fiction Author

With your positioning statement, marketing strategy and campaign plan, and customer personas now defined, you are on your way to building a rock-solid marketing program. The next logical step is to build your website. As the saying goes, "If you build it, they will come," but with a website, unfortunately, it's not that easy.

It's true that if you build a website and add content you will get traffic, but you don't want just any traffic. You want the right traffic, which will come from having the right content optimized with the right key terms. You want your defined customer personas to find your website when they are searching on keywords related to your company's solutions. To ensure that your website pops up in the top search results, you need to focus on keywords your personas use that lead to search results that include your products, services, or technologies.

➔ **Look for data in chapter 9 that shows what lead form fields engineers are most likely to complete.**

Search engine optimization (SEO) is not black and white. It takes time, patience, and a lot of trial and error. Google and other search engines are very particular (and very quiet) about what they allow to rank in the search engine results page (SERP). They have spent a significant amount of time and money ensuring that the sites that get credit truly deserve that credit for their quality content and relevant messages. You can, however, take a specific and strategic approach to SEO that will help you gain the search engine visibility that your website deserves. The first thing is to remember the people you're trying to reach, and the second is to follow a methodical approach, which I'll go into below.

> *While 92 percent of all traffic on Google is driven by page 1 search results, only 5 percent of engineers say they stop on page 1. In fact, more engineers will go 10 pages or deeper than will stop on page 1. We now have proof that engineers really are different!*

SEO for People

Google's ranking algorithm is developed with its customers, not your website, in mind. To ensure the billions of Google customers using its search engines are satisfied with their search experience, Google bases its algorithm on what it calls SEO for People. Unlike traditional SEO methods that rely solely on tactics to convince search engines to rank a website based on a keyword, more modern SEO practices aim to provide an easy way for searchers to find what they need and have a pleasant user experience once they find it. With this in mind, some have even started calling SEO by a new name: Search Experience Optimization. In an article called "How People Interact with Search Engines,"[1] Moz Marketing, a thought-leading company specializing in SEO practices, explains SEO for People this way:

> **"One of the most important elements to building an online marketing strategy around SEO is empathy for your audience. Once you grasp what the average searcher, and more specifically, your target market, is looking for, you can more effectively reach and keep those users."**

[1] moz.com/beginners-guide-to-seo/how-people-interact-with-search-engines

Google has incorporated measurements in its algorithm that help it "decide" if customers are happy with its ranking on a given term and with your content. One measure is the use of a website's bounce rate based on how the visitor interacted on the site. Google Analytics defines bounce rate as the percentage of visitors who visit one page and leave after only that page. According to Evan Bailyn, author of *SEO Made Easy*, "A bounce rate of 40 percent is good for a B2B site. Anywhere from 25 to 50 percent is normal."[2] If the bounce rate for a website is low, the Google algorithm interprets this to mean that the searcher found a term that Google offered in its results to be useful, clicked on it, and continued to browse the site, therefore, finding it relevant. Adding bounce rate as a weight in the algorithm to rank websites is just one of hundreds of tweaks Google has made to its algorithm, and more are to come.

All of these small and complicated paths and tweaks to the ranking algorithm underscore why you should not attempt to trick Google with tactics intended to convince it to rank your page high. You may be able to fool it for a time, but you can bet that any trick will be foiled by Google eventually. Instead, think the way your audience thinks when choosing terms and optimizing your site, and be patient. It can take up to six months or longer to see results from your SEO efforts, and by results, I mean traffic and leads and not necessarily ranking on page 1. With the right keywords and a consistent flow of new optimized content written for people, not search engines, you will start to see these results, and winning in search will have been worth the wait!

Keyword Planning: Balance Science with Instinct

The process of earning a consistent flow of the right traffic to your website starts with SEO. With keyword analysis and content

[2] firstpagesage.com/seo-blog/seo-faqs/whats-good-bounce-rate-b2b-site

optimization for these keywords (discussed in chapter 7), you greatly improve the chances that your website and content will be found by the engineering customer personas you want to attract. The foundation for SEO is keyword planning and the following steps will help you set up your SEO foundation.

Step 1: Research Keywords

The keyword selection process starts with research and prioritization. Engineers, scientists, and similar technical audiences are often very specific in their searches. They are determined to find exactly what they need and often employ the well-known approach of "long tail"[3] searching by using multiple, specific words in their search phrases, as shown in the graph below. As a marketer, you should in turn use long-tail keywords in your SEO plan to improve the chances that your site will be found by your target audience and not by a broader audience who may not find your information relevant. As you get

B2B Long-tail SEO

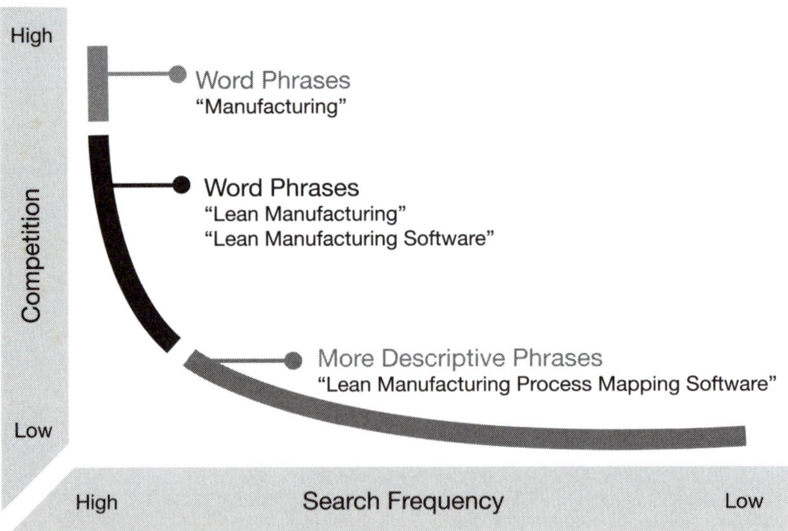

Use descriptive long-tail keywords to reduce competition and help ensure your site is found by your specific audiences.

[3] en.wikipedia.org/wiki/Long_tail

more descriptive in your keyword phrases, the search frequency decreases but so does the competition for that keyword phrase (and the relevance to your company's offerings, specifically).

This long-tail approach is ideal when targeting technical audiences, who have unique behaviors when it comes to search and how deep they will go to find what they need. To illustrate the difference in search behavior on Google for the universe of all searchers versus a Google searcher who is an engineer, compare the data from two studies.

Data in the first study by Chitika[4] found that sites listed on the first Google search results page generate 92 percent of all traffic from an average search. The percent of total traffic on Google from sites listed on page 2 drops off a cliff, generating just under 5 percent of Google traffic from search results. In contrast, nearly 70 percent of the 705 engineers who responded to the Marketing to Engineers 2014 study by TREW Marketing and CFE Media indicated that they will go three pages or deeper in their search results to find the information they're seeking. So, while 92 percent of all traffic on Google is driven by page 1 search results, only 5 percent of engineers stop on page 1 In fact, more engineers will go 10 pages or deeper than will stop on the first page of search results. Though the first study looks at real search data on Google and the second is the engineers' opinions of their online search behavior, the two data points do paint a contrasting picture that's important to understand. We now have proof that engineers really are different! And we need to be smart in how we market differently to them. This means your web pages and content must include specific and relevant multiword phrases. To find these keywords and phrases, you have to do your research and prioritize those that are aligned with the greatest opportunities for your business and that will generate the right traffic from your technical personas.

[4] chitika.com/google-positioning-value

Percentage of Google Traffic by Results Page

91.5%

Chitika Insights 2013 Study

A June 2013 study by Chitika Insights found that page 1 search results in Google drove 92 percent of all traffic for the average search.

Percentage of Google Traffic

Page 1	91.5%
Page 2	4.8%
Page 3	1.1%
Page 4	0.4%
Page 5	0.2%
Page 6	0.2%
Page 7	0.1%
Page 8	0.1%
Page 9	0.1%
Page 10	0.1%

How Many Pages Engineers Will Go on Google

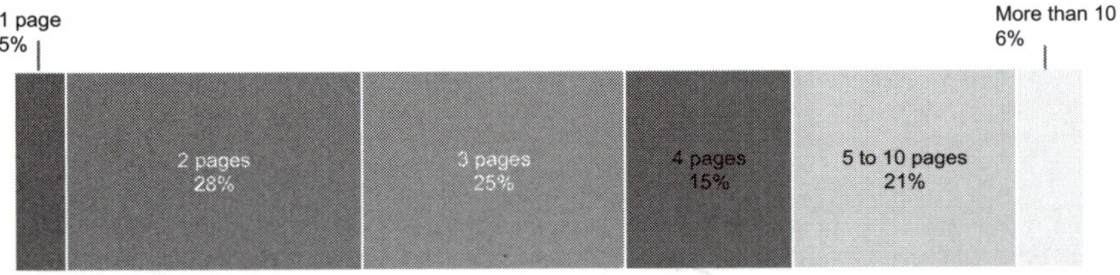

Marketing to Engineers 2014 Study

The Marketing to Engineers 2014 study by TREW Marketing and CFE Media found only 5 percent of engineers stop at page 1 of search results and more than 75 percent indicated they will go to page 3 or higher.

When thinking about which keywords to start with, put yourself in the shoes of your engineer persona searcher and answer these questions:

- **Who You Are**—How do your target customers describe what your products are or the nature of your services?
- **What You Do**—How do they describe what your products do or how your services are implemented?
- **Whom You Serve**—How do your customers describe themselves and their technical needs? Searchers want to know that your

company has experience serving their industry and application, so you need to know how they self-identify.

- **Pain Points**—How do your customers describe the problems they are trying to solve?
- **Purchase Intent**—How do your customers indicate that they intend to purchase?

Considering these questions, let's take an example of a company that makes computers and is trying to differentiate from its competition to attract the most relevant visitors. They may use the following keywords across six main categories on which their buyers search:

- **What It Is**—6-core desktop and 12-core computer
- **What It Does**—animation desktop, 3D-rendering computer, video-editing PC
- **What It's For**—AutoCAD computer, Autodesk PC
- **Who It's For**—computer for architects
- **Specific Features**—liquid-cooled PC
- **Buying Intent**—render farm services or render farm price

You can incorporate a few other steps, considerations, and tools to round out your keyword selection process. One is to ask your sales force to share the words they hear customers using to describe your offerings, or ask how they would describe the pain points their customers are trying to solve with your products. Also, consider variations of words a searcher might use, such as "ATE" versus "automated test equipment." After the keyword analysis, you'll be able to determine the most common ways people search on a term or phrase so you don't miss certain search traffic.

Use this process to develop your first set of potential keywords. You should end up with a list of about 10 to 20 important keywords or phrases per product, service, campaign, and so on. When you are finished with the analysis, you will narrow it down to about five to 10 terms per area.

Step 2: Gather Search Data

Once you have an initial list of keywords, you need to crunch the numbers to determine search volume, competitiveness, and your website's current performance in light of the chosen keywords. Later, you'll analyze the numbers against the relevance of the term to your company in order to pinpoint the terms you want to pursue. Your goal is to find the least competitive keywords that will draw the most relevant traffic to your site.

You can choose from several effective tools for SEO keyword analysis, selection, and performance measurement that range from no to some cost. I'm going to cover two here: one free and one paid. I'll show both so you know what to expect in terms of features as you increase your investment in tools.

Google AdWords Keyword Planner

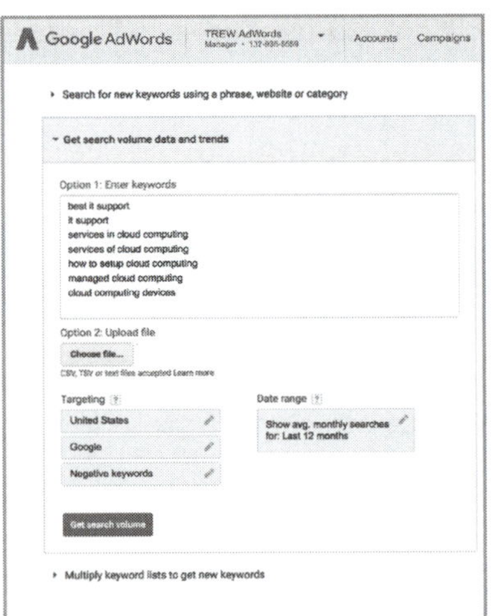

Enter keywords into the Google AdWords Keyword Planner to see search volume data for each keyword.

The first tool, Google's AdWords Keyword Planner, is an effective free resource for gathering data on monthly average search volumes in Google by keyword. To find the search volume, you enter the keywords you want to analyze in the Keyword Planner tool home screen, and it generates a report that shows you the average monthly searches for that word. A note of caution when using this tool: the report will also include data on competition and suggested AdWords bid prices for paid search, not organic. But you should use a different tool to get accurate data on organic search competition. This is where the second tool comes in.

> *Your goal is to find the least competitive keywords that will draw the most relevant traffic to your site.*

To illustrate the features of a paid tool, I'll refer to the SEO environment inside a popular marketing automation software platform, HubSpot (marketing automation is described in more detail in chapter 11). Other similar tools provide a varying degree of functionality and likewise vary in price, and blogs by SEO experts like one from Blue Mountain Media[5] are published regularly that offer insightful reviews and advice about the latest SEO tools. In HubSpot's Keyword tool, you can find a monthly search number for specific keywords that is an average and approximation of multiple sources for how popular each keyword is. This tool not only provides data to help you analyze the estimated organic competition but also gives a rating for the level of difficulty for the organic competition of that keyword.

There are many ways to measure the level of competition, or difficulty, and tools are changing often. Google's tool currently uses a level of competition rating of low, medium, or high (based on a numeric calculation between 0 and 1), and HubSpot uses a proprietary algorithm with a scale from 1 to 100 to estimate the difficulty of getting a page with that keyword to rank on the first page of Google search engine results. The higher the number, the greater the difficulty. For example, a score above 70 is considered extremely difficult to rank for on page 1 of Google. Using a tool like HubSpot, you can focus on keywords with low difficulty between 0 and 40 and then move to 40

[5] bluefountainmedia.com/blog/10-seo-analysis-tools

through 60 and so on. This tool, and others like it, also allows you to track your current page rank for each keyword and increases and decreases in rank with simple red or green arrow indicators.

HubSpot Keyword Grader

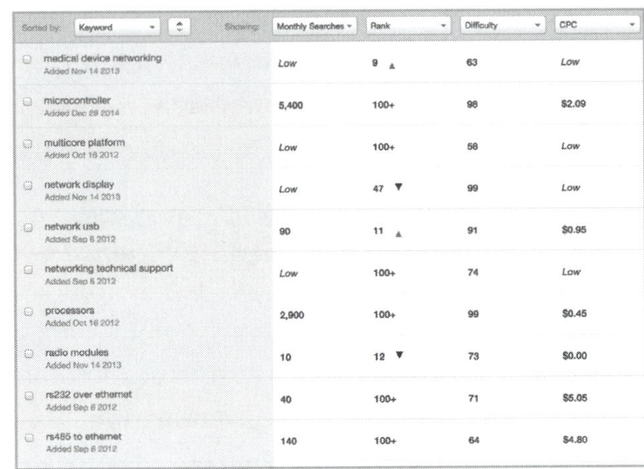

Sorted by: Keyword	Monthly Searches	Rank	Difficulty	CPC
medical device networking Added Nov 14 2013	Low	9 ▲	63	Low
microcontroller Added Dec 29 2014	5,400	100+	98	$2.09
multicore platform Added Oct 16 2012	Low	100+	58	Low
network display Added Nov 14 2013	Low	47 ▼	99	Low
network usb Added Sep 6 2012	90	11 ▲	91	$0.95
networking technical support Added Sep 6 2012	Low	100+	74	Low
processors Added Oct 16 2012	2,900	100+	99	$0.45
radio modules Added Nov 14 2013	10	12 ▼	73	$0.00
rs232 over ethernet Added Sep 6 2012	40	100+	71	$5.05
rs485 to ethernet Added Sep 6 2012	140	100+	64	$4.80

The Keyword Grader feature in HubSpot helps you determine difficulty for keywords and monitor ongoing SEO performance.

Step 3: Select Your Keywords

To select your keywords, you need to weigh three variables: (1) the search volume of the keyword, (2) the level of difficulty for ranking, and (3) the relevance of the term to your company and target audience. A common mistake when choosing keywords is focusing on those with the highest volume of Google searches. As described earlier, broad, high-volume keywords are nearly impossible to rank on the first few pages of search results, and they often won't attract the right traffic anyway.

Instead, with the long-tail approach, you should be prepared to sacrifice search volume for relevance, which may mean selecting keywords or phrases with a lower average monthly search volume. This will improve your page ranking for the terms that are most important to your company and draw higher quality, targeted traffic to your site.

One company, Crank Software, did just that. An embedded graphical user interface (GUI) solutions company, Crank set out to refine its keywords and attract more targeted, high-quality traffic to its site. Its personas are R&D and user interface (UI) designers of embedded devices such as in-car graphical displays and animated GPS systems, and its primary product is Storyboard Suite software for animated device UI design and development.

After conducting a full analysis of its keywords and search engine optimization performance, the Crank team found that the site was optimized for "GUI design" and "GUI software" keywords, both

Case Study: Long-Tail Keywords

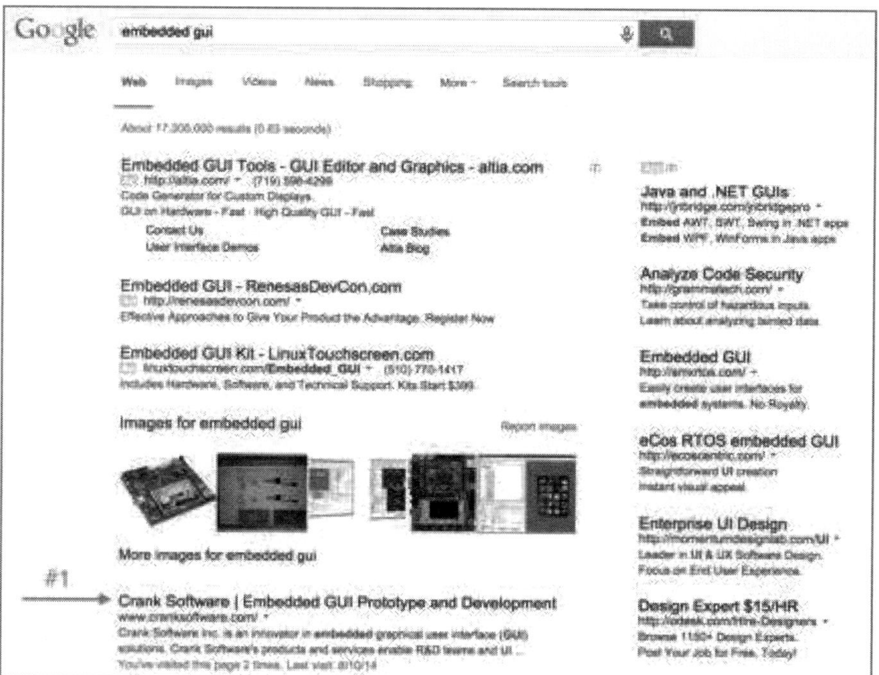

Crank Software increased its rank from page 3 to the top search result on page 1 by refining selected keywords to ones with less competition and lower volume.

broad and highly competitive areas of search. By adding "embedded" and "prototyping" terms to the "GUI" words, Crank increased its traffic dramatically as its search rank improved from the third page to the No. 1 search result on the first page of a Google search for "embedded GUI."

You don't have a hard and fast rule to follow for selecting terms based on one variable or another; rather, you have to weigh all three to find the right balance that leads to the best keywords for your business. In some cases, you might find it reasonable to pursue a term that has a high level of competition because it has a high search volume and is relevant to your website and audience. For instance, the term "Internet of Things" fits in this category: a high search volume (40,500 monthly searches), a high level of competition, and high relevance.

On the other hand, you might sacrifice search volume by selecting a much more focused, long-tail term because it is relevant and the competition is low. The phrase "Industrial Internet of Things" matches this scenario: lower search volume (480 monthly searches), a low level of competition, and high relevance. In the end, you must weigh the variables and combine data with intuition to finalize your keyword selection.

Example of Keyword Search Results

Term	Average Monthly Search Volume	Level of Competition	Relevance to the Company
Internet of Things	40,500	High	Medium
Industrial Internet of Things	480	Medium	High

To select search terms, weigh search volume with competition and relevance.

When you complete your analysis and select your keywords, group them into two primary categories based on these three criteria of search volume, competition, and relevance: priority keywords and tier-two keywords. You may also want to document the terms that are so broad or so competitive that, after your analysis, you determine they should not be a priority.

You can create simple tables with your final keyword analysis selection using priority and tier two categories to help organize and prioritize your list.

Priority Keywords

Keyword	Average Monthly Searches	Competition	Relevance
High consequence area analysis	25	Low	High
Current interrupter	10	Medium	High
Atmospheric corrosion	90	Low	High
Internal corrosion	30	Low	High
High energy surge arrester	110	Low	High
Risk intelligence platform	50	Low	High
Emergency flow restriction device	55	Low	High

Tier-Two Keywords

Keyword	Average Monthly Searches	Competition	Relevance
Pipeline compliance system	10	High	Medium
Cathodic protection	4400	Medium	High
Leak survey	20	Medium	High
Pipeline compliance	10	Low	Medium
Solid-state relays	590	High	Medium
Pipeline integrity management	110	High	High
Pipeline risk assessment	20	Medium	High

Use simple tables like these with data from tools like Google's AdWords Keyword Planner to categorize your keywords and rank them according to search volume, competition, and relevance.

Step 4: Monitor Performance, Continuously Improve

Once you have selected your keywords, you need to optimize your content, both existing and new, to ensure that search engines rank your company as highly as possible when potential buyers search on those keywords. Chapter 7 includes details on keyword implementation and content optimization.

Once you've optimized your content, you need to continuously monitor performance, tweak existing keywords, and add new ones. Google indexed 67 billion[6] web pages in 2014, and millions more are being added on a weekly basis, including from your competitors who are trying to get ahead of you. Keyword performance is a long-term journey, and regular monitoring is critical to keep track of changes and make updates to stay ahead of your competition and improve your performance.

Keep the following considerations in mind as you continue to monitor your SEO performance, evaluate your keyword selection, and implement optimization.

- **Be authentic by remembering SEO for People**—Your content should be first and foremost authentic and not sprinkled with forced words or repetitiveness.
- **Optimize page titles and tags**—Weave keywords in the page titles and metadata so search engines and searchers alike understand what your site is about (discussed in detail in chapter 7).
- **Focus**—Narrow in on one keyword for each interior web page.
- **Provide clear direction**—Give content writers a list of the keywords you're targeting so every new piece of content strengthens your SEO performance.

[6] statisticbrain.com/google-searches

- **Be topical**—Create web pages, such as solutions, industries, or product applications, that can be used to strengthen optimization of key terms.
- **Remember graphics and photos**—Visual content is powerful for SEO. Using keywords in the photo alt tags on your blog and web pages tells Google what the picture is about and helps ensure that your site shows up on the Google images SERP.
- **Cross-link on your domain**—Linking to your pages from other pages on your internal site, such as from the site-wide footer or from related blog posts on products and services pages, helps search engines identify what your content is about and creates a better user experience for visitors.

Use Keywords in Blog Categories

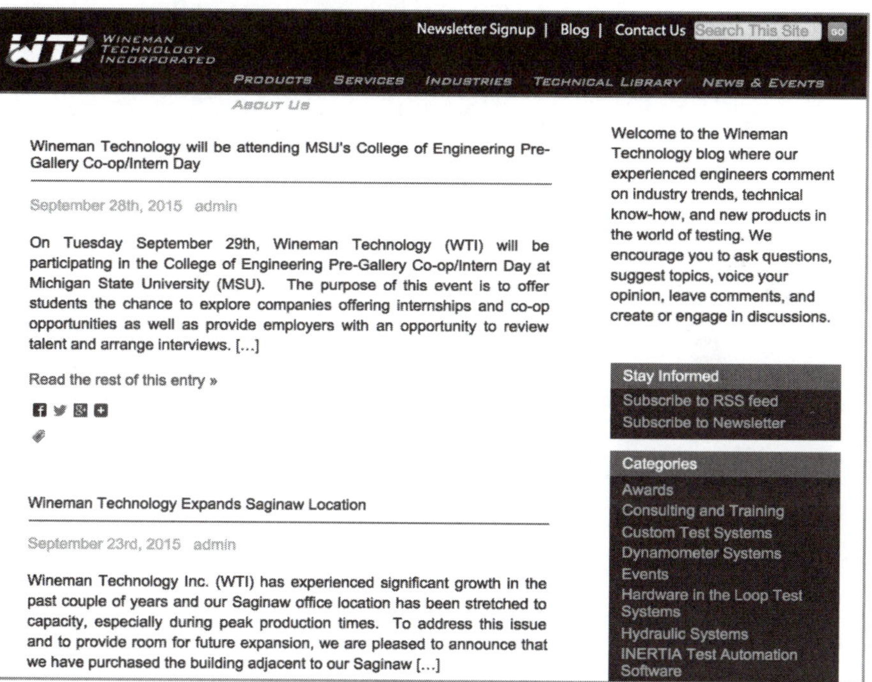

By using keyword topics for blog categories, Wineman Technology helps readers find relevant information and search engines find its site for these topics.

- **Blog**—Blogging (discussed in more detail in chapter 7) is critical for driving new and repeat traffic to your website. Though most engineers have no interest in blogging, as I'll explain in chapter 7, by creating new blog content, you can target new keywords, increase your site's page count, position yourself as a subject-matter expert in specific areas, and significantly increase traffic and leads.
- **Add categories and tags to blog posts**—Tagging and categorizing your blog posts by keyword topics helps users find relevant content and helps search engines find content related to the keywords. When you add a category to your blog post, the category keyword appears in the URL, which helps Google find your content based on keywords.

SEO Attracts More than Search Traffic

As you embark on your SEO journey, remember that the end game is not just rank. By using the SEO strategy I've described here, you will enhance your company's brand, attract the *right* visitors to your site, provide an easy way for them to find what they're looking for, and ultimately develop trust through relevant, high-quality content that results in capturing them as leads. Content is the most important asset to a search marketing strategy, and SEO is what helps searchers find your content.

Many different tactics are involved in optimizing content for search, and, as I mentioned earlier, various tools make it easy and efficient to implement SEO. By balancing search optimization between your goals and the needs of searchers and search engine requirements, you'll get not only clicks but the *right* clicks. This will lead to more engagement from your web visitors and longer-lasting results with better measurements of what resonates with your audience. It takes time, and you can't trick Google, but when SEO is done right, it's worth the wait.

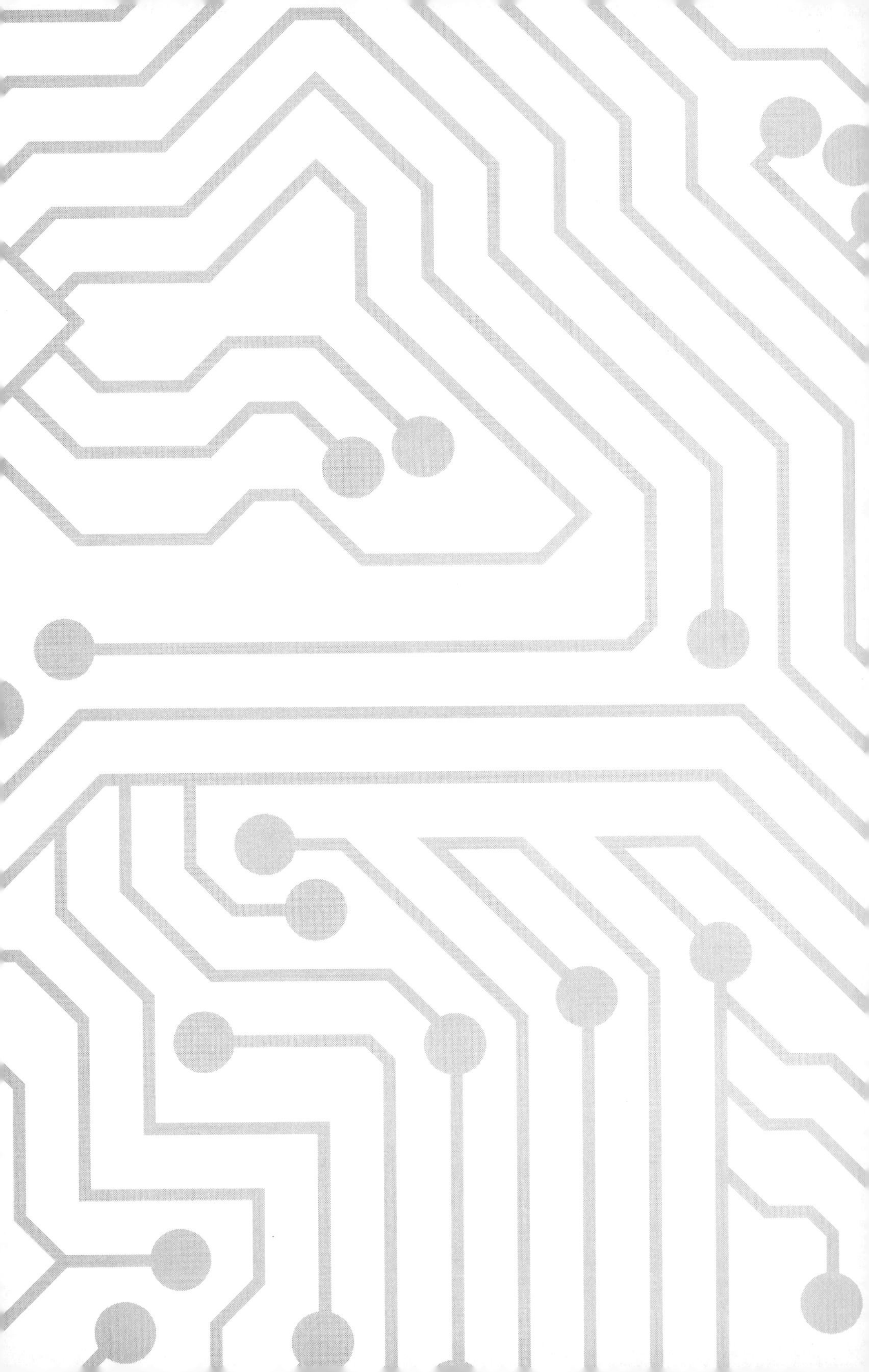

Chapter 5

DESIGN YOUR WEBSITE

The Hub of Your Inbound Marketing Program

"The human foot is a masterpiece of engineering and a work of art."

– Leonardo da Vinci, Artist, Mathematician, Inventor, and Writer

Your website serves many roles in your organization, from your company storefront to a customer support resource to a recruiting center, to name a few. From a marketing standpoint, it is the hub of all your activities and the main vehicle for generating leads and creating your online branding experience. It has the

Think of your website as a 24-hour-a-day marketing employee, who is always ready to communicate your brand value and generate leads.

unique ability to serve as both an outbound and inbound marketing tool, as a way to communicate your brand image to your audiences, and as a response mechanism for prospects interested in learning more about you. You can think of your website as a valuable, 24-hour-a-day employee in your marketing organization. It's always on, always ready to communicate your brand value, and always focused on generating leads.

As mentioned in chapter 1, in both the Marketing to Engineers 2014 study and the Smart Marketing for Engineers 2015 study, engineers said search engines are their preferred method for finding information. These results underscore that investing in your website is THE single most important marketing investment you can make.

However, many engineering and scientific companies have websites that do not effectively engage their personas. Some typical reasons include the following:

- The site is outdated visually and navigationally and doesn't offer updated information.
- The content is low in quality or not useful for the target audience's needs.
- The site fails to attract leads or search traffic.
- The company's brand and value are not well-represented.
- The site doesn't allow visitors to interact with the company online.

Building a truly effective website requires many elements: a clean and mobile-friendly design, intuitive navigation, informative graphics, clear company positioning, well-structured code and sitemaps for SEO, and compelling, succinct, up-to-date, and optimized content. In addition, the site must serve many distinct visitor groups, including existing customers, prospective buyers, partners, prospective employees, the media, etc. Creating a website that incorporates all of these elements, for all of these audiences, can take months to complete and requires many steps and skills. It also requires a significant investment. The costs to create it vary widely. For a small investment of several hundred to a few thousand dollars, you can get a website up and running quickly but you're going to be locked into functionality and design. If your company is just starting, that may be where you need to begin. As you mature, your offerings grow, and your need for functionality and security expands, so you're more likely to require a custom website that matches the specific needs of your company. Investment in a custom website can range from tens to hundreds of thousands of dollars. To determine the best approach and investment level for your company, consider your needs for the next two years to define your website strategy.

Define Your Strategy

A big mistake many companies make when redesigning their websites is to jump headfirst into the design phase before ensuring that their web strategy is well-defined. This can lead to a site that doesn't fit the company's needs or its customers' needs, and one that fails to help achieve marketing goals. Following a deliberate, proven process, beginning with strategy definition, is the key to a website redesign that fully engages your visitors and helps push your prospects down the funnel to increase leads and sales. As I recommended in chapter 2, develop your business goals and marketing plan before jumping into campaigns and tactics. Using this method, you can create a web strategy that aligns with business and marketing goals and that considers your audiences' needs. This step is critical before you start thinking about aesthetics, page layout, or website functionality.

To define your web strategy, you first need to determine the top goals for your site. All other activities involved in website redesign will fall into place more easily if your goals are clear, straightforward, and agreed on by key stakeholders in the organization.

For its goals, you may want your website to:

- Quickly and effectively communicate who your company is, what it offers, and how it's different from competitors
- Immediately offer visitors information they want and need
- Help search engines find your company
- Capture quality leads and serve as your prospect-nurturing engine
- Help build thought leadership and credibility for your company
- Demonstrate your company's expertise and offerings

As you consider your goals, look at other websites and consider what you like about them. Ask others on your team to do the same. Document likes and dislikes and what you want to "creatively swipe" for your website. The next step is to prioritize your site's visitors. First and foremost, you need to build your website in a way that is useful to the buyer personas you developed in chapter 2. Note who they are and what they care about, and refer back to your selected keywords from chapter 4 to determine which tasks or information will draw them to your site. Both personas and keywords are key tools in guiding you through the process of organizing your web pages, site sections, and content offerings. In addition to personas, you may have visitor groups such as the media, technology or funding partners, government agencies, etc. Prioritize these groups and make sure your website is built with the highest-priority groups in mind.

Once you've prioritized your visitor groups, you need to develop a site map. Generally called "information architecture," this map helps define the relationship between different content types and pages as

Example of a Site Map

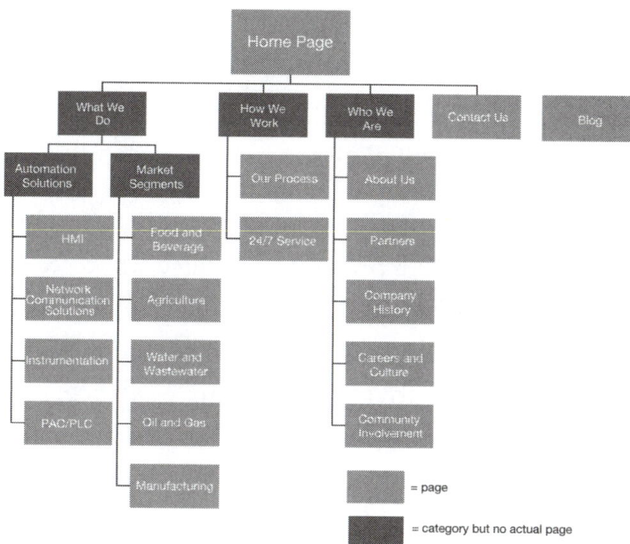

Site maps help define different web content, pages and visitor paths through your site, starting with the home page, and branching out to each site section offered in your global navigation.

well as the paths to reach specific pages. Your site map starts with the home page and then branches out to each site section offered in your global navigation. Below each of those branches, add the lower-level pages you plan to include in each site section.

When designing the information architecture for your site, remember these five tips:

1. **Be customer-centric**—Make the user experience simple and effortless with site structure and labels that make sense to your customer for easy navigation to topics and pages.

2. **Design for the 80 percent**—Develop a site architecture that addresses the majority of your buyer personas rather than getting distracted by corner-case scenarios.

3. **Consider your goals and your page ranking**—The way you organize the information on your site should correlate with your web marketing goals, including how best to improve your search engine results rankings by ensuring you are using the right keywords in your site map.

4. **Use card sorting**—Consider a card-sorting exercise with a few key customers who represent your personas to see how they naturally categorize your content. Have your users generate a category tree with index cards that represent web pages on your site without providing them any guidance, so you can see where users might organically anticipate that they would find particular information. This helps guide your categorization and site hierarchy moving forward, and sheds light on the best way to organize your pages so your customers find what they want quickly and easily.

5. **Outline your proposed site map**—Create a visual outline to show how all pages on your site will be grouped and how they relate to one another. If you are redesigning an existing site, outline your original structure and eliminate, add, and shuffle pages to ensure you have a clean structure.

Create a Content and Layout Blueprint

With your site strategy in place, you need to create a blueprint for both content and design. For content, you need to prioritize the high-level elements you want most prominent on your home page and other key site pages. A common mistake is the "kitchen sink" phenomenon: trying to get too much content on the home page, which results in a cluttered experience that requires users to work too hard to get to the right information. If your content and message priorities are crystal clear before the design phase, your site hierarchy and page layouts align much better with your goals.

Page Description Diagram

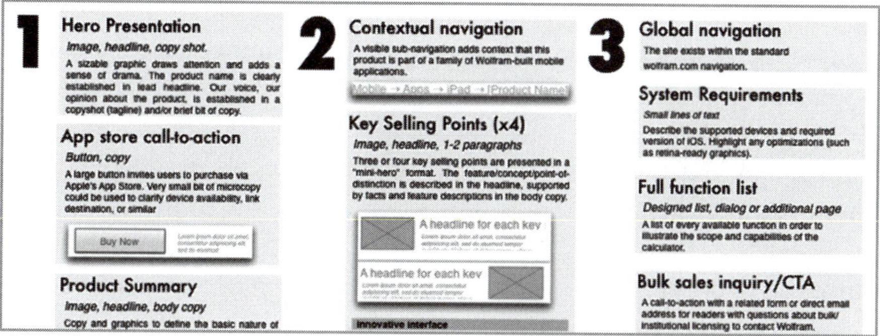

Create a page description diagram to prioritize your high- to low-priority web content.

An effective way to prioritize content is to use a page description diagram for your home page and other key site pages. The page description diagram helps you visually prioritize the messages or types of content you want users to see or click on.

Follow these three steps to complete a page description diagram:

1. For each of the main pages of your site, starting with your home page, list the content elements you want to place on that page and write a brief description of each. This could be content that exists today or content you want to create in the future.

2. Prioritize these content items into three columns: a highest-priority column for must-have content, a medium-priority column for really great content to have if you can fit it in, and a low-priority column for nice to have but not critical content.

3. Ask three or four others from your leadership, sales, and marketing teams to complete the same exercise. You can have them do this separately and then compare answers and work through discrepancies, or you can do it together and debate differences until you have a final completed diagram. Either way,

you will find it is a productive, efficient way to identify and prioritize the most important content, not to mention a valuable opportunity to glean what others in the company view as most important so you can sign them up as content authors later!

I will go into much more detail about content planning, creation, and optimization in section 2.

Once you've prioritized the content you want to highlight on your website, building your page layouts, or web templates, is the logical next step. It is at this point that you need to decide if you can use a templatized approach to sufficiently meet your web goals or if you need to customize your approach. If you decide you do not need to customize, I recommend you select a WordPress[1] theme with templates that best match your web needs. Taking this approach is straightforward, and you can find many resources online to guide you through the process. If, on the other hand, you decide to take a custom approach, the next step I recommend is to develop wireframes. Wireframes are simple layouts that help you plot the location of content on each web page or in each site section, and should be created before you go into the design phase of the site. Wireframing has four main benefits:

1. It allows you to conceptualize what should go on each page before the designer starts logging hours.

2. It helps you think through content decisions visually and try out different approaches quickly and easily.

3. It results in a more efficient design process with fewer modifications.

4. It provides the designer with a clear idea of which content is most important, which leads to a design that is closer to the end result much earlier in the process.

1 wordpress.com/website

The focus of a wireframe is the content, arrangement, and sizes and proportions on each page. Wireframes do not include any colors, images, fonts, or other design elements. Think of them as blueprints. Unless you have e-commerce or a highly transactional site, start with wireframing three to five web page templates. You improve efficiency and site usability if you create templates you can repurpose on different pages of your site rather than creating one for each page.

Wireframes may sound complex, but, in reality, the process can be as simple as sketching out the content elements for each page on a piece of paper or a whiteboard.

Wireframe Example

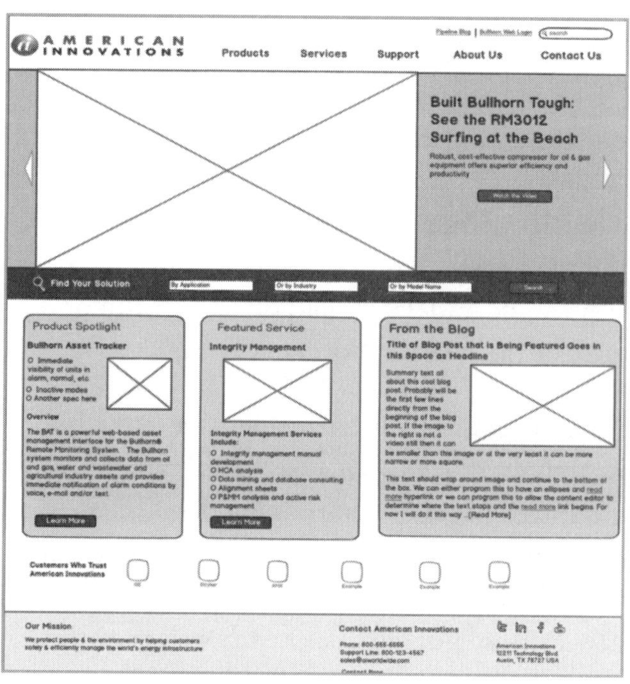

A wireframe is like a blueprint, that serves as a simple layout plotting the location of content and images before design begins.

Creating them should be straightforward and, dare I say, one of the more unemotional parts of website planning. Using wireframes strips away any focus on design elements and allows you and your team to focus solely on the page structure and the content types you'll place on a page.

You can amp up your wireframes by turning them into working prototypes of your site. Many popular wireframing tools such as Balsamiq[2] and Axure[3] offer prototyping functionality that allows you to conceptually build out the site. You can link up your wireframes so that click-through navigation is possible to get a feel for the flow of the site, and you can build out your site hierarchy and global navigation using these prototypes. The result is a group of wireframes that represent not only your site's layouts but also the structure and flow for the end user. Prototypes allow you to test-drive the site before any actual programming takes place and make modifications easily to achieve the flow and user experience you desire. This is especially useful for heavily transaction-oriented sites, such as e-commerce sites, and other complex web applications.

When developing your site templates, consider usability data from trusted sources to determine how people use the web. Then apply that knowledge to your content placement. If you haven't conducted your own website usability study, you can find insightful and practical advice from outside sources. For example, Jakob Nielsen, a pioneer in web usability research, has been studying how people interact with the web since the mid-1990s and offers a wealth of research on his website[4] for the Nielsen Norman Group.

Research groups like this are continually collecting data to track behaviors such as how web users' eyes scan a page. You can apply this learning when laying out web pages or determining the placement of headlines, images, and calls to action to ensure your design makes it as easy and natural as possible for web visitors to scan content quickly and effortlessly. To this end, make sure each web page that serves as an entry point to your site is brief and impactful because, as Nielsen has found, you have very little time to capture a visitor's attention:

---

[2] balsamiq.com
[3] axure.com
[4] nngroup.com

- You have only about five to 20 seconds to pique web visitors' interest.
- Web visitors read only about 20 percent of the words on a page.
- Users tend to gaze more at brief headlines in large fonts than at any other words on a page.
- Where there are multiple paragraphs, users read the first one the most.

With very little time to capture the interest of your busy and distracted audience, don't waste it with too much text or small fonts. The shorter and more actionable your headlines and the easier they are to read, the greater your success at communicating your message.

The Marketing to Engineers 2014 study further reinforced this. Respondents indicated their preference on web pages is for images and graphics, short paragraphs, and moderate bulleted lists versus longer, detailed paragraphs. As visitors go deeper into your site, you can take greater liberties to go more in-depth with longer, more detailed paragraphs. Ideally, you should reserve longer paragraphs for long-copy pieces such as white papers.

Home Page Design Example

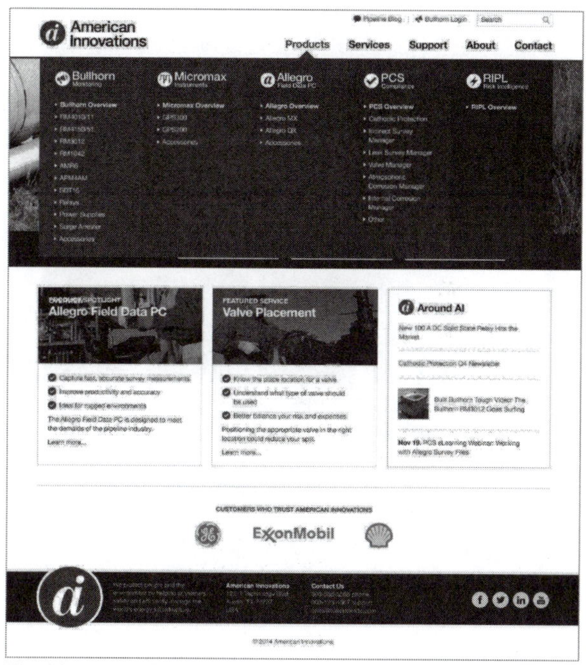

The American Innovations website uses a clean, multicolumn visual layout to help users quickly and easily locate the information they seek.

Web visitors read only about 20 percent of the words on a page.

Now It's Time to Design

With your website strategy, information architecture with prioritized content, and wireframes complete, you are ready for design. Considering eye-tracking data and knowing you have only a few seconds to pique visitors' interest, you need a clean design that visually reinforces your brand position and makes it easy to quickly find relevant information.

Engineers' Preferred Web Page Content Structure

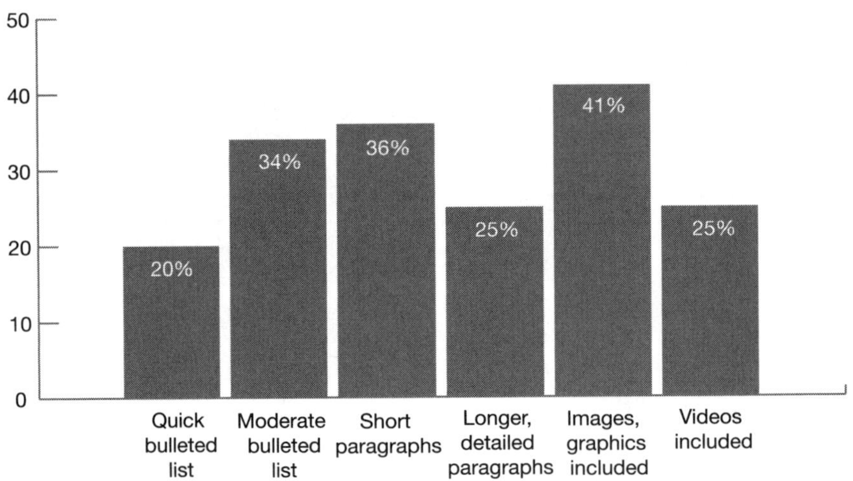

When engineers were asked their preferences for online content structure, they most preferred images and graphics, short paragraphs, and moderate (versus quick) bulleted lists.

Your website is your brand online, and, to this end, it should incorporate the visual and textual elements of your brand style guide, including colors, fonts, and other design elements. You may use several creative ways to incorporate your brand in the site design, whether it is a header color, a color on the global navigation bar, or even a background color, to truly stand out. As you design the interior pages of your site, the look and feel should be consistent across each page. For example, if you feature blog posts on each page, the posts should always be in the same place with the same design elements throughout the site.

Home Pages

The home page must convey your unique value to prospects in just a few seconds and compel them to learn more about your products or services. Staying disciplined and communicating only a few things on your home page is one of the toughest parts of web design. Refer back to the home page description diagram you completed earlier to categorize high-, medium-, and low-priority content. Consider how you can focus the design of your home page around your highest-priority content or messages.

A common and effective way to do this is using large, visual hero graphics with dynamic content offerings that are highly visual but also offer a peek into your business, such as an impactful quote from a key customer, a bragging point about your work in a specific industry, or simply a new product promotion. Compared with large areas of static text, a hero graphic, or a large, colorful banner area stretching across the top half of your home page, can add depth and dimension and compel visitors to learn more about your company while instantaneously providing them with a "feeling" about your brand.

Navigation

With your key messages prominent on the home page, be sure to also create clear navigational paths that help your target audience find relevant information quickly. Label your services and products

Examples of Large Hero Graphics

Focus home page design around your highest priority content to direct imagery, navigation, and calls to action into the site.

in a way that makes sense to your personas. Be cognizant of how many clicks your web visitors must make to reach the core pieces of information and content, including your key product information or service offerings. Consider your most valuable lead-generating content and make sure it's not buried too deeply. Instead, offer it in relevant places along the visitor's path through your site.

Making these decisions helps shape your site global navigation, the menu that is constant throughout the site and serves as a quick roadmap for visitors. The global navigation is critical to a site's usability and success in driving visitors down key paths, and the way you build its structure and links can have a real impact on site results.

Many sites now employ mega-menus in their global navigation. A mega-menu is larger than a typical drop-down menu and incorporates helpful categories and visual cues for users to more easily find information on your site.

Incorporating mega-menus offers real benefits to your site's usability such as:

- Making navigation options easier to peruse because the menu displays everything at a glance. This ensures users can see all pages available in a given category.
- Providing room for short descriptions of your offerings. This is beneficial if your user is new to your site and your services/ products.
- Allowing you to visually emphasize relationships between your offerings. Regular drop-downs don't allow you to group content into separate bins or demonstrate relationships between offerings.
- Accommodating different font sizes and colors, which helps you visually distinguish different levels and categories. You can also opportunistically include images to enhance an offering's description or drive the user's eye to something important.

The mega-menu approach allows you to present your navigation options to your web visitors in a visually appealing way that a traditional drop-down menu cannot achieve.

Use Product Descriptions versus Model Numbers in Navigation Structure

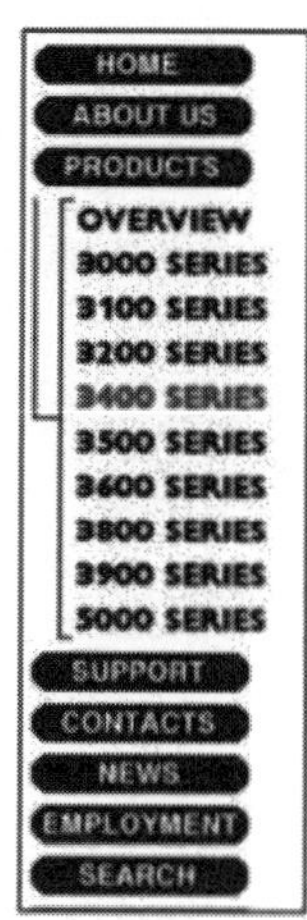

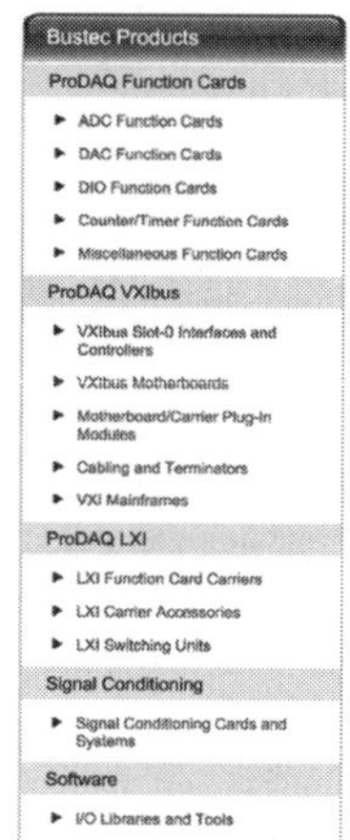

Use descriptive product and service labels your personas understand (right) versus internal model numbers (left) to make it as easy and quick as possible for web visitors to find what they need.

Mega-Menu Example

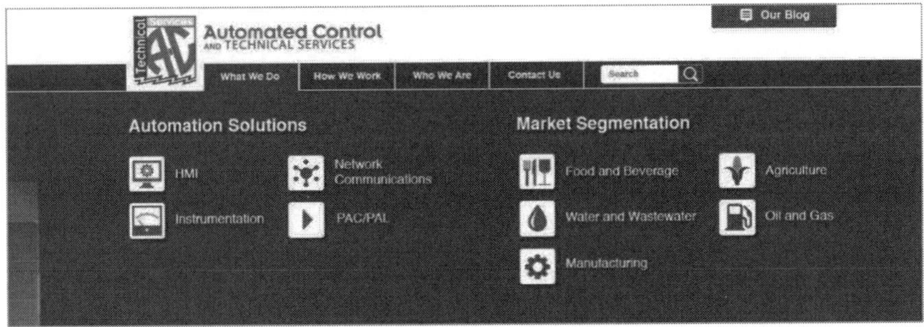

A large mega-menu includes categories, imagery, and even calls to action inside the drop-down box to help web visitors quickly navigate to the information they seek.

Generating Design Concepts

A word of caution to the engineers who are leading their company's website redesign project and working with a graphic designer: avoid dictating design elements such as fonts and use of accent colors, moving around elements in the approved wireframe, changing design direction mid-project, and second-guessing the design approach and strategy. This not only causes graphic designers to lose their drive and enthusiasm but also risks the design appearing disjointed and patched together. As a result, it can derail your entire website project. If design starts to go awry, consider first revisiting the defined strategy and page description table that prioritizes content and reviewing the approved wireframes before getting into colors or font styles. This ensures everyone is grounded in the same strategy that led to the design ideas and results in a more cohesive design approach. If your graphic designer does not follow this process, make sure you do.

Request at least two different design concepts for your site's overall look and feel. If your budget allows, ask for three. This gives you the opportunity to see different approaches, colors, and styles applied to the same strategy and wireframes. You may like certain elements from each design, and though you must choose just one of these concepts for the next round of design, you can often borrow elements from all of the concepts for your final design. Always begin design with the home page and, once the home page is in a good place visually, create graphic comps for the interior page templates based on your wireframes.

Imagery

One of the most important aspects of design is the imagery you use. The quality of your imagery reinforces the power of your brand, and the content of the imagery tells the story of your brand. Whether you opt to use your own images or stock photography, the images you select should directly relate to the page content and enhance what you want to communicate. An image of two people in front of a computer doesn't mean anything if it doesn't relate to surrounding content on that page. Investing in accurate, high-quality, relevant images adds to your site's attractiveness and relevance.

Ideally, you should have photo shoots completed and imagery selected by the next design review so you can see the real imagery in the final design and make tweaks to images and/or the web design before calling it final.

Design for Speed and Mobile

Studies have shown that if a visitor to your site has to wait for a page to load, he or she is more likely to leave. One study by Red Gate made this conclusion: "…frustration develops after a second or so of waiting. If a user is required to wait between five and 15 seconds, there is a significant chance that a user will abandon a website rather than wait for the information. Any wait beyond that is highly likely to cause the user to abandon the site."[5]

[5] simple-talk.com/dotnet/.net-tools/the-cost-of-poor-website-performance

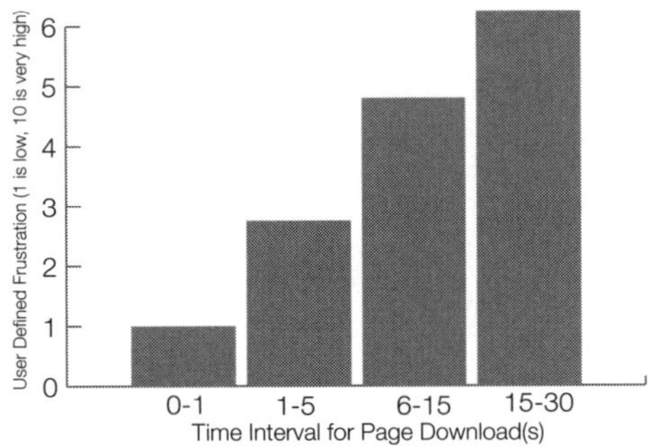

Red Gate Software

Users are more likely to abandon a website if they have to wait between 5 and 15 seconds for the page to load.

With this in mind, you need to pay close attention to the technologies your designer and web programmer may be using and how they are implementing them, such as JavaScript that executes when a page loads or the incorporation of many images on a given page. These elements may be necessary for your site, but you should ensure images aren't heavy and JavaScript is used only when necessary. In addition, embedded videos that are set to autoplay can also affect page load times. You should test download times if you plan to use these elements and consider making features like video play optional. This may mean users must click on a featured video to watch it rather than having it start automatically, but the payoff is a shorter page load time, creating a better and faster user experience.

Server speed is another indicator of site speed, and companies that use their own service must upgrade their web servers as part of their website investment. Keep speed in mind and make sure you communicate to your web designer and developer early in the process that you want your pages to load as quickly as possible. If you anticipate users from other countries accessing your site frequently, consider both the average Internet connection speed in key countries as well as how slow the content will load coming from your server, which may be thousands of miles away from those users. If you have a large group of users in other countries, you may want to consider upgrading your server to a global content delivery network, which is a collection of web servers distributed across multiple locations to deliver content more efficiently to users. If you don't have the budget or bandwidth to upgrade your server, just remember that the faster your site loads for you, the faster it will load for everyone.

Another important part of your web design is ensuring your site displays well on a mobile device such as a smartphone or tablet. Responsive design, which ensures your website automatically and dynamically adapts to the varied sizes of mobile display screens, has become a critical web investment given the rapid adoption of mobile devices. This became especially apparent following Google's announcement in April 2015 that it would expand its "…use of mobile-friendliness as a ranking signal. This change will affect mobile searches in all languages worldwide and will have a significant impact in…search results."[6] All businesses now have a new critical reason to ensure their sites are responsive: Google will penalize them if their sites are not.

Now it's critical that your website be responsive, and it's important to plan on this during the web design stage because it requires additional design time, programming work, and quality assurance (QA) testing upon implementation. Responsive design may increase the price of a web redesign by 30 to 40 percent, but it's an investment you must make if you want your site to perform well on Google. By making this investment, you also ensure a better mobile experience for your visitors and set your company up for success as engineers expand their use of mobile devices for work-related research.

[6] googlewebmastercentral.blogspot.com/2015/02/finding-more-mobile-friendly-search.html

Content Management System: Build a Site You Can Keep Fresh

Once your website launches, it requires ongoing attention to keep content fresh and compelling. Consider it a living document and schedule frequent content updates to successfully meet your marketing and business goals. Companies that update their content frequently not only enjoy more repeat visitors but also consistently rank higher in search engine results, which fuels more website visits and site popularity.

If your website is difficult to update because the process is cumbersome or requires a programmer's time to make changes, you'll be less nimble and effective in keeping the site fresh and updated. Many companies use a web content management system (CMS) to maintain their sites, but not all CMS platforms are created equal, and the options can be overwhelming.

There are three types of web CMS platforms:

1. Off the shelf, such as HubSpot's COS or Ektron
2. Open source, including WordPress and Drupal
3. Fully customized and coded exactly to your site's needs and specifications

You must consider several factors when selecting the best web CMS for your site, including:

1. **What level of functionality do I have or need on my website?**

   A simple, small website may have only text and images that require little to no customization or sophistication on the part of its CMS platform. In this case, a simple off-the-shelf CMS or an open-source platform is a good option. Requirements such as interactive forms, data flow to back-end systems, "product quickfind" search functionality, or multiple, detailed page layouts demand a more customized installation and sophisticated functionality.

2. **How many staff members will update content on the site, and what is the approval process?**

   In most cases, a few people may be updating your site and need the required skills to do so. However, if you have a large number of content publishers and require approvals before content goes live, consider a CMS that includes built-in workflows so you can manage reviews and finalize content efficiently. A CMS workflow helps you track content production through each step of the process and notifies each person working on the content when it's time to review it. For example, when a content producer updates a page and saves a draft version of it, the workflow sends an email to her supervisor to review the page and approve/push live or decline the change.

3. **What server is my site running on?**

   Some CMS platforms are built in ASP.NET and require a Microsoft server and licensing to run properly. Many other CMS programming languages, such as PHP and Python, are server-independent and run best on LAMP servers (LAMP is short for Linux, Apache, MySQL, and PHP, an open-source web development platform).

4. **How will I handle bug fixes or modifications to site functionality?**

   The programming talent you have on staff plays a large role in influencing your web CMS platform. For example, if you have an in-house programmer who knows PHP, you should consider an open-source CMS that runs in PHP. If you don't have a programmer on staff, you might consider an off-the-shelf CMS with built-in programming support, or think about outsourcing to a knowledgeable and reliable marketing agency with web expertise and a programmer on staff who can manage your site's required updates and programming tweaks.

5. **What is my budget?**

   CMS platform prices vary widely. For a few thousand dollars, you can make minor customizations to an open-source platform like WordPress or a moderately customized CMS. Or you can pay a six-figure price tag for a sophisticated off-the-shelf or fully customized system with e-commerce, dozens of ready-made design templates, multi-language functionality, and back-end integration.

Your budget alone should not define your CMS choice but should be considered alongside your site needs and requirements. Open-source CMSs appear free on the surface, but the total cost quickly rises when you decide to customize to get the site looking and working the way you want it to. However, open-source and custom CMS platforms for which you own the source code do not have significant, mandatory ongoing costs and don't require you to use the same programmer for every future modification. Evaluate the trade-offs to ensure you make the right decision for your company's website.

Go the Distance

Follow this methodology to create a website you and your target technical audiences will love. Each step of the process is critical, from developing a strategy and site map tied to marketing goals to designing a highly usable website with distinct branding to selecting a CMS that meets your business and technical needs.

Your initial investment in developing a high-quality website may be substantial, but the ROI comes from your ability to make your site work for you over the long term. If your website is the valuable, 24-hour-a-day employee in your marketing organization, you can't just let it perform on autopilot. As with any employee who requires your time and attention to grow and succeed, you need to consistently invest in your website by adding fresh content and staying on top of user trends such as mobile adoption, browser usage, and screen resolutions. This effort will help keep your website, your most critical marketing employee, armed for success.

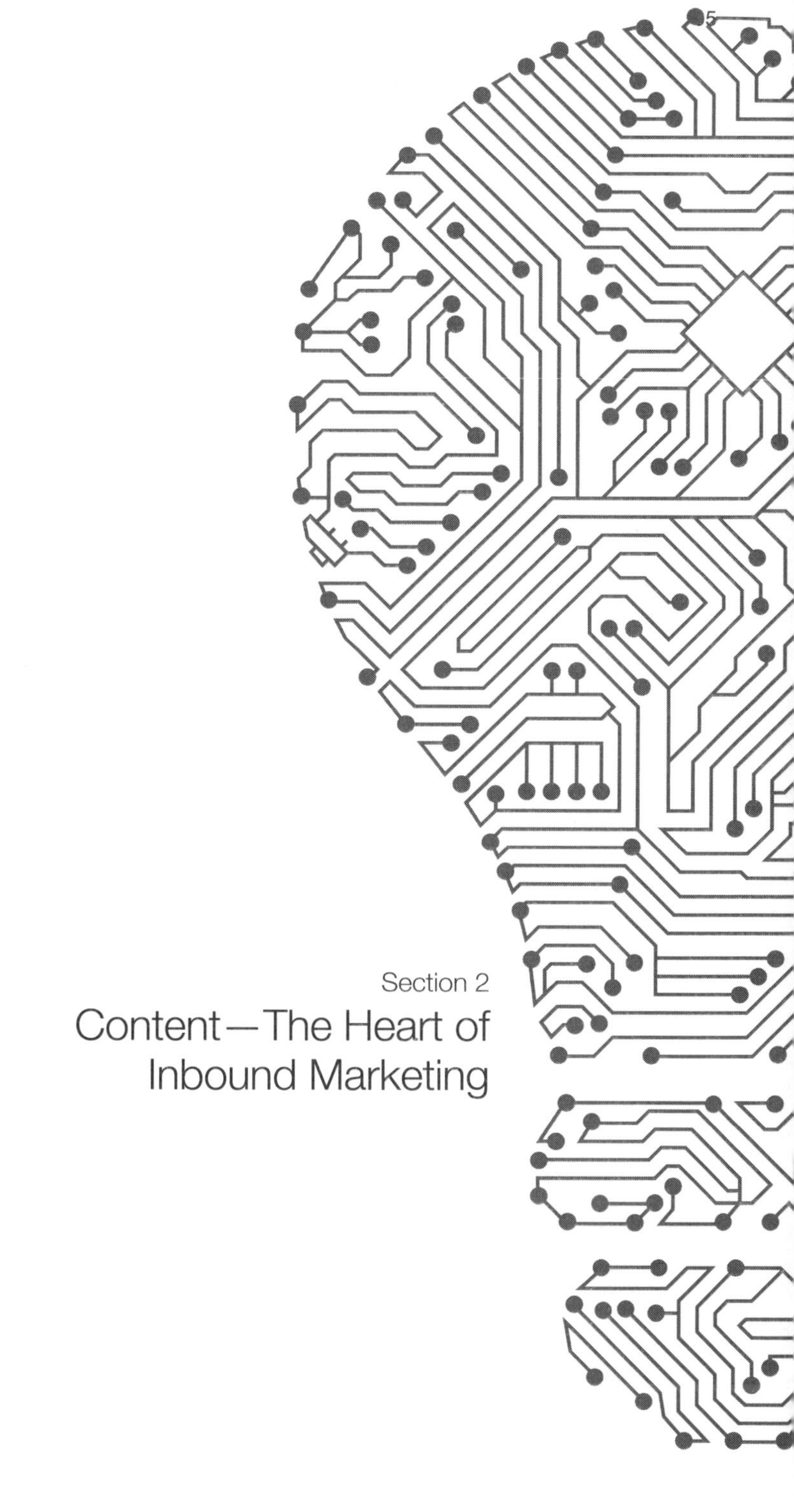

Section 2

Content—The Heart of Inbound Marketing

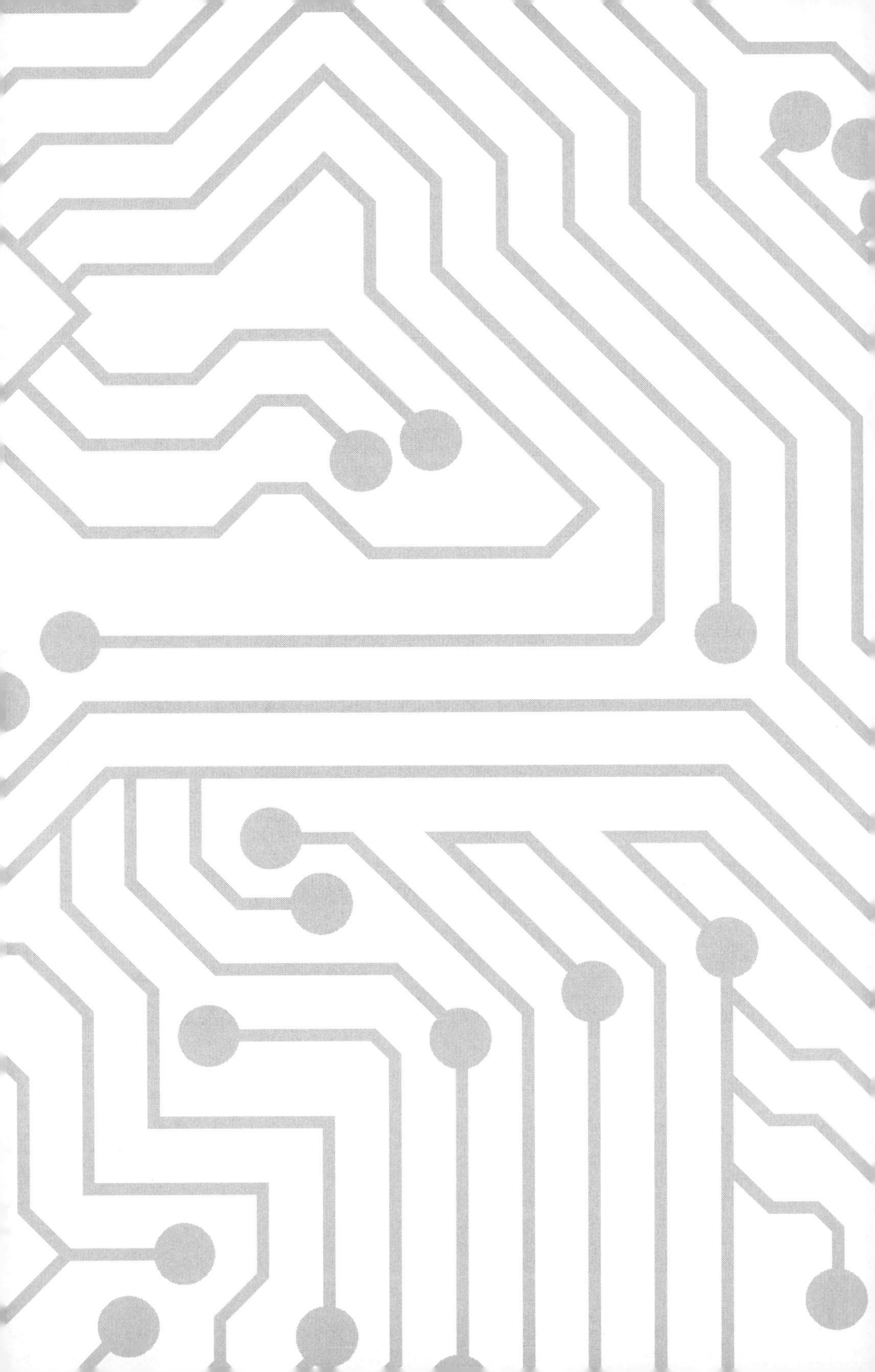

Chapter 6

DEVELOP YOUR CONTENT PLAN

Map It along the Funnel

"History will be kind to me, for I intend to write it."

– *Winston Churchill, British Prime Minister and Nobel Laureate*

In the old days (a.k.a. before Google), sellers controlled marketing. We pushed our important messages to people at times we chose and with methods we dictated, through printed catalogs, ads, and direct mail and at trade shows. We decided which, when, and how prospective buyers should listen to us, and we could predict with reasonable accuracy the expected return on an investment and when that return would be realized.

Enter Google. Now marketers have to worry about SEO rankings and monitor search ads, build strategies for social media, and on top of all this try to respond to an ever-changing algorithm constantly tweaked by Google. It's become much more difficult to predict what the outcome will be and when it will come from these digital channels.

The power has shifted. Buyers are now in control, powered by Google. They decide what to search, when to search, and what to click on. It's now on us marketers to ensure they find our companies and clients when they're searching, to interest them enough to spend time on our websites, and to convince them to begin a relationship.

Content Is the Heart of Inbound Marketing

Content is the heart of your inbound marketing program. It's how new people find your company from searches, it educates prospects and compels them to complete lead forms, and ultimately it builds trust between your business and your prospects and customers.

Unlike many other marketing activities, such as a trade show booth torn down at the end of a show or search advertising with benefits that end the second the money stops flowing, content lives on indefinitely. You face an up-front cost to create content, but through optimization and promotion, it can generate new interest and leads for years to come.

Marketing to a technical audience requires an understanding of the types of content engineers need and where, why, and how they look for and use this content throughout the buying cycle. At TREW Marketing, we have worked together with industry partners to research this and learn how engineers find, use, and engage with content. It is well known, for example, that high-quality, accurate content is important to attract technical target audiences and build trust and credibility. As already shared, the quantitative research we have done has reinforced hypotheses and provided enlightening new findings.

Engineers Prefer Companies Who Produce Content

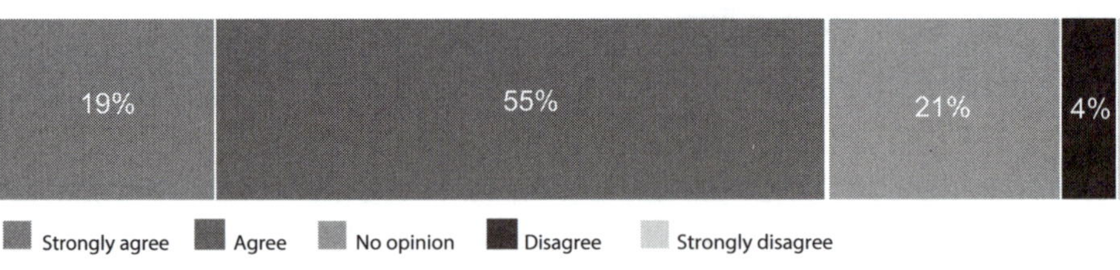

Marketing to Engineers 2014 Study

When prompted with "You are more likely to do business with a company that regularly produces new and current content", 74 percent of engineers agreed or strongly agreed.

As a reminder, in the Marketing to Engineers 2014 study by TREW Marketing and CFE Media, when asked where they go to find information to help them do their jobs, the more than 700 engineers who responded indicated they go to Google first (87 percent) followed by vendor websites (84 percent). More surprising was learning that nearly 75 percent of engineers are more likely to do business with a company that regularly produces new and current content.

➔ **Go to trewmarketing.com/smartmarketingforengineers to download the complete research studies referenced throughout this book.**

What types of content do engineers value most? We studied this, too, and found the four types of content engineers gave the highest ranking of "Very valuable" to are product information (55 percent), white papers (37 percent), case studies (30 percent), and webcasts/webinars (28 percent). These four types represent "on domain" content that lives on your website, and you control when, what, and how to create and promote it. You develop product information and write white papers, you develop application stories with your customers, and you produce webinars that go in-depth on specific topics of interest to your customer personas. Once you market that content, visitors find it through search and come to your website, i.e., your domain, to learn more.

If the value engineers place on regularly producing the four content types previously mentioned isn't enough encouragement for you to create and refresh that content, another study shows the value engineers place on vendor-created content over any other. In the Smart Marketing for Engineers 2015 study by TREW Marketing and ENGINEERING.com, when asked what content engineers trust the most, the top choice was content written or published by engineering experts at vendor companies. Based on this data, we know our technical customer personas value doing business with companies that produce high-quality content; they're searching for it on Google and vendors' websites; they prefer product information, white papers, case studies, and webcasts; and they trust it most when it comes from our engineering experts.

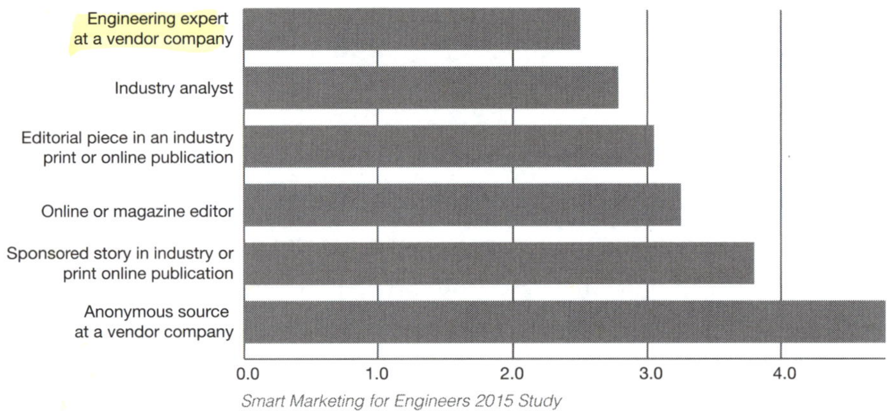

Engineers surveyed indicate they trust content written by an engineering expert at a vendor company above all others.

This data begs the question of whether you are committing enough time to content marketing. Is content at the center of your marketing program? Do you put as much or more of your budget into content marketing as you do trade show marketing, search engine optimization, or online advertising? Do technical subject matter experts (SMEs) in your company help develop content? To get the most out of your marketing program and effectively fuel growth, content MUST be at the heart of your marketing plans. It is through content that you will drive traffic, generate leads, and create qualified opportunities for sales.

A key reason why so many companies do not commit to high-quality content development is because it takes time to do well. To create content your technical customer personas value, and that is as good or better than the best content already available, you must ensure it is well written, technically accurate, informative, and trustworthy. You also need to make sure your competitors can't easily re-create it. The only way to achieve this is by committing completely to the highest quality and working with a select group of SMEs inside your company. Unfortunately, their time is incredibly valuable and in high demand.

The burden is on you, the marketer, to ensure that every minute of time these high-value resources spend on content is maximized. By building trust between marketing and SMEs, you ensure that the SMEs will be more likely to help you in the future. The best way to do this is three-fold:

1. Create a content plan along the funnel that maps to the buying cycle.
2. Make sure your content plan aligns with your campaigns and selected keywords.
3. Repurpose, repurpose, and repurpose to extend your investment.

Let's dive into the first two elements of content planning and the tools and processes you can use to develop the most efficient and effective approach. The next chapter covers the importance of repurposing and amplifying your content, or, put another way, treating your content like a product.

Mapping Content along the Buying Cycle

Engineers and scientists are searching for information throughout the entire buying cycle, from the initial research "awareness" stage at p of the funnel to the "opportunity" stage at the bottom, where they make a purchase decision.

Your plan should outline content that engages prospects throughout this funnel. To create this plan, start by mapping out content ideas that follow the marketing funnel. In the first column, include the campaign, product, service, industry, or audience persona. From section 1, you have the campaigns your team will focus on (chapter 2), your customer personas defined (chapter 3), and your keywords selected (chapter 4). Use this information to brainstorm content offerings you can develop for the top, middle, and bottom of the funnel.

Content Plan Along the Funnel

Product, Service, or Persona	Stage of Funnel	Offer	Call to Action
Product: vehicle simulation software	Top of the funnel	Vehicle simulation landing page	GM case study, demo video
	Middle of the funnel	Software demo video	GM case study, trial
	Bottom of the Funnel	30-day free trial	Contact us
Service: engine test stand integration	Top of the funnel	Guide to engine test	Lubrizol case study
	Middle of the funnel	Lubrizol case study	Getting Started video
	Bottom of the funnel	Getting Started video	Get a quote
Persona #1: automotive OEM owner	Top of the funnel	Ground transportation landing page	Ford case study
	Middle of the funnel	Ford case study	Services brochure
	Bottom of the funnel	Automotive services brochure	Contact us
Persona #2: automotive OEM chief engineer	Top of the funnel	Ground transportation landing page	Ford case study
	Middle of the funnel	Ford case study	Vehicle test systems white paper
	Bottom of the funnel	Vehicle test systems white paper	Talk to an engineer

Create a table like this one to map your content by campaign, product, persona, etc., along the funnel.

Use these questions to spark ideas:

- What tough questions do your customers consistently ask you?
- What are the top three or four current trends that are relevant to your products or services?
- What are common challenges you see customers face that you could explain to help others avoid, evaluate, or work through?
- What are the business risks associated with the application areas you work in and what can you share about how to mitigate these?
- What does your company do better than your competitors that your prospects need to know?
- What competitor weaknesses or gaps in the market can you educate your prospects about?
- What real-world examples can you share to illustrate your expertise?

As you brainstorm your content, be sure you have a variety of "free" and "gated" content. Free content is available to visitors without their completing a form, such as top-level web pages, case studies, blog posts, and news releases. Gated content is higher-value or premium content visitors can access only after completing a lead form, such as technical white papers, webinars, e-books, and software downloads.

For each stage of the funnel, identify an offer or a next content piece with a corresponding call to action (CTA). By doing this, you create a path for visitors to find your company, learn more by reading your free content, then select other content CTAs that may be free or gated, and continue this process of learning and engaging as they move down the funnel. We call this a closed-loop web experience, where you provide more content offers on each web page, blog post, and landing page that give users options to continue to learn more and stay on your site.

Let's walk through the vehicle simulation software product in the first row of the table above to see how it works. In the first row, the campaign is called "Vehicle simulation software." At the top of the funnel, the content offer is the main software landing page. You could add other free content to this list such as blog posts and product-related news releases as well as feature tables and screen shots.

The top of the funnel features two content CTAs. One is a free case study and the second is a gated software demonstration video. The video serves as the middle-of-the-funnel offer, the lead conversion content that compels visitors to move down the funnel by expressing further interest and a willingness to complete a form to learn more. In this example, the company has provided enough free content for visitors to learn about its software and dive in deeper with the software video. The two software video follow-on CTAs are another free case study and a gated 30-day software trial.

As you complete this table, you naturally find gaps in your paths. This tool helps you see where these gaps exist specifically, by campaign and/or by stage of the funnel. To fill these gaps and complete your content plan along the funnel, continue the brainstorming process from above, consult with your sales engineers, and go back to your keywords, persona pain points, and other related information to spark further ideas. Consider having an intern sit in on several new customer meetings and note topics that the customers were most interested in. Though you may think it's the same topic you talk about all the time, it may turn out to be a subject that many engineers and target customers struggle with.

If you are just starting out with content planning, the minimum annual content publishing output you should strive for to see results from your investment includes the following:

- Two customer-named case studies (or four unnamed case studies)
- Two pieces of gated content (e.g., white papers, e-books, webcasts, etc.)

- Three news releases
- 12 blog posts
- Four web pages, such as for products, services, etc.
- Four e-newsletters

As you brainstorm, consider a variety of media types. Remember, some people prefer written content such as blog posts and white papers while others are more visual and prefer images such as detailed block diagrams, infographics, or application photos. Still others want to watch short product demos or webcasts.

One of the toughest content challenges technical companies face is securing approval from customers to talk about how the company's products or services helped solve their problems. Four of the most common reasons for this are:

1. The salesperson does not want to ask the customer until the work is done or the product is fully in use, and then too much time goes by. The customer has moved on and it's too late to ask.

2. The customer won't allow you to share the application due to confidentiality reasons.

3. Your salesperson doesn't have the time or is not willing to ask the customer.

4. You can't get your customer to respond or take the time to help you.

Try these three tips to get around these hurdles:

1. **Interview Sales**—Consider interviewing your salesperson or engineer working on the account and write up a short (100- to 250-word) description of the application without naming the customer or including any confidential information. Though having a customer

name in your case study is ideal, especially if it's a large, recognizable company, it's equally compelling to have multiple unattributed application examples. There is power in numbers, and if the specifics of the challenge and solution are included, you can effectively establish credibility and prove your expertise without having to name the customer. Below are examples from ECS, a systems integrator in process manufacturing. ECS consumer brand clients often do not allow publication of their applications.

2. **Time the Ask**—Train your salespeople to ask for approval to publish a case study when their customer is asking something of them. For instance, maybe their customer is asking for a price discount or on-site training or out-of-scope support during installation. There's no better time to ask for something of them as when they're asking something of you. It gives your salespeople some ground to stand on and creates a fair exchange between parties. The next time a customer asks for a 10 percent discount, tell your salesperson to negotiate 5 percent plus a case study instead!

3. **Help Customers Promote**—Often your end customers are seeking visibility for their work and welcome partners publishing case studies about them. Seize the opportunity when your application is strategic to their company and they are seeking publicity about its success. Maybe your product is embedded in their product and they want partners or suppliers to talk about their technology and the importance of the end product. Maybe your customer's new manufacturing line is state of the art, and they want your company, which implemented the systems integration, and others who contributed to talk about the innovation inside. If you are working with government organizations, consortia, or academia, they will want to demonstrate tax dollars at work.

Unnamed Customer Case Study Examples

Bringing Process Control into the 21st Century

PLC-5 processors provided a great hardware solution for process control in their day, but faster, more adaptable technology has now made them obsolete. A $500 million food manufacturer in the southeastern United States recently engaged ECS to migrate its PLC-5-based soybean refinery operations to the newer ControlLogix platform. We teamed up with an industry-leading process systems builder to migrate the controller hardware and I/O points. In addition, the company followed our recommendation to upgrade the human-machine interface (HMI) software on operator terminals to achieve immediate improvements in network performance and reduce long-term support requirements.

Experience makes the difference in systems integrator selection

Our client isn't the only food manufacturing/refining company migrating a PLC-5-based operation to ControlLogix, and we're not the only systems integrator the company could have chosen for the project. But we won the business because of the faith the company's process systems builder had in ECS's Total Process Automation methodology, and because of our extensive experience and engineering resources. A 38-year history in process automation and a deep team of engineers put us in a strong position to respond quickly to meet the company's needs now as well as provide longer-term support for its rapidly growing operations.

Going above and beyond project requirements

One customer hired ECS to migrate the controls hardware and software, including PLC-5s and I/O, but we were able to do far more by implementing new HMI software. In addition to providing a redundant server solution and thin client operator terminals throughout strategic process areas, we upgraded the HMI component to the FactoryTalk View Site Edition (SE) client/server operator interface. This change in HMI provided a more comprehensive visualization of operations and eliminated intermittent networking errors the company had been experiencing.

A significant reduction in future support needs

The FactoryTalk View SE operator interface that ECS recommended has eliminated the need to support multiple isolated HMIs. As a result, the company's process control workstations will require less maintenance over the long term. The migration has also resulted in fewer unexpected alarms and shutdowns, which has in turn increased system availability and decreased support requirements. The company has contracted ECS repeatedly since the conclusion of the project to extend the new process control system to other areas of the company and expand the benefits of the system throughout its facilities.

Case studies from ECS Solutions, ecssolutions.com/case-studies

Content Calendars

With your content plan defined by campaign and stages of the funnel, an effective and easy-to-use tool to help you organize and prioritize your content creation is a content calendar. Created and managed simply in Microsoft Excel, a content calendar is broken down into the four quarters or 12 months of the calendar (or fiscal) year and defines the following:

- Channel
- Content type
- Topic

- Publish date
- Author
- Reviewer
- Audience persona
- Keyword(s)
- Sales funnel position

With your content mapped along the funnel and calendar developed with timing and authors assigned, you need to make sure the hard work of creating this high-quality content pays off by driving traffic to your website and generating leads via your gated content. The next chapter focuses on the importance of optimizing, amplifying, and repurposing your content to make sure each piece is developed with the best chance of being found when your prospects search.

Content Calendar Example

Channel	Content Type	Topic	Publish Date	Author	Reviewer	Audience Persona	Keywords	Sales Funnel Position
Blog	Blog	Greenfield vs brownfield data centers	Jan-15	Tim	Morgan	IT Managers	greenfield vs brownfield	Top
Blog	Blog	Announcing FEDC	Jan-15	Randy	Andrea	All	fiber cabling data center	Top
Blog	Infographic	Cross-promotion with TIA	Jan-15	Brad	Andrea	All	TIA in cabling	Top
Blog	Infographic	Splits options	Jan-15	Tim	Morgan	All	split cabling	Top
Blog	Blog	Operational: brownfield data centers	Apr-15	Tim	Morgan	Designer/Architect	brownfield data center cabling	Top
Blog	Blog	Operational: Greenfield data centers design	Apr-15	Nick	Johanna	Designer/Architect	greenfield data center design	Top
Blog CTA	Slide deck	FAB overview -- incorporating graphics from infographic/videos	Jan-15	John	Randy	All	use of data center cabling	Middle
Blog CTA	White paper	FAB overview	Jan-15	Brad	James	All	uses of data center cabling	Middle
Blog CTA	White paper	The state of data center footprints -- Greenfield vs Brownfield	Jul-15	Tim	Nick	IT Manager, Designer/Architect	data center footprints return on asset	Middle
Blog/Website	Video	Cabling management feature	Jan-15	Randy	Johanna	All	fiber cabling data center	Middle
Blog/Website CTA	Feature Graphic	CTA graphics (unlimited)	Jan-15	John	Randy	One for each persona	n/a	Top
Blog/Website CTA	Video	"How to improve your data center return on asset"	Feb-15	Nick	Johanna	IT Managers	data center return on asset	Middle
Blog/Website CTA	Video	Case study interview with customer	Feb-15	Randy	Andrea	IT Managers		Middle
Collateral	Feature Graphic	Product flyer graphics	Jan-15	Nick	Tim	All	n/a	Top
Social Media	Feature Graphic	Social media graphics (banners, profile pics, backgrounds)	Jan-15	Randy	Johanna	All	n/a	Top
Website	Case Study	American	Jan-15	John	James	IT Managers	uses of data center cabling	Middle
Website	Feature Graphic	Home page graphic B	Apr-15	Randy	Andrea	All		Top
Website	Feature Graphic	Home page graphic C	Jul-15	Nick	Tim	All		Top
Website	Webcast Series - 1	Feature 1	May-15	Tim	Morgan	IT Manager		Bottom
Website	Webcast Series - 2	Feature 1	Jul-15	Randy	James	Designer/Architect		Bottom
Website	Webcast Series - 4	Trends in fiber enclosures for greenfield data centers				All		Bottom

Use a content calendar to organize and track the completion of all your content by publish date, author, channel, keyword, etc.

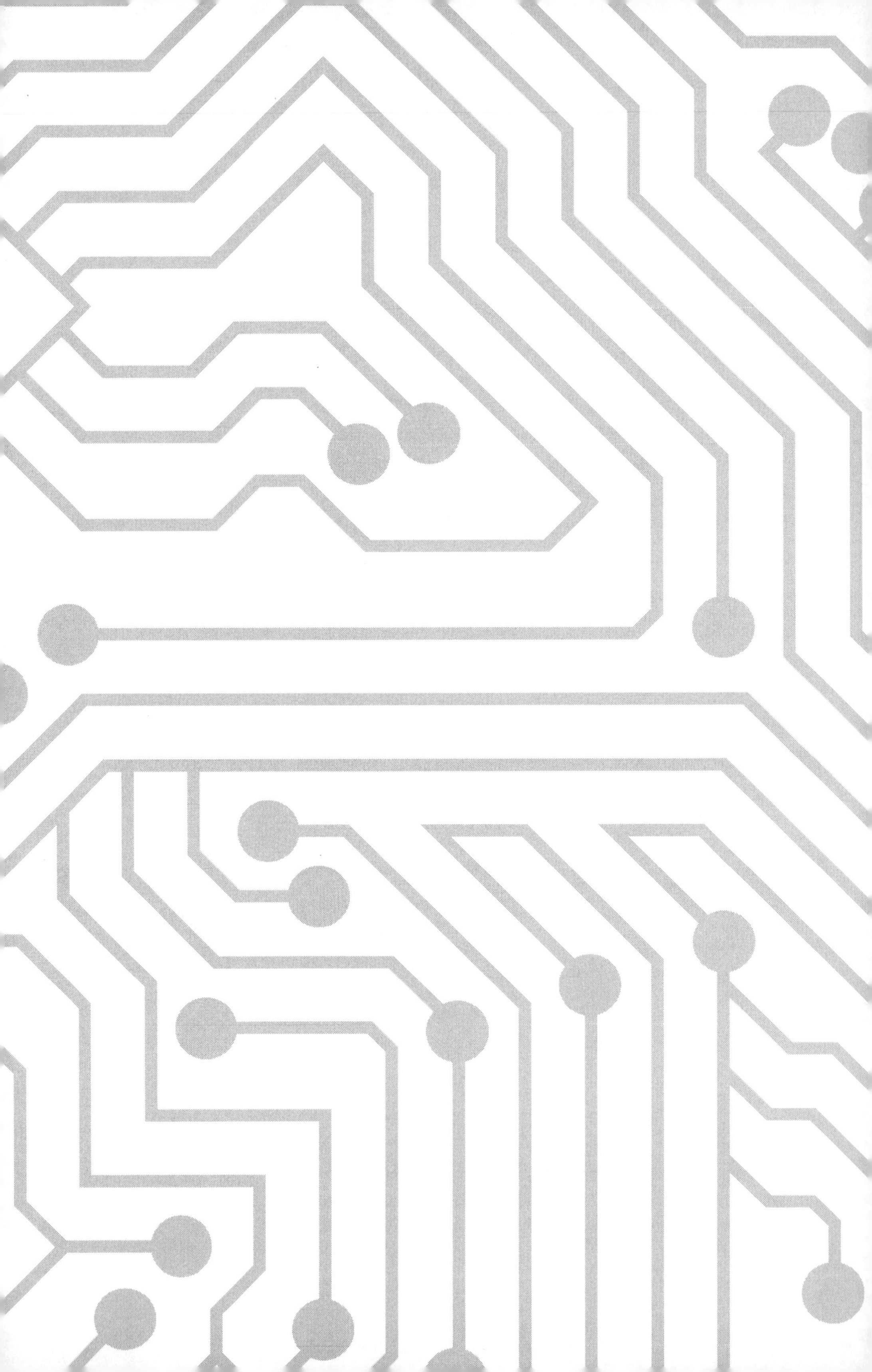

Chapter 7

TREAT YOUR CONTENT LIKE A PRODUCT

Optimize, Amplify, Repurpose, and Repeat

"Engineering-driven companies falsely assume that because they build it, the industry will magically become aware and be willing to buy it."

– Brian Lawley, author of The Phenomenal Product Manager, former President of the Silicon Valley Product Management Association

The chapter you just read, chapter 6, is one of the most important in this book. Content is the heart of inbound marketing. Content is king. Content is the fuel that drives modern marketing. No matter what outbound or inbound channels you're using—trade shows, web, email marketing, PR, social media—you can't expect a return for your efforts today without high-quality content being at the heart of that effort.

With your content plan now in place, you need to make sure your customer personas searching for your keywords, services, products, and expertise find your content instead of your competitors'. You need to treat your content like a new product, market it across multiple channels, and optimize it with the keywords to ensure it gets found.

Content marketing can be broken down into three steps: (1) optimize, (2) amplify, and (3) repurpose. You should repeat these steps with all content you create, so that over time you rank higher and higher in Google for the keywords you most care about, your web traffic increases, your leads grow, and your marketing program generates a consistent and predictable level of awareness and demand for your business.

Step 1: Optimize Your Content

The immense and growing competition on search engines today is illustrated by the number of searches and pages indexed on Google. In just six years, from 2008 to 2014, the number of daily Google searches more than tripled, from 1.75 billion to nearly 6 billion. That translates to 3,986,111 searches per minute. That's 66,444 searches per second. In this same time period, the number of pages indexed by Google increased by over 500 percent, from 11 billion to 67 billion. If that's not competition, I don't know what is! Don't be discouraged by this data, though. The good news is that you don't want all these billions of people to find your company; you want only your targeted customer personas to find you through the specific content that is most relevant to your business. To do this, you need to optimize your content for those people.

This is where the good news continues. First, you already have the keywords you selected in chapter 4, so you know the words and phrases you want to get found on. Second, we know engineers will go much deeper in Google to find the specific information they are seeking. So, if you create high-quality technical content, treat it like a product and use content marketing best practices. Over time, you have a good chance of your personas finding it.

You need to follow a series of steps to optimize your content on your website, from the elements of the web page where you promote the piece to the elements in the piece itself, including the title, body content, and PDF document properties. Though SEO techniques are always changing and Google and other search engines are always tweaking the weight placed on different aspects, certain elements of your website are critical to optimizing your keywords. Google spiders look for these elements as they crawl a site or web page, and they greatly impact your SEO performance. Additionally, pay attention to the formatting suggestions below to further optimize your elements.

- Meta description
  - Use keywords as close to the beginning of your meta description as possible
- Heading text
  - Include keywords in header tags that match your content
  - Always include an H1 tag
  - Bold heading text for a better user experience
- Links
  - Use internal links to link pages on your website with the same keyword
  - Use external links to link pages on your website to pages on other credible websites with the same keyword
  - Include keywords in your link anchor text
- Page titles and page URLs
  - Keep keywords to the far left
  - Stay under 60 characters (including spaces) for both title and URL length
  - Use specific, long-tail terms
- Text formatting
  - Use bullets
  - Bold where appropriate
  - Italicize where appropriate

- Images
  - Match your image to your content
  - Include keywords in the image alt text
  - Use keywords in the anchor text for linkable images
- Navigation
  - Consider keywords in navigation headings

These optimization elements have remained mostly constant through the years of the ever-changing Google and SEO scene, albeit with variations in priority. To stay abreast of SEO best practices and search engine algorithm changes, I recommend visiting these sites regularly:

- Moz[1]
- TREW Smart Marketing Blog[2]
- Google Webmaster Central Blog[3]
- HubSpot Marketing Blog[4]

As mentioned in chapter 4, where I described SEO for People, Google's ranking algorithm is developed with its customers in mind, not your website. Remember this as you consider SEO performance; it's more than just the elements of content and website optimization listed above. It's also how you present your content, such as how easy it is for searchers to find what they need and, once they find it, how pleasant the user experience is across platforms (on mobile, for example).

By incorporating the elements above, staying abreast of the constantly changing best practices, and keeping SEO for People in mind, you will be on the right track to seeing the SEO results you want.

---

[1] moz.com
[2] trewmarketing.com/smartmarketingblog
[3] googlewebmastercentral.blogspot.com
[4] blog.hubspot.com

Step 2: Amplify Your Content

We know from physics that energy and amplitude are related. As stated on physicsclassroom.com, "The amount of energy carried by a wave is related to the amplitude of the wave. A high-energy wave is characterized by high amplitude; a low energy wave is characterized by low amplitude."

Applying this physics analogy to content marketing means you need to add energy to your content to make each and every piece a high-energy wave with high amplitude. Two optimal channels to amplify your content are blogging and social media.

The Amplitude of a Wave Is Related to the Energy That It Transports

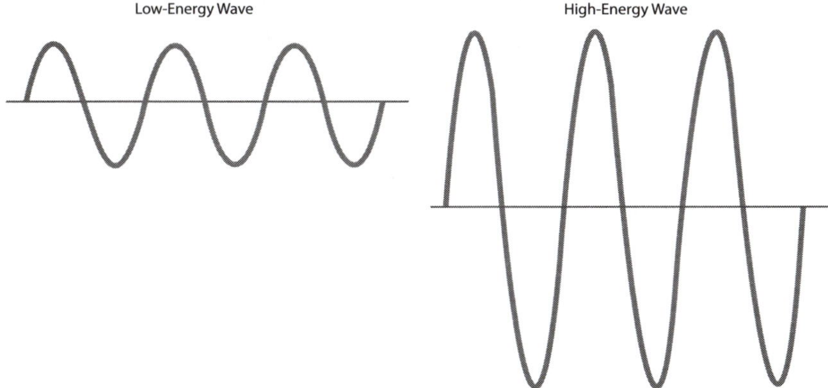

Just as more energy in a wave increases its amplitude in physics, amplifying your content through more channels and cross-promotion drives increased awareness and traffic.

Blogs

According to marketing automation company HubSpot, B2B companies that blog generate 67 more leads per month than those that do not.[5] By blogging about your new content and including links to your free and gated content throughout your posts, you amplify your content and drive awareness of your company among your customer personas. When aligned with your keywords and content-along-the-funnel plan, your growing indexed blog pages become a major online highway to your company.

Companies That Blog Generate More Leads

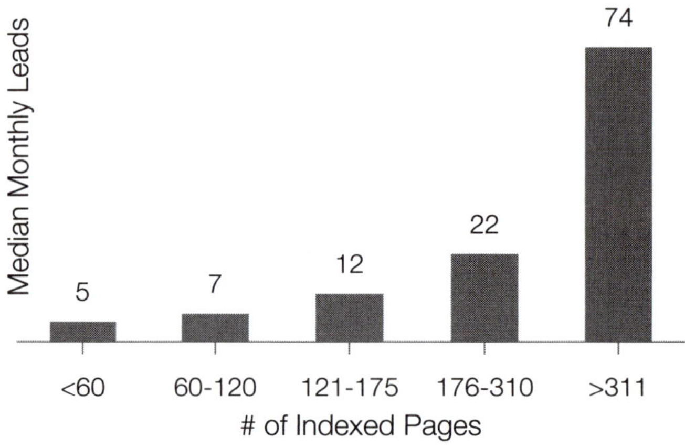

HubSpot State of Inbound Marketing Lead Generation Report

Studies like this one from HubSpot show companies that blog generate more leads than those that don't.

Most small- to medium-sized businesses don't often add new web pages once a website redesign goes live. Product companies will create new pages when products are introduced, but new page creation is much less frequent between product launches. For services companies, new pages are almost non-existent since service offerings

[5] cdn2.hubspot.net/hub/53/docs/resellers/reports/state_of_inbound_marketing.pdf

rarely change, and new pages are limited primarily to news, awards, certifications, etc. When a site becomes stagnant, Google crawls it less often since its spiders see the same content repeatedly with no change. The easiest path to consistently increase the number of your indexed pages is through blogging, and that's just one of the benefits of this amplification channel.

Many companies don't start a blog because of the necessary time commitment or because they just don't believe it has value. Business leaders and engineers often see blogging as a waste of precious time that could be devoted to product or service delivery, new business development, and many other business demands. They believe blogging will be ineffective and get lost in the information overload of the Internet. This could not be further from the truth.

As an example, take my company, TREW Marketing, a marketing services firm targeting three primary personas, two of which are

Case Study: Increased Blogging Drives 400% Growth in Leads

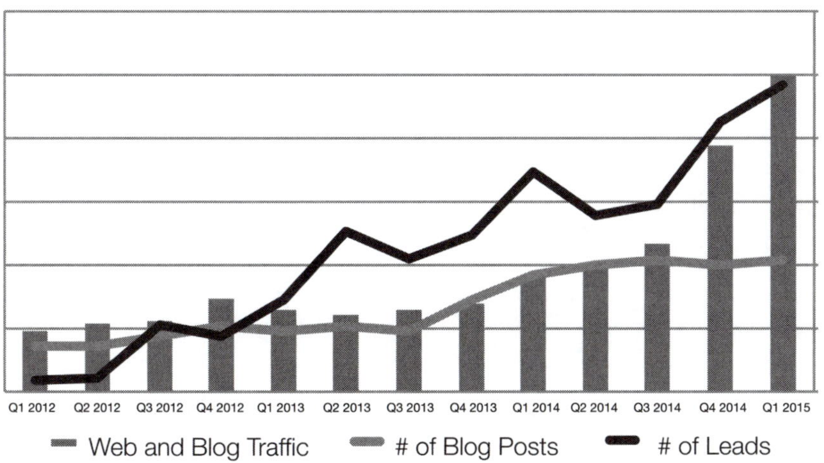

TREW Marketing doubled blog frequency and, as a result, traffic quadrupled and leads tripled.

degreed engineers or scientists responsible for marketing at their companies. When the business first started, we could commit to only two posts a month. After three years, the team began blogging weekly, and the results could not be ignored: the increased frequency of blog posts directly correlated with an increase in website traffic and leads. More and more prospects now find the company's website through the blog. With such proven success, a year later, TREW doubled the frequency of posts again to twice per week. As a result of doubling blog posting frequency, traffic has quadrupled and leads have tripled.

The reason blogs are such an effective amplifier is because they deliver fresh content regularly. This attracts:

- Search engines because each post represents another page that can be indexed for a specific topic or keyword and fed to others searching that phrase
- Prospects because it helps them learn from you and understand what your customers do
- Customers because it helps them stay up to date with product or service offerings and strengthens their perception of you as a thought leader and expert in the specific areas they care about

Your blog can direct traffic to specific content and other parts of your website so prospects can find even more information including products, services, case studies, and white papers. By coming to your blog and clicking on links in your posts, leads proceed down your marketing funnel at their own pace, and you serve up more and more content at each new page.

For example, when you have a new white paper, blog about it by sharing some of what's inside, and point to the landing page where a reader can get more information and download it. Share your company news on your blog and include links to relevant content such as case studies or videos. You can even repackage a series of blog posts into a gated piece of content that serves as a middle-of-the-funnel CTA to use in other channels such as an e-newsletter or sales follow-up.

In the past, a primary method of building thought leadership and awareness with a targeted audience was through coverage of your company in technical trade publications. However, with the consolidation of print media and one editor doing the job many used to do, it has become more and more difficult to garner press coverage. Though successful technical industry journals still publish in print and online today, and though investing in PR to build relationships and secure coverage for your company is likely a sound investment, with a blog, you can publish on your terms about the topics you deem important and relevant, with your keywords embedded. You essentially become your own publisher, posting content that educates your prospects and shows them that you understand the challenges they face while providing valuable solutions for their applications. It also is a generous way to help prospects and the larger community learn from you. This builds trust, which is the cornerstone of any relationship.

If this is not proof enough, another reason to blog is because engineers have told us they trust content from engineering experts more than any other type of author (discussed in chapter 6). Engineers want to hear from engineers, and a great way to share your knowledge and build trust with your target personas is through your own blog.

To engage your readers and subscribers and provide fresh content for the Google spiders to crawl and index, you should blog at least once a month and more frequently if possible. As you saw with the earlier example, the more frequently you blog, the more pages you'll have indexed with search engines, which improves the chances you'll be found and see steady and increasing traffic and leads.

> **"Search engines have used links as votes—representing the democracy of the Web's opinion about what pages are important and popular."**
>
> **– Moz, SEO Service Provider and Thought-Leading Website**

Another powerful result of blogging is the backlink traffic you gain when others link back to your content. Critical to strengthening your SEO performance, backlinks are created in two primary ways. The first is guest blogging, where you or others at the company write a blog for another site to offer expertise, insights, and opinions. When you post on other blogs with links back to your site, not only do search engines give you more popularity points, but you expand your audience of readers by writing on other relevant blogs that also attract your customer personas. The second way is to invite experts outside your company to be guest authors on your blog. Their loyal readers will likely visit your site to see what their familiar author penned and become engaged with your content if they find it relevant and helpful. Guest bloggers will also link to their post on your site from their websites and social media pages, which drives further backlinks to your site from theirs.

Social Media

The second optimal channel to use to amplify your content is social media. For many technical business leaders, social media is near the bottom of the marketing priority list, right along with blogging. They can't justify the time and don't understand how much the value of social media has increased since Mark Zuckerberg created Facebook for other college students in his Harvard dorm room. They don't invest in social media because with the many options available, they don't know where to start. Social media channels like YouTube and Vine are dedicated to video, Pinterest and Instagram are for pictures and photos, Google+ and Twitter are for microblogging, and LinkedIn got its start as a site for job seekers and finders.

Though the value of social media is measured by many aspects, first and foremost, it is an engine for links back to your site. SEO experts like Moz (moz.com) have been studying and sharing best practices for years on the power that links pointing back to your site have on your SEO performance. Matt Cutts, a long-time Google insider, writes a popular blog (mattcutts.com/blog) to frequently share insights on Google and SEO. Links from other sites back to your site indicate to Google that other relevant sites believe your content is valuable. By distributing your content on popular social media platforms like LinkedIn and Twitter, you expand the number of people seeing your content and, in turn, the likelihood more people will link back to the content on their social media and other online platforms. This happens through messages such as retweets on Twitter or posts on LinkedIn.

I mentioned earlier that a benefit of guest blogging is the links back to your site. Though these backlinks boost your popularity on Google, and you should try to do this as often as possible, they take time and therefore occur less frequently. By complementing your less frequent, more time-consuming guest blogging efforts with frequent, quick amplification of your content and your company on the most effective social media sites, you cast a much wider net to grow your visibility and potential for backlinks. Also, social media is in your control. Just like blogging on your site, you can post on topics most relevant to your company, using your keywords, as often as you choose. Additionally, because this channel is social by nature, you can engage with specific audiences to target your efforts.

In the B2B marketplace, the use of social media is quickly gaining momentum. In a 2015 study by the Content Marketing Institute

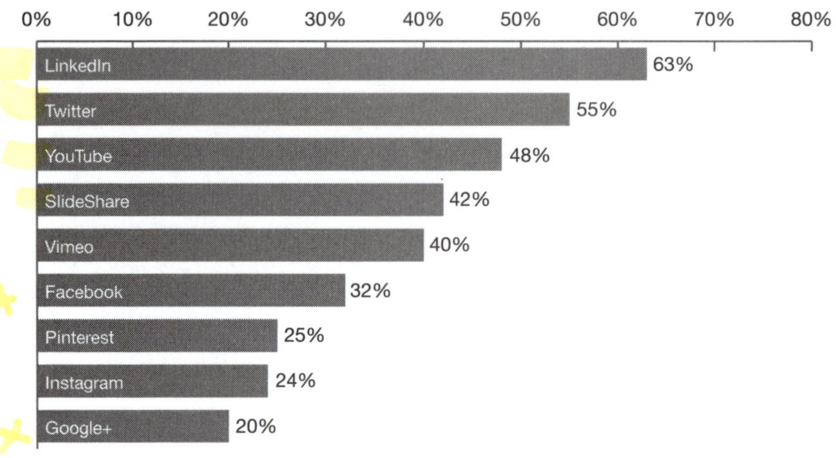

2015 B2B Content Marketing Benchmarks, Budgets, and Trends—North America

B2B marketers said LinkedIn and Twitter are the most effective social media platforms and Google+ was the least effective.

and MarketingProfs[6], marketers said they use an average of six social media platforms, leading with LinkedIn and Twitter. The same study also asked about social media platform effectiveness, and, again, LinkedIn and Twitter ranked highest. In looking at engineers' use of social media specifically, according to a study by CALGAVIN[7] released in 2013, the No. 1 reason engineers use social media is for learning. This is followed by their use of social media to find products and white papers. Specifically looking at finding new products, the number of engineers using social media for this purpose more than doubled from 2012 to 2013.

You don't have to post your content on all the popular social media sites. It's better to amplify and engage on a few than to have many set up and ignore most of them. If you have to start with one, that's OK. Start with LinkedIn and expand to Twitter when you're ready.

[6] contentmarketinginstitute.com/wp-content/uploads/2014/10/2015_B2B_Research.pdf
[7] calgavin.com/2013/01/engineering-social-media-survey/

The first step with each of these channels is to make sure they look as polished as possible by including your corporate logo and brand colors, completing the About Us section, and adding appropriate contact information. The images and text should match those on your website.

To attract your target audience, you need to get connected with others. For LinkedIn, start by connecting with company employees, business partners, vendors, and customers. For Twitter, search your industry hashtags, or keywords, using the Twitter search field, and follow relevant users in the technical community who are likely to follow you back.

Once the social media foundation is set, a company may let the accounts sit silent for months because next steps are unclear. Remember the goal is to be found, so staying active and intentional drives the best results. Part of being intentional is keeping in mind that the tone and audience for each platform varies, so you'll want to customize your posts for each platform.

For instance, your posts on LinkedIn should be mostly professional and educational in nature, and include links to your website to read more. For Twitter, you only have 140 characters so using shorthand words and symbols is accepted along with a friendlier, more casual tone. On Facebook, focus your posts on events, interesting pictures, and stories or insights on your company culture and milestones. Decide on a frequency you believe you can stick to, and develop a weekly posting plan with topics while keeping keywords in mind. Start small with a few posts daily (or even weekly) and increase the frequency once the processes are in place. Map out content for the first month, measure it, analyze it, and then find ways to improve for the next month. Include posts on industry topics that are trending, your new or existing content, upcoming trade shows or events, and blog posts. For example, once you have created content such as news releases, case studies, videos, and new web pages, use social media to amplify that content to your target audiences. For events such as industry trade shows, plan tweets announcing your booth demos, important news, or product launches. Consider what attendees will want to hear, monitor the event hashtag to see what others are posting about, follow and engage with the media who are attending, and add to the conversation with relevant information.

With social media, you can't sit back and be silent; that will not help you get found. Rather, chime in by retweeting, favoriting, or commenting on conversations and topics for which you are an expert and on which you have opinions. It is social media after all—the value is in the sharing and the conversation. And when appropriate, provide social media users with additional information about your site or blog where you discuss a topic in more detail. For technical companies, having engineers serve as advisers for the social media plan is helpful because they can provide specific answers to technical questions and watch for certain topics being discussed that your company should have a voice in.

Many larger companies dedicate a percentage of an engineer's (or engineering team's) time to addressing technical questions/comments that come through social media. This interaction both addresses customer needs in an efficient, quick-response manner and humanizes the company by making customers feel less like they're dealing with a large corporation.

Remember, people who ask questions through social channels expect immediate answers, so consider using free tools like TweetDeck or marketing automation software to help you monitor and stay on top of the social conversations. You can also take advantage of a growing set of low-cost tools like ManageFlitter to efficiently build a following and Social Oomph to efficiently schedule posts, track keywords, and manage engagement such as @mentions and retweets.

I discuss marketing measurement in chapter 12, but I include specific metrics for social media here because there is more confusion about ROI for this channel than others. You can use many metrics to measure the effectiveness of social media, but below are the most important ones:

- Interest shown through clicks on the stories you post
- Engagement measured by retweets (RTs), likes, comments, and shares, which amplify your social media message, almost like a personal referral for your company
- Reach based on the number of friends, followers, and subscribers your social media channel has
- Traffic from social media posts to your website, providing insight into which social media sites your visitors are most often coming from and how effective your posts, content, use of hashtags, and images are on the various social media outlets
- Time on site from traffic that comes from social media to see how interested those social media visitors are in your offerings versus visitors from other sources
- Customer retention and advocacy if you use your social media account for technical support; measured by the number of support questions your company addressed on social media

Based on the data you collect, you can adjust your strategy to concentrate on one social media channel over another, reduce resources, switch up CTAs where needed, modify your tone or approach for a particular site, and encourage employees to maintain and expand their own social networks to further amplify the company and its content.

If your company is not already leveraging blogging and social media to amplify content, you are missing traffic and lead opportunities and run the risk of being left behind while your competitors become stronger. If you have to pick one to start with, prioritize blogging. It will drive much greater traffic, and you need blogging, and content, before you can further amplify and engage on social media.

A final, very important channel for amplifying your content is email marketing, including segmented email marketing and e-newsletters. These are so important that I've dedicated an entire chapter to them (chapter 10).

Step 3: Repurpose and Repeat

High-quality content takes time to create, and when you treat that content like a product and put a marketing plan around it, it becomes what I like to call a content annuity: the gift that keeps on giving for years to come. With the significant investment of time required to create a white paper or webcast, for example, it's not enough to share it on a few LinkedIn groups, write a blog post about it, or email your database once or twice. With this minimal effort, you cannot compete in the Google universe with billions of new indexed pages going live each year. Moreover, you get minimal return on your investment by using it only once or twice, and you leave the door wide open for your competitors to be found by your customer personas before you are.

By adopting the approach of treating your content like a product, for which you repurpose the original content into many different formats and amplify it across multiple channels, you maximize your investment and greatly increase your SEO performance. One piece of well-written, well-placed content can have multiple uses and surprising longevity. For example, writing a 2,000-word white paper is approximately a 25- to 35-hour project and includes a marketing writer partnered with your subject-matter technical expert. The project may take up to two months to complete, from initial brainstorming and research to writing several drafts to creating images or taking new photos to finalizing it through multiple reviews to ensure readability and accuracy.

If you simply publish this white paper on your website, share it over the next week or two, and then leave it alone, your ongoing investment will give you a return of a small surge of activity and then quickly dissipate. Why? Because in the two weeks of minimal effort you made to market that new white paper, Google indexed a staggering 2 billion, 576 million, 923 thousand, and 80 web pages (yes, that is how many new pages are added to the Internet in a two-week time period). This is a losing strategy.

All that work and investment will be wasted because the competition is intense. You can't stop there; you have to beat the drum and repurpose the content across formats and different types of media. For instance, turn your 2,000-word white paper into a three-part blog series with a CTA at the end of each post to drive people to the full white paper. These posts could be 300 to 500 words each pulled largely from the gated white paper. In this way, your blog serves to whet the appetite of the web visitor with high-quality technical content that took you only a short time to re-create. By offering a small portion of the white paper for free on your blog, your visitor doesn't have to commit to completing a lead form up front. Instead, you offer valuable information showing off your engineers' expertise, strengthening your company as a go-to resource for valuable information all while improving your SEO.

On your social media channels, you can create 15 to 20 posts or tweets for the first couple of months with key sound bites from the full paper. Then, continue to amplify via your blog and social media throughout the next year. Turn your white paper into a pared down PowerPoint presentation, post the presentation on SlideShare, and link to the landing page for the full paper. Feature it in your next e-newsletter and create a segmented email marketing campaign to a small portion of your database that specifically cares about your white paper topic. Find relevant blogs or partner sites where you can guest blog about the topic with a CTA pointing back to your white paper for further reading.

I'm just getting started with the ideas for repurposing. You can also turn the content of the white paper into a video, webinar, and/or presentation with tags and metadata that search engines will see. You can post these on your website as well as on social media channels such as YouTube or SlideShare for further amplification. You can bundle your content with other relevant content on the same subject and create a separate CTA that is a "getting started kit" or "knowledgebase pack" for that industry or application area.

The ideas for repurposing this 25-hour investment in a white paper are almost endless. Just as a product launch plan doesn't stop with the news release but rather spans a year or more, your content marketing plan needs must include repurposing to give each piece new life and maximum return in the form of traffic and leads.

And repurposing is not limited to content on your site. For example, consider an in-depth, highly technical contributed article published in a publication by an expert engineer at your company. You can turn this piece into a gated white paper with a lead form to generate leads (with sufficient modification of the published version), promote it in the company's e-newsletter, turn it into multiple blog posts, amplify it via LinkedIn and other social media outlets, and turn it into a presentation for a technical industry conference. By leveraging this high-value effort by an expert engineer on the research and development team in one country, you can treat the content like a product and extend its life and global reach across channels over time to help the company get found and convert leads. More importantly, the repurposed content creation and promotion effort can be done in a fraction of the time required to create this content from scratch since it was all leveraged from the original piece.

A note of caution about repurposing: By repurposing, I do not mean duplicating. If you simply duplicate content across web pages and on your blog, Google will, at a minimum, direct traffic to the page it deems to be the most authentic original page and ignore the others. In the worst-case scenario, if Google perceives the content to be intentionally and deceptively duplicated, your site may be removed from search results. A common scenario that is not deceptive, but that requires caution when implementing, is when you want to repost content from another site to yours. For instance, if you guest blog on an external site, such as another vendor or publication, and you want to publish that same, or very similar post, on your site, that is acceptable, but Google recommends using what is called canonical URLs.[8] The opposite is true if another site wants to repost content originating from your site. When reposting content that is the same, or very similar, be sure to follow Google best practices to ensure you don't unintentionally hurt your SEO performance.

By treating your content like a product through optimization, amplification, and repurposing, you will greatly increase your chances of beating your competitors on Google and turn your single pieces of content into content annuities that deliver maximum return through high-quality traffic and leads on your site.

[8] support.google.com/webmasters/answer/139066?hl=en

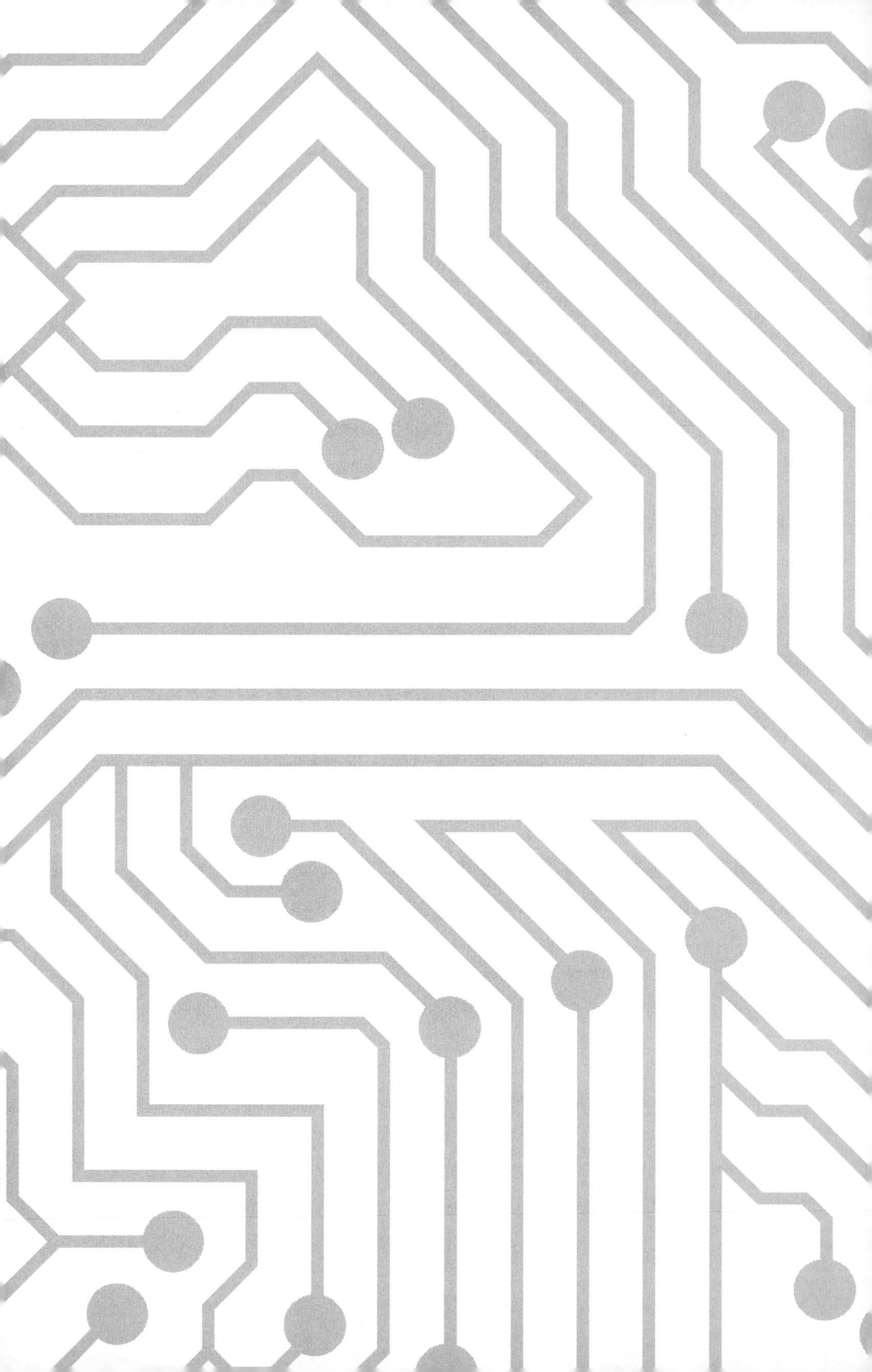

Chapter 8

CREATE HIGH-QUALITY TECHNICAL CONTENT

Top 4 (+1) Content Types Engineers Prefer

"What we usually consider as impossible are simply engineering problems... there's no law of physics preventing them."

– Michio Kaku, Physicist

Highly skilled, educated engineers are masters at seeing through fluff, finding inaccuracies, and separating good from great content. As content creators, however, most engineers lack confidence in their writing and persuasive communication abilities or in their ability to create high-quality content. Engineering schools do not provide much writing training. In fact, of the 125 credit hours required to receive a four-year degree in electrical and computer engineering at The University of Texas Cockrell School of Engineering, students spend only up to 4 percent of their time in a writing-related class.

Therefore, I thought I needed to include a chapter dedicated to content development best practices and tips based on my 20+ years of experience creating, reviewing, editing, and marketing highly technical content targeted to engineers and scientists. In this chapter, I will discuss research-based findings on what engineers care most about in their content and give practical information on how to develop the preferred content types.

Engineers are creative, observant, and analytical. They have a high bar for quality, and, when it comes to marketing, they are often quick to scrutinize design and words. They don't want gimmicky slogans but proven fact. Their trust of companies that provide concise and objective content that includes sufficient, credible data and supporting imagery will grow over time and help them take action or move forward in their research. Fact-based, straightforward analysis that directly relates to and aligns with a specific challenge makes up the most effective content you can provide your technical audiences.

However, the top challenge I hear about when working with technology companies is finding the time and talent to produce content their target audiences will engage with and trust. This was reinforced in the same 2015 B2B Content Marketing Study by the Content Marketing Institute and MarketingProfs referenced in the last chapter. Across industries, producing engaging content is marketers' top challenge with 54 percent of respondents rating this a

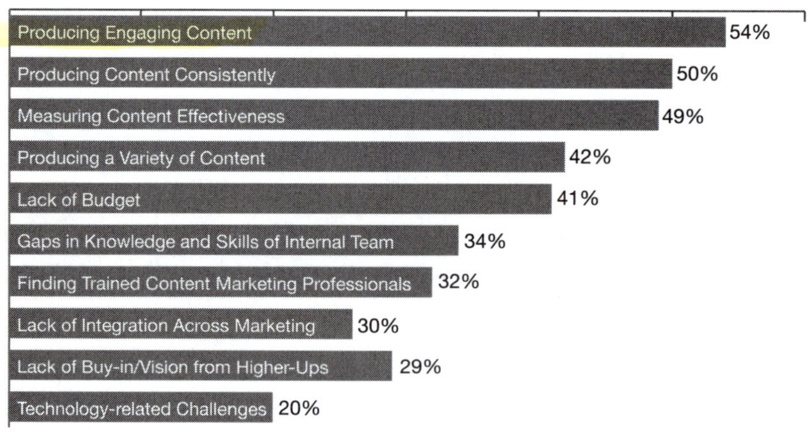

The top challenge of B2B marketers over the past five years has remained producing engaging content.

four or five, with five representing "Very Challenged." For marketers targeting skeptical engineering audiences with high expectations for technically dense and accurate content, producing engaging content becomes exponentially more challenging. The next biggest challenge is producing this engaging content not just a few times but on a consistent basis.

> *For marketers targeting skeptical engineering audiences with high expectations for technically dense and accurate content, producing engaging content becomes exponentially more challenging.*

Other research, however, gives insight into how marketers can overcome these challenges and succeed when producing content targeted to engineers. As I shared earlier, an encouraging finding from the Marketing to Engineers 2014 study by TREW Marketing and CFE Media showed that engineers will go many pages deeper than the average searcher on Google to find the information they need. A

Most Important Aspects of Content to Engineers

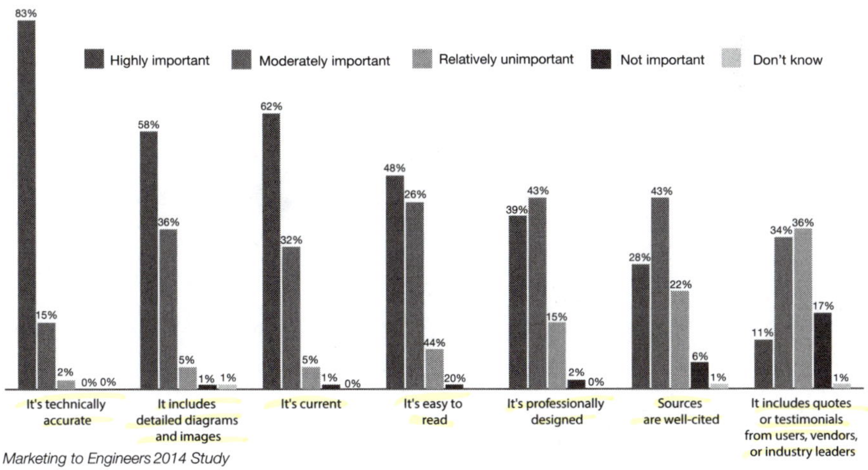

Marketing to Engineers 2014 Study

The three most important aspects of content that engineers look for are technical accuracy, detailed diagrams and images, and current information.

second encouraging finding showed that nearly 75 percent of engineers are more likely to do business with a company that regularly produces new and current content. To take it a step further, the study asked what aspects of content are most important to engineers. Respondents said the most important aspect is that it's technically accurate with the next most important aspect being that the content includes current information with detailed diagrams and images.

From this data, we can conclude that engineers will search relentlessly to find high-value content, they are more likely to do business with companies that are regularly producing new and current content, and they value content that is technically accurate and current and that includes images and diagrams. So the data shows that marketers' biggest challenge is producing engaging content and doing it consistently. For marketers targeting technical audiences, this data helps justify the importance of investing in content and directs our efforts toward producing the content engineers most value.

➔ **Download all the studies mentioned throughout the book at trewmarketing.com/smartmarketingforengineers.**

The next challenge, though, is knowing what type of content to produce. As discussed in chapter 6, from this same study, the content types engineers gave the highest ranking of "Very valuable" to are product information (55 percent), white papers (37 percent), case studies (30 percent), webcasts/webinars (28 percent,) and videos (23–26 percent). These five types represent "on domain" content that lives on your website, and you control when, what, and how to create and promote it. You develop product information and write white papers, you develop application stories with your customers, and you produce webinars and videos that go in depth on specific topics of interest to your customer personas.

Content Types Engineers Value Most

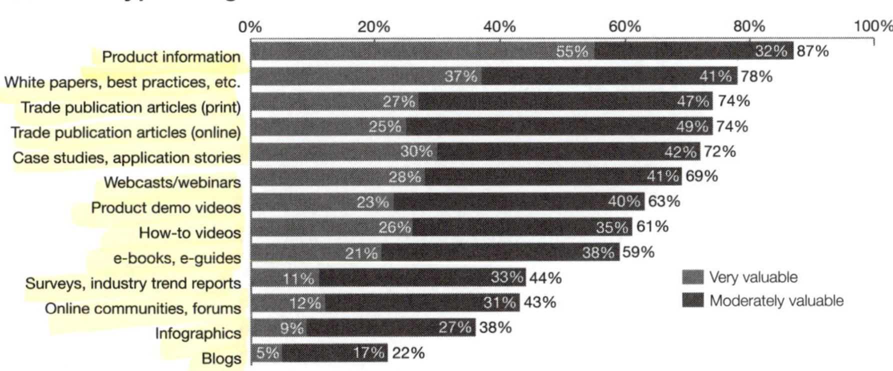

Marketing to Engineers 2014 Study

In looking at content types engineers said were "Very valuable," the highest ratings went to product information, white papers, case studies, webcasts, and videos.

Let's take an in-depth look at four of the more challenging content types of these five engineers say they prefer. As a bonus, I also discuss the development of a core presentation, which is critical to ensuring your company, products and services are presented consistently.

1. White papers

2. Webcasts

3. Case studies

4. Videos—product and how-to

5. Core presentation

Although product information was the top preferred type, I don't include it here since most engineers are comfortable creating data sheets and specifications material. Though not all of these content types are written documents, per se, they all require the same creative organization that is core to any writing project.

Access example white papers, case studies, videos, and other content types discussed here at trewmarketing.com/smartmarketingforengineers to help you create your own.

White Papers

White papers are a valuable source of technical content for your audience that can position you as an expert in a specific field. They are engineers' most preferred content type, preceded only by product information. Unlike general marketing content, white papers include a deep level of technical detail and may also include how-to guides, visual diagrams, and even mathematical formulas about a relevant industry issue, product feature, or technical subject. White papers are one of the most common lead-generating sources of content for technical companies, and engineers expect to complete a lead form to access them. I'll discuss lead forms in more detail in chapter 9.

The following seven steps can help you write a high-quality white paper.

1. Outline your content.

To make sure you provide adequate detail for your white paper, outline your content first, including the following recommended sections:

- **Introduction**—Briefly define the topic.
- **Challenge**—Describe the reader's pain points.
- **Overview**—Summarize what the paper will cover and define key terms.
- **Body**—Discuss the industry issue, technology, or product feature, including your solution or resolution to the challenge and related benefits. Include quantifiable expected results, if applicable.

- **Call to Action**—Clarify what you want your reader to do next. Examples include watching a video, visiting specific areas of your website, or requesting a product demo.

As you're outlining your white paper, keep in mind that the final length should be between 1,500 and 2,500 words.

2. Include images.

When asked to rank the importance of different aspects of technical content, engineers listed "detailed diagrams and images" as the second most important aspect behind technical accuracy. Spending time selecting or creating new images for your white paper is time well spent. Using graphics helps a reader visualize what you are explaining. For a white paper on an industry topic, you may want to use graphs or charts; for a white paper on a product or technology, use models, diagrams, or screen shots to illustrate your points. Aim to include five to eight images with captions.

3. Wait for your pitch.

If you are writing a white paper about an industry trend or a technical subject, you may be tempted to quickly dive in and explain how your company or product can address the topic. Wait until the end of your white paper to mention your products or services, and do it in general terms rather than with a direct sales approach. This way, you successfully establish your expertise and develop the need for your product or service before you introduce it.

4. Review your work.

Take a break and read your draft when you return. Think about your audience members and how they approach your content. If they aren't familiar with the technology you reference, make sure you address it thoroughly at the beginning of the paper. If your audience likely knows a lot about the subject, don't labor over unnecessary details.

To edit your content, read it backward: read the last sentence, then the second-to-last sentence, and so on. This is a tedious process, but it can help you catch missing or superfluous commas and spelling errors because you are able to read for grammar and punctuation without your mind jumping through the ideas and flow of the paper. Throughout the content creation process, from outline to final product, have one to two other subject-matter experts as well as an outside writer or editor review it. It's always best to have a few more pairs of eyes to provide an outside perspective.

5. Give it curb appeal.

Engineers like to read clean, well-designed content. Don't forget to give the white paper a design that makes it inviting to read, and be sure it is branded according to your company style guide (see sidebar "Why You Need a Style Guide").

6. Use your content.

Once you've written your white paper, make it work for you by using it as a CTA for other marketing activities. For example, you can link a white paper that explains how to use a specific product feature on that product's web page. This shows customers that you can provide more expertise in specific technical areas such as a product feature, industry trend, or technical process.

7. Study others.

If you need further inspiration, read white papers from the technical companies you admire and trust most. See how they write and present a topic and work in their services or products, and note the images they use and how they have designed their papers. On this book's web page (trewmarketing.com/smartmarketingforengineers), you can access examples of well-written and well-designed white papers to reference as you create your own.

Customer Case Studies

Case studies are one of the most preferred content types in the survey, along with product information, white papers, and trade press articles. Engineers want to hear how others have benefited from using your products and services. Case studies not only improve the sales process by reducing perceived risk but also allow customers to help tell your story.

The following five tips can help you efficiently secure and effectively maximize your customer case studies.

1. Prioritize the most impactful case studies.

Anyone who has worked on case studies knows they take time—time to get a customer to agree to the project, time to develop the content, time to review, and time to approve, which is often the longest step. With this time investment, you need to prioritize those case studies that will have the biggest influence on your target audience. The criteria for prioritization varies by company and may include customer name (if it's a well-known, respected company), industry, use of specific products or services, or application.

2. Streamline the process.

One way to speed up the process of securing a case study or even just a quote is to draft it yourself. Your customer can review and modify your draft as desired or provide new content. Most of the time, assuming your draft is accurate and PR and legal teams don't have to get involved, the customer will approve it with little or no changes.

3. Tell a simple, visual story.

Create a case study that is easy to read and informs your audience with relevant and specific information. You have only a few moments to catch your prospective customer's attention, so the case study needs to be immediately interesting and informative with a strong benefits-oriented headline, interesting images, a simple and clear opening and closing, and relevant content to the reader.

4. Budget time for the approval process.

Securing approval for a case study can be tricky and time intensive. At a minimum, it can be difficult to get customers to take time away from their priorities to review your content. In larger companies, the review and approval process takes even longer because of the need to include PR and/or legal staff in the loop. To simplify this process, consider including the case study in your customer's sales contract. By doing this, when the time comes to work on the case study (usually when the application is implemented and the customer is confident in the finished project), it becomes their contractual responsibility to work internally to secure approval. A great time to consider taking this approach is when your customer is asking you for something, such as additional training, price discounts, or on-site support. Decide what you're willing to give on price or margin in return for the completed case study and then write it into the contract so what both parties agreed to give the other is clearly documented.

5. Leverage your work.

Once you have an approved case study with a strong, benefits-oriented headline, compelling images, and a simple, clear story that is targeted and easy to read, you need to maximize all of your hard work. Include your case study and/or quote on related pages of your website, in your next conference call script if you are a public company, in relevant sales visits, in your core slide deck, and in relevant areas of your web-based demos and training materials.

On this book's web page (trewmarketing.com/smartmarketingforengineers), you can access examples of well-written and well-designed case studies to reference as you create your own.

Webcasts

Webcasts, also called webinars, are unique in that your prospects can hear from a subject-matter expert without talking to anyone. By registering for or attending your company's live or recorded webcast and listening to you for 10 to 30 minutes, prospects express a real interest in you. That's a long time. Webcasts are lower in the marketing funnel because prospects will not spend 30 minutes with you after just learning about your company. So, when they sign up for a webcast, you know they are further down the funnel in their consideration of your company. With a prime opportunity on your hands with a qualified lead, you need to make sure your webcast is informative and professionally delivered, and that you are communicating with attendees before, during, and after the event.

In the Smart Marketing for Engineers 2015 study by TREW Marketing and ENGINEERING.com, engineers ranked the following as the most preferred features that make webcasts more worthwhile:

1. Real-world examples

2. Images and diagrams

3. Pre-webinar agenda/explanation of what you will learn

With this in mind, use the following tips to create and deliver a top-notch webcast.

Create your presentation.

1. Adhere to presentation best practices, stay under eight words per bullet, and use fewer than eight bullets per slide.

2. Graphics are better than bullets. Videos are better than photos. Think demos and be dynamic!

3. Your slides will likely be rendered smaller to the viewer than how they appear on your desktop, so use at least an 18-point font and ensure any graphics are large and crisp enough for viewing through a web browser.

4. Each slide may take from two to five minutes, so plan your time wisely. Keep the presentation to between 20 and 30 minutes. You can even do 10- to 15-minute webcasts as long as you set expectations with your audience about the level of detail you will cover.

5. Keep in mind the definite limit to the attention span of an online attendee. Consider what incentives you can use with attendees to keep them engaged throughout the entire webcast. This could be a mention at the beginning and/or throughout of key information, drawings, and/or trends or data you'll share soon or at the end.

Deliver your presentation.

1. Conduct a run-through to ensure you are comfortable with your webcast delivery platform (GoToWebinar, WebEx, etc.). Practice transitions if presenting with partners or a moderator.

2. Make sure you are in a quiet room free of background noise, echoes, and co-worker distractions.

3. Turn your mobile phone off. Use a headset for clear audio.

4. Log in at least 20 minutes early so participants can arrive before the event starts.

5. Don't read your slides verbatim. Use the bullets and images on your slide to tell a story and help the viewer understand what's most important.

6. Vary your vocal volume by using voice inflection and speak a bit louder and slower than your normal pace. Select a speaker whom your audience will easily understand and avoid speakers with heavy or foreign accents.

7. Check in with your audience. Since you don't have the benefit of seeing when your audience is disengaged, bored, etc., schedule specific pauses in your presentation where you can poll your audience for their interest or comprehension.

8. If you allow attendees to ask questions during your webcast, have a colleague monitor the questions and then, if time permits, answer them at relevant intervals during the presentation or at the end.

9. Create a Q&A document with answers to the questions asked during the webcast and use it as a next-step CTA in your follow-up email to registered attendees.

10. Record the live event and archive the recorded version as an on-demand webcast for ongoing lead generation.

Go to trewmarketing.com/smartmarketingforengineers to access an example of a highly effective webcast produced by Wineman Technology, which specifically targets engineers in the automotive, aerospace and defense, and off-highway industries. Similar webcasts have generated over 150 leads in less than a year.

Video

Video is an affordable and effective content type for marketing your company and products. On the web, video is more likely to win a first-page Google rank, resulting in anywhere from a two- to six-fold improvement in conversion rate. In a 2014 Aberdeen study, The Impact of Video on the Hidden Sales Cycle,[1] researchers found that website lead conversion rates for video users are 40 percent higher than for those who consume non-video content (4.8 percent versus 2.9 percent). When you extrapolate that to thousands of visitors during a given year, you can see how your lead numbers start to significantly increase when you add video to your content mix.

You can create different types of video, depending on your marketing and campaign goals. I explain five of the most common video formats below. You should offer most videos as free content, but you will want to put a lead form in front of them sometimes, especially if they are longer, in-depth, or how-to videos.

1. Interviews

Interviews with your internal staff can humanize your company and brand and build credibility. These can be interviews with technical industry experts who are company partners or subject matter experts on your engineering team. The interviews should focus on a trend or a product that they specialize in and should be kept short at ideally two minutes or less.

2. Testimonials

Customer testimonial videos provide third-party validation of your company, products, and services in the market. Because you're putting your customers on camera, you need to show them in the best possible light. Hire a videographer and find a well-lit, quiet room to conduct the interview, ideally at the customers' locations, so you can take footage of their application and facilities if permitted. To minimize the time your customers need to spend on their testimonials, don't ask more than five questions total and keep the interview to less than 30 minutes if possible. This will force you to ask

[1] aberdeen.com/research/9788/RR-Video-Hidden-SalesCycle.aspx/content.aspx

the most compelling questions and keep your post-production editing time down. To develop the questions, think about what you want your customers to say. Then develop questions that will prompt them to cover the topics you want in the final video. Provide your questions in advance and let the customer add any he wants to answer. The more involved the customer is, the better the quality and authenticity of the final video. When edited and final, these videos should be limited to three minutes and ideally less than two minutes.

3. Product Overview or Demo—Short

Introductory product overview or demo videos serve to visually show a product's most important features and benefits along with a quick explanation. In the first 20 seconds of the video, the viewer should learn who your company is and what your product does. In the next minute, you should briefly explain three or four key features and benefits. This keeps the video moving at a fast pace so the viewer stays engaged. These videos should be less than two minutes, and they are best implemented as animations to keep the quality and energy level high versus relying on a person to narrate and manually walk the audience through the product. In addition to one overview or demo video, you may consider creating separate shorter videos (under one minute) on each of the product's main features so prospects can quickly learn about the features they care about most before deciding to watch the entire product video.

Software

Overview or demo videos allow prospects to view the environment, functions, and features of your platform. They are best implemented as animations to keep the quality and energy level high, but they can also be done onscreen in the actual software environment with a narrator who walks through the software features. If you use the latter approach, your biggest challenges will be keeping the pace brisk and visual examples engaging.

Hardware

Overview or demo videos give viewers the opportunity to see a product up close and understand how it's used in the field. These videos can have a narrator on screen who points out key physical features as the camera zooms in. You can also implement hardware demos like software videos: show product images on screen as the narrator provides a voiceover.

4. Product Demos—In-Depth Whiteboard

Sometimes videos need to be longer, such as when a product is transformative to an existing market, or when you are introducing a process innovation that changes the way an application has been executed for many years. This is often an optimal time to use a whiteboard approach. Using a whiteboard style creates a fast-paced, technical feel to the video while visually explaining complex ideas. This approach requires a professional videographer to capture a subject-matter expert whiteboarding the topic live. From there, work with the expert to create a storyboard (visual outline) and script that, once approved, manifest into a fully animated, educational video.

5. How-To Videos

The more specific your how-to topic, the more powerful the impact and the more likely it will rank high in a natural search for specific, long-tail terminology. For example, imagine that you search on Google for the make and model of a washing machine to troubleshoot a broken feature. You then find a YouTube how-to video of your exact machine having similar issues (down to the same strange sounds). How-to videos can work for hardware, software, or systems, and they show the viewer how to set up a product, use a certain software feature, or put a system together. Today, some of the most-watched videos on YouTube are how-to (how to play the guitar, how to add memory to your PC, etc.) and this same approach applies to technical products as well as services. For instance, you may create videos on how to decrease application time through programming tricks or on common mistakes or even on fails during hardware system setup. These can be compelling enough to be put behind a lead form.

A Core Presentation

One other content type that is a smart marketing investment and often a source of frustration for executive business leaders or engineers in business development or marketing is a well-designed, cohesive corporate slide deck. A compelling deck of presentation slides can help efficiently and clearly tell your company story and lends itself to planned (versus last-minute) customization for many different audiences and speaking opportunities. Think of the 80/20 rule: though 20 percent of your slides may need to be customized (with, for example, application-specific use cases or relevant customer examples), 80 percent can be reused as-is across all audiences (company, products and services, technologies, customer examples, etc.). By reusing content as much as possible, you increase:

- **Efficiency**—Rather than starting from scratch for each presentation, save time and remove irrelevant slides and/or make minor adjustments to increase relevancy for specific audiences. Every reuse is time saved. You can even put the core presentation on your website or on LinkedIn (through SlideShare) for additional exposure and to strengthen your SEO.
- **Consistency**—By using slides with the same wording, imagery, and data instead of creating new ones for each presentation, you are more likely to remain consistent with your message. Also, by being consistent, you're able to more confidently equip new staff or leadership to give an external presentation that accurately depicts your brand.

- **Impact**—Because of the thoughtful, creative, and thorough work you put into the core presentation, your slides are more compelling, professional, and accurate. Your presentation will have a much greater impact than a set of slides you throw together at the last minute prior to a big opportunity.

You may think a core presentation sounds like a great idea on paper, but you're not sure about the process. The following eight steps will pay dividends in efficiency many times over:

1. Audit what you have.

Look through current presentations you've created and pull out the slides you like or think have potential. Start with four to six presentations or other documents to use as source material for the first draft of a core deck.

2. Hone your core messages.

Remove content that is ambiguous or goes off on a detailed tangent. Paste this information in the notes and know you can always put some of it back as needed.

3. Outline all possible audiences.

You will likely be presenting these slides to customers or prospects who fit your personas. How do you need to modify them for each persona? How much overlap is there between audiences? For instance, you may be speaking to mid-level engineers in one presentation and C-level executives in another. For the engineers, you'll want to beef up on technical and feature-rich slides with specifics about topics such as cabling setup, communications, GUI, and sensor-level connectivity. For the executive-level audience, you'll want to discuss costs, benefits, and your proven track record.

4. Review and perfect each slide.

Go through each slide thoroughly and cut down the text as necessary. Add images to help illustrate key points, clean up bullets and font sizes, and edit for spelling and grammar.

5. Get everyone on board.

Core presentations can have a long life only if everyone is working from the same deck. Key internal groups, such as sales, company leaders, and R&D, may need to weigh in to get the content and messages right.

6. Test and rework.

Give the presentation a few times to varied audiences, and then tweak it based on feedback from those initial run-throughs.

7. Integrate into your marketing mix.

Through the presentation development process, you may end up changing some wording, images, or other elements. Make sure you incorporate these changes in other media vehicles such as your website. Take the time to update pages and keep messaging consistent across channels.

8. Study others.

If you need further inspiration, look up slides from technical companies you most admire and trust. See how they present their company, position themselves, and address the industry and trends. Also note what images they use and how they designed their presentations.

Why You Need a Style Guide

Companies looking to further their business and their brand rely on corporate style guides to provide a professional look and feel to their content. In the absence of a style guide, your logo usage, messages, or tone of voice may be inconsistent. As a result, a reader has less trust in your company, and is less likely to consider or prefer you over others who create well-branded content and experiences.

When customers see a news release on your product, then later a video about a new product, and even later an article about your company, and all of them have the same tone and style, customers easily recognize that each piece of content is from your company. Those reminders help customers continue to build a positive image of your company.

Note the following four benefits to editing with a corporate style guide:

1. It helps keep customers engaged.

If your text is garbled and difficult to get through, you will lose your potential customers to a competitor within seconds. Clearly written content allows your customers to glide through your information, pinpoint what they need, and enjoy a positive experience with your organization and brand.

2. It helps you save time by reusing your own content.

You may have written a news release about a product and then several months later needed a bulleted list of features to put on that product's landing page. If your news release is edited using your corporate style guide, you easily can drag and drop the features list from the news release to a new web page without having to rework the content.

3. It makes third parties more likely to publish your content.
Because the web contains so much information, journalists look for well-written content they can place in their stories. When those stories are published on their news outlets, you reach a new segment of potential customers. If your content is poorly written and confusing, it's easy for a journalist to pass over your company and move on to a competitor instead.

4. It improves your brand awareness.
When your information is well-edited and adheres to a corporate style guide, it has one voice. This helps your customers quickly recognize your organization and your products or services. Without the use of a style guide, each time a potential customer sees your content, it's like they are seeing a new company. Customers won't know what to expect if they come to you for business.

Engineers trust content from expert engineers at vendor companies over any other type of author. They go to Google more than any other source for work-related information, and they search deeper through results than the average searcher. Engineers are also more willing to do business with companies who regularly produce new and current content. And these content types—white papers, case studies, webcasts, and videos—are what they prefer to consume most in their research over other content types. Now you have your content plan along the funnel, have a methodology to follow to market your content like a product, and you know which types of content to prioritize.

With your marketing foundation in place, and the heart of your inbound marketing program centered on content, you are ready to put this content to work to drive results for your company and scale for growth.

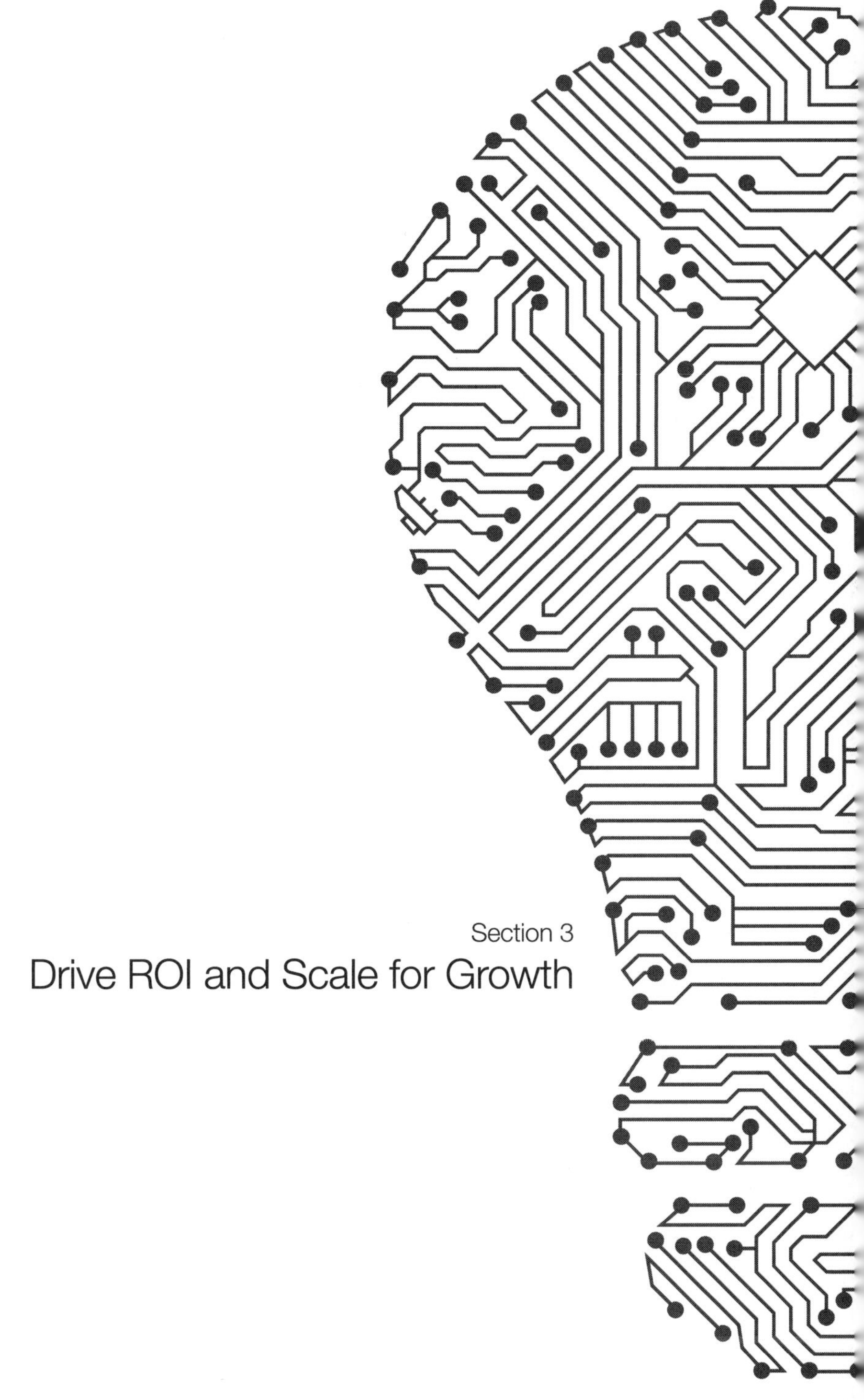

Section 3

Drive ROI and Scale for Growth

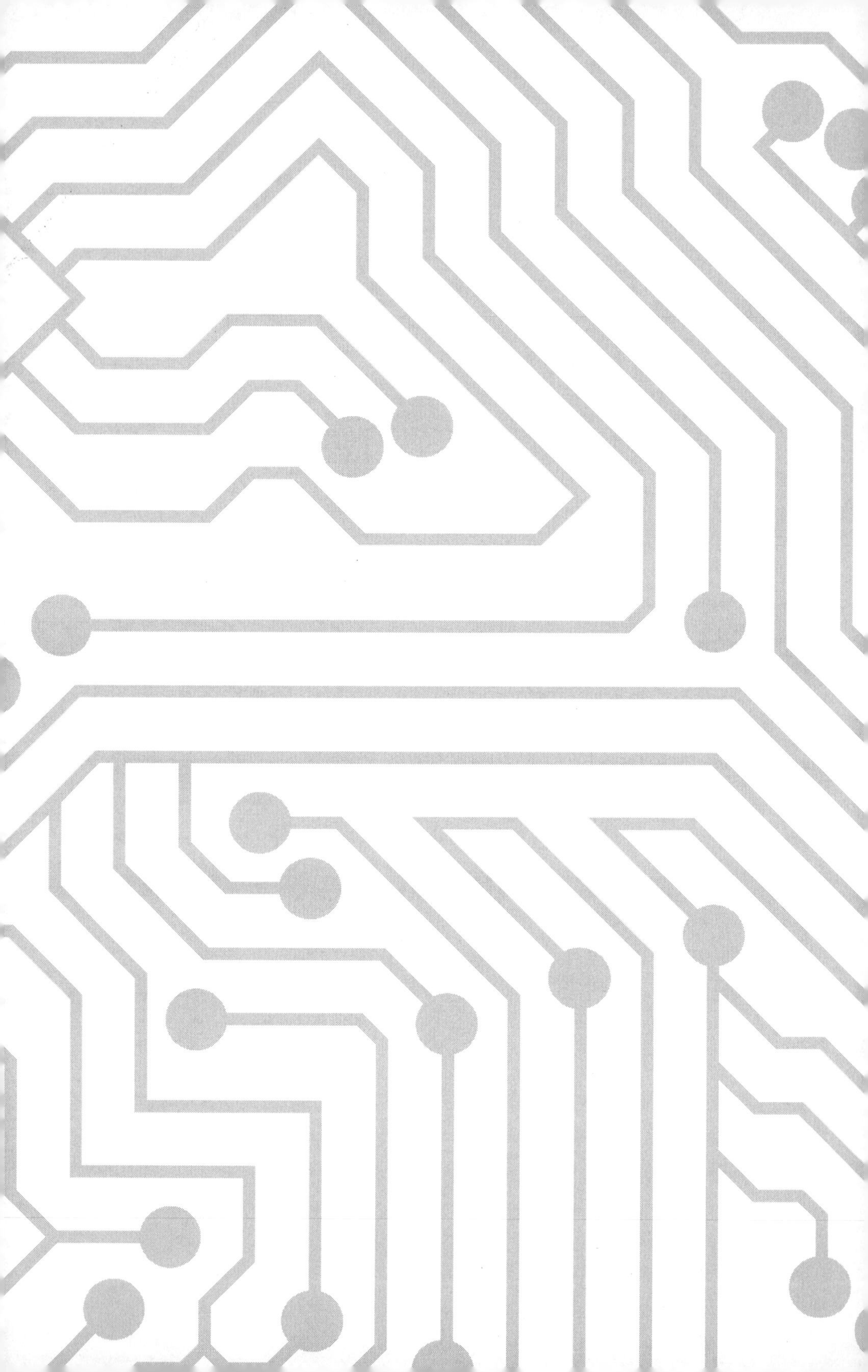

Chapter 9

GENERATE DEMAND ONLINE

Steps to Effective Lead Conversion

"Design is not just what it looks like and feels like. Design is how it works."

– Steve Jobs, Cofounder of Apple Computer Inc.

As the months pass with consistent marketing of your high-quality content across channels through optimization, amplification, and repurposing, you will begin to see a noticeable increase in new visitors to your website. Increasing traffic is the first step in improving ROI, but traffic alone doesn't generate demand. You need to turn that traffic into leads. How do you do that in a manner that builds trust with your visitors instead of turning them off? Start by providing visitors multiple paths and offerings to follow, including free and gated content, and pointing them to opportunities to become a lead.

As I already explained, introductory content is generally high-level information that you want everyone to be able to access freely. Top-level web pages, news releases, blog posts, short videos, company and product collateral such as data sheets, and case studies should be free because they help people learn more about your company, products, and services in the awareness and education phase. They are also expected to be free since these types of content tend to be shorter and introductory in nature and, therefore, less intensive to create.

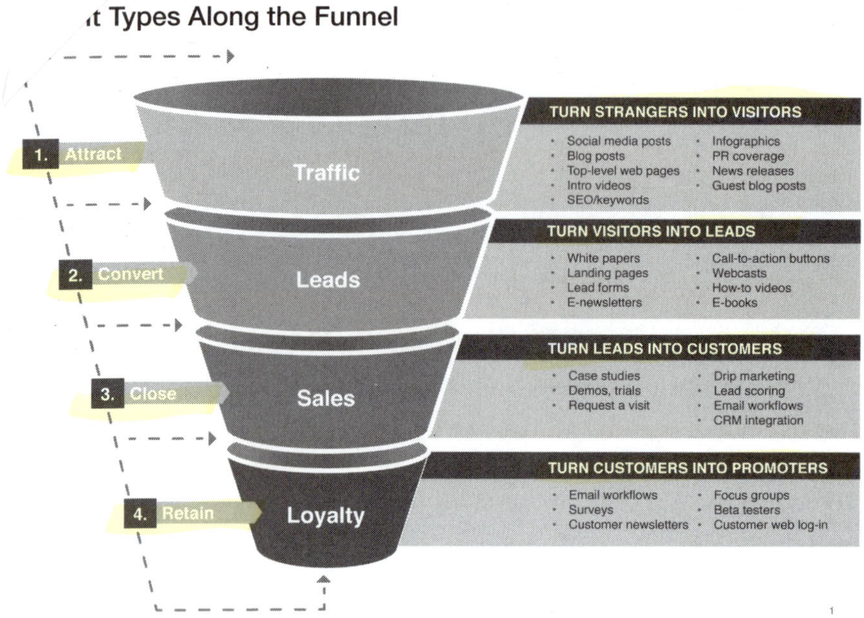

t Types Along the Funnel

1. Attract
Traffic
TURN STRANGERS INTO VISITORS
- Social media posts
- Blog posts
- Top-level web pages
- Intro videos
- SEO/keywords
- Infographics
- PR coverage
- News releases
- Guest blog posts

2. Convert
Leads
TURN VISITORS INTO LEADS
- White papers
- Landing pages
- Lead forms
- E-newsletters
- Call-to-action buttons
- Webcasts
- How-to videos
- E-books

3. Close
Sales
TURN LEADS INTO CUSTOMERS
- Case studies
- Demos, trials
- Request a visit
- Drip marketing
- Lead scoring
- Email workflows
- CRM integration

4. Retain
Loyalty
TURN CUSTOMERS INTO PROMOTERS
- Email workflows
- Surveys
- Customer newsletters
- Focus groups
- Beta testers
- Customer web log-in

1

Using free content at the top of the funnel attracts traffic and brings visitors to your website. When visitors reach your site, use gated content to convert them to leads.

In contrast to this free content, as you move down the funnel from attracting traffic to converting leads, your offers should be gated or premium content that features more in-depth, technical information. As the perceived value of a piece of content rises, so does the amount of personal information a web visitor is willing to share to access it. In deciding the value of your content, one rule of thumb is to think about the level of technical effort the content took to create. Did it require the involvement of subject-matter expert engineers? Is it more in-depth than your free content? Does it offer valuable how-to information or technical tips or trends that your audience desires and can't easily find elsewhere?

Examples of premium content include:

- Technical white papers
- Thought leadership trend pieces
- E-books
- Tutorials
- Webcasts/webinars
- Research reports and surveys
- Resource kits with multiple pieces of content
- Online training or course material
- Online software evaluations
- Technical project-related templates (e.g., reference designs)

Because producing premium content requires a significant time investment, and because readers expect the quality will be high, they will be open to the idea of "give to get" by completing a lead form. By putting a lead form in front of your premium, gated content, you create opportunities to generate leads. In addition to new leads, you build credibility as a knowledgeable leader in your field and continue engaging with customers who are further down the marketing funnel. Readers who find your introductory free content relevant and informative will dig deeper into your site to discover what else you have to offer that helps them do their jobs better, faster, and cheaper (later in the chapter, I share data on which lead form fields engineers are most likely to complete to access gated content).

→ **Read in chapter 11 how to implement progressive profiling using marketing automation software to gather information about your leads over time in a non-intrusive, user-friendly manner.**

Convert Leads with Winning Landing Pages

An effective way to generate leads from gated content is to create a landing page, also called a lead capture page, where visitors learn about the content before they fill out a form to download or view it. Simple and attractive landing pages that won't turn away doubtful engineers and skeptical scientists don't display a "kitchen sink" of embedded links web visitors may be interested in. Instead, they feature the one piece of content, one main image of the content, and one main CTA: the download button.

The key ingredients to a highly effective landing page that "sells" your gated content to your web visitors include:

- Page title and detailed subtitle highlighting the offer
- Brief and compelling one or two paragraphs followed by a bulleted table of contents, list of key information, or list of benefits the reader will gain from the content
- Short lead capture form prominently placed above the page fold or in the sidebar
- Clickable CTA text or button that pops off the page, incorporates actionable language, and draws the visitor's eye
- An image of the professionally designed cover of the content offer
- A bonus free offer, such as a short embedded video that further explains the content (optional)

➔ Visit trewmarketing.com/smartmarketingforengineers to see examples of landing pages following these best practices.

Think of your landing page as a living document. Allow it to run at least a month and track visits and conversion rates before making changes. Try one or two changes at a time to improve page performance, such as changing out the image, the page headline, the placement of the bullets, or the number of fields in your form (discussed later in this chapter). Also make sure the page is optimized for related keywords just like any other web page.

Guide Visitors with Effective Calls to Action

A key element of a high-performing landing page is the call to action (CTA). A CTA can be clickable text or a visual cue such as a button that leads visitors to take a specific course of action or next step. CTAs highlight your most important pieces of content and provide a logical progression of actions down the marketing and sales funnel. Without this textual or visual guidance, visitors may become discouraged by not being able to quickly find what they're looking for and leave the page, or worse, your website.

Example Call-to-Action Buttons

Download Now	Subscribe	WatchNow

Call-to-action buttons are effective ways to draw the visitor's eye to an action and should be kept simple and specific.

For CTAs to be effective, they must be simple, obvious, and specific. People must notice them, quickly understand what they're about, and find them compelling enough to click on them to get what they offer. CTAs should feature the following characteristics to offer the most impact:

- **Well designed**—For visual CTAs such as buttons, use simple but visually pleasing graphics with high-contrast colors so the button stands out from the background.
- **Obvious**—Make sure the CTA looks clickable by using an underlined hyperlink or an image that changes the cursor into a pointer hand whenever you mouse over it.
- **Actionable**—Label your CTA button with an action-oriented, imperative verb that tells people exactly what to do and makes it clear what they're getting. Examples include "Download White Paper" or "Start Your Trial." You can also create urgency by adding words like "now" or "today."
- **Specific**—New visitors to your website are unlikely to bypass the early stages of the funnel, move immediately to the bottom, and complete a Contact Us form. You should provide specific CTAs throughout your site and allow visitors to slowly build trust in your company as they read, learn more, and progress down the funnel. By offering specific CTAs throughout the funnel versus just one bottom-of-the-funnel offer like a Contact Us form, you will generate more leads and create a multifaceted web experience that your diverse audience of web visitors will appreciate and value.
- **Well placed**—The best locations for a CTA are prominently above the fold (do not require scrolling down to see), so web visitors see it immediately when they come to the page, and at the end of the page to guide readers who want to know "what's next?" CTAs in sidebars don't perform as well as in the center of the page because web visitors tend to ignore them.

"Sidebars are horrifically ineffective places to promote your call to action, engagement items, or social media channels. Like most things, sidebars used to work but not anymore. Why? Well…your readers are ignoring them."

– Stan Smith, Founder, Pushing Social

Lead Capture Form Fields: How Many and Which Ones?

Though we know engineers and scientists seek accurate, research-based content, we also know they are skeptical of filling out lead forms for fear of being marketed to. They are more likely to complete a lead form to access content if they perceive it is valuable and useful to their jobs. In the Marketing to Engineers 2014 study, more than two-thirds of respondents indicated they were willing to provide such details for webcasts or webinars, product information, and white papers/best practices content.

Content Types Engineers Will Complete Lead Forms For

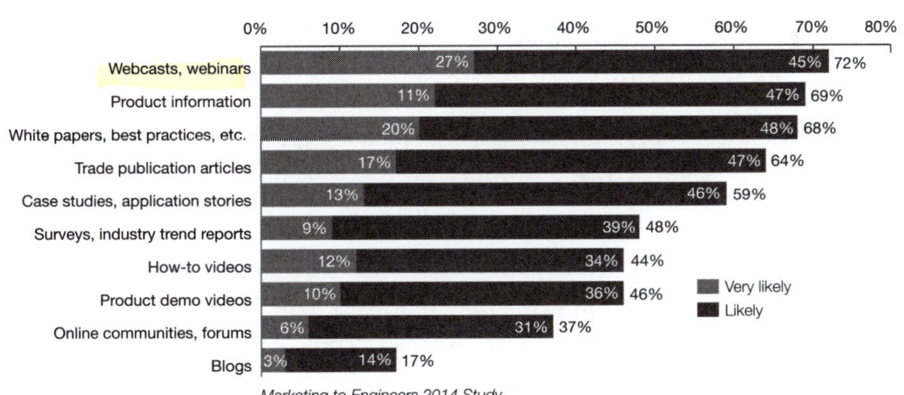

Marketing to Engineers 2014 Study

Respondents were most likely to provide basic contact information to access webcasts and webinars (72 percent); product information (69 percent); and white papers, best practices, etc. (68 percent).

You can show product information in many types of content, from product flyers to in-depth, 20-page data sheets. From the survey data, it is clear engineers highly value this type of information. Though it appears engineers are willing to complete a lead form to access product information, I do not recommend you gate this type of content. Most technical companies do not gate this type of information, and you certainly don't want to have a barrier to yours when your competitors offer it for free. This high in the funnel, you are trying to build trust with prospects not turn them away or make them work for product information. If you do decide to gate this type of information, you can always remove the lead form if you observe high bounce rates on the page.

Though nearly 60 percent of respondents indicate they are likely or very likely to complete a lead form for a case study, I don't recommend you gate this content, either. You want your prospective customers to be able to hear from your existing customers about their successes with your products and services without adding any barriers. Engineers indicated they would not be as likely to complete a lead form for content types such as industry reports, videos, online communities or forums, and blogs, which is an indication that these types of content should also be free.

Just like landing pages, lead capture forms need to be clear, simple, and concise. Studies from companies such as Marketo[1] have shown that longer lead forms have lower conversion rates than those with simple landing page descriptions and forms. To produce the highest landing page conversion rate and the lowest bounce rate (i.e., when the visitor comes to the page and leaves without completing a lead form), you need to ask for the information your visitor is willing to give and no more. What fields should be required versus optional or removed? When asked in the Marketing to Engineers 2014 study, engineers gave answers that are specific and actionable, with three

[1] marketingexperiments.com/blog/internet-marketing-strategy/lead-generation-testing-form-field-length-reduces-cost-per-lead-by-10-66.html

distinct groups of lead form fields. In the first group, five fields (first name, last name, work email, company name, and job title) are all more than 70 percent likely to be completed, which is notably higher than the rest. In fact, first and last name fields are more than 80 percent likely to be completed. In the next group of four fields (industry, product interest, company address, and work phone number), the likelihood of field completion drops below 50 percent. The final group drops by another 13 percent, with form fields including phone, website, and purchase timeframe having only a 27 percent chance or less of being completed.

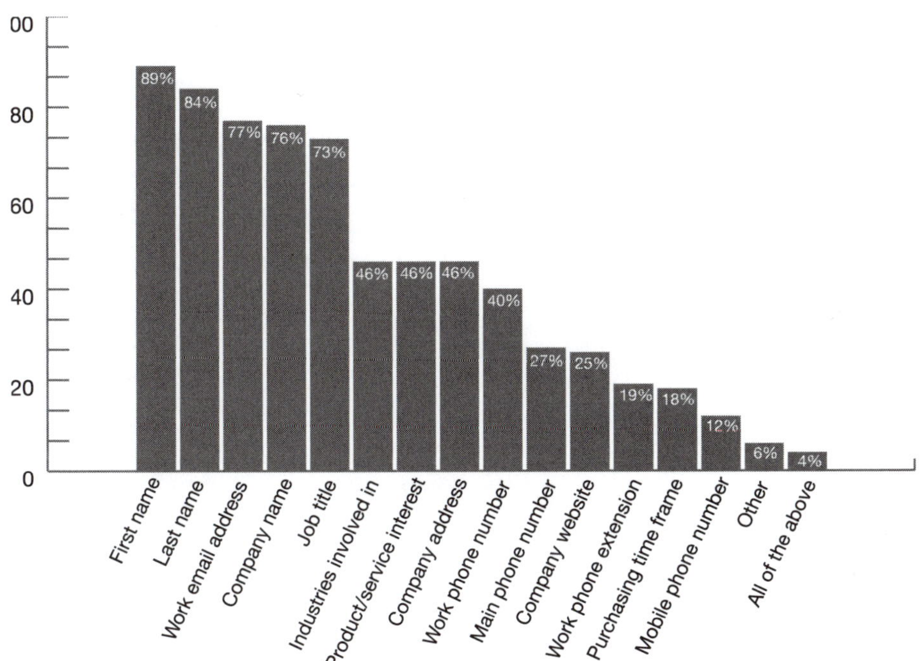

Marketing to Engineers 2014 Study

Engineers are most likely to complete five lead form fields: first name, last name, work email, company name, and job title.

This information helps you determine which fields to use on your lead forms to drive the highest conversion rates on your landing pages. But if you shorten your lead forms to get the best conversion rate, how do you capture the rest of the information? You know you can't ask for it all at once, but you'd like to know more than name, email, company, and title. By using marketing automation software such as HubSpot, Marketo, or another leading platform, you can gather lead information over time using progressive profiling features. I discuss this in detail in chapter 11.

Though engineers and technical business leaders in charge of marketing regularly express their skepticism to me about using lead forms on their websites for fear they will anger visitors, the truth is web visitors will complete them. If engineers perceive the gated content you are offering is highly valuable, they will give their information to get yours. Gated content has many flavors, from white papers to webcasts to technical project-related resources, but if a prospective customer is going to give you his information to get your information, how you "sell" the information on your landing page, how well the piece is designed or produced, and what lead form fields you require him to complete are critical elements to driving a higher conversion rate from visit to lead.

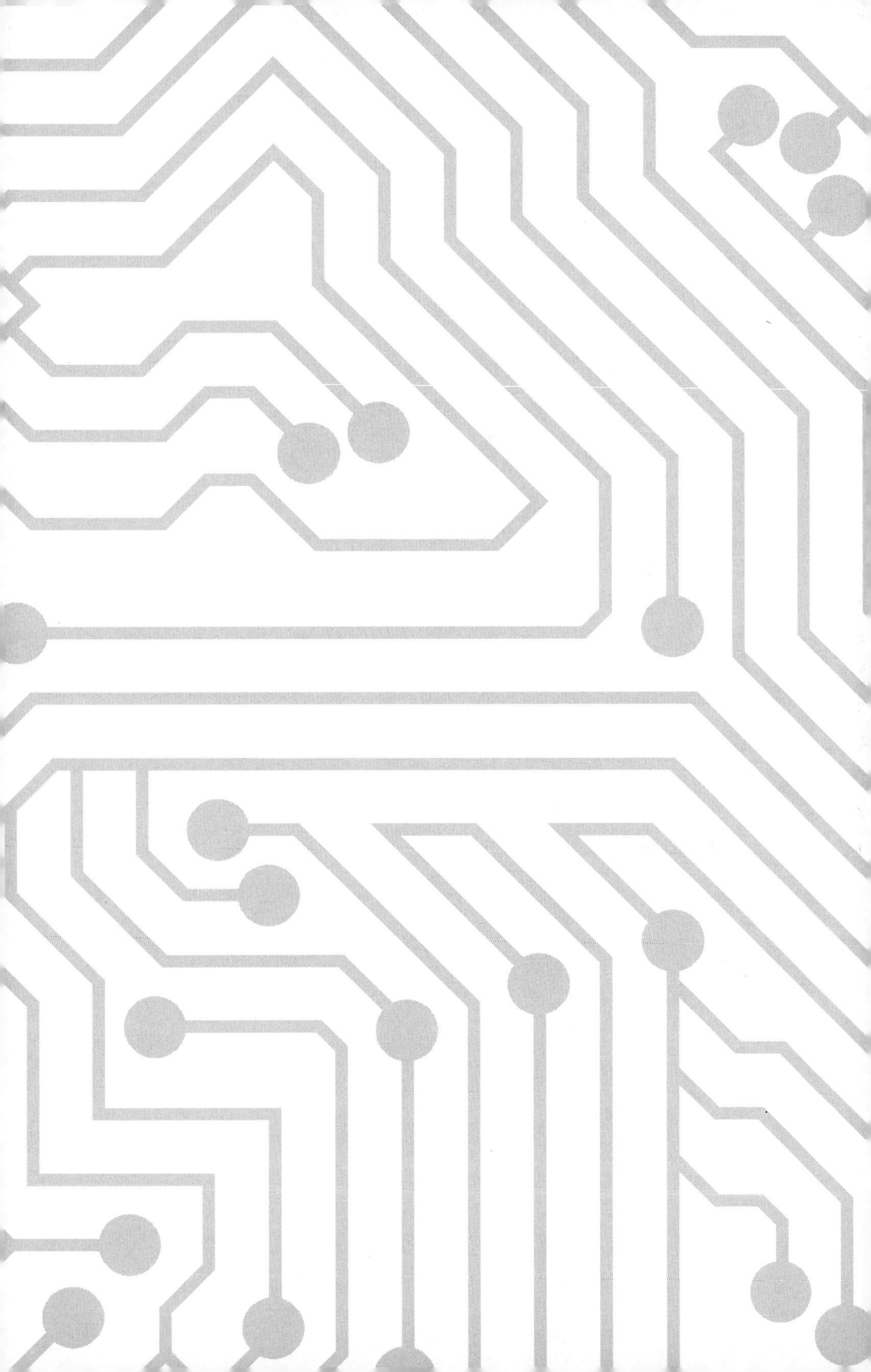

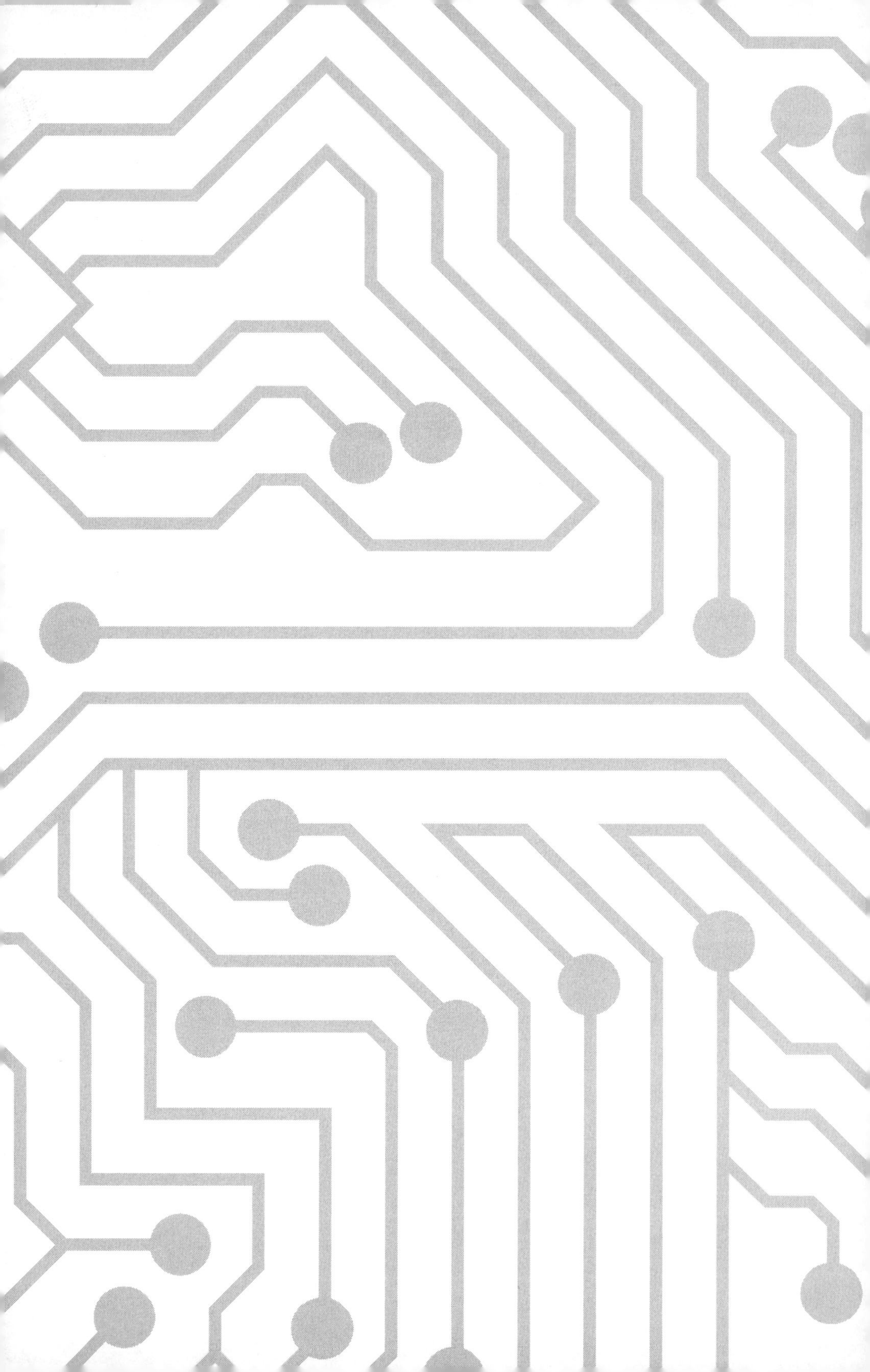

Chapter 10

NURTURE LEADS TO BUILD TRUST

Deliver Qualified Leads to Sales

"In my intercourse with mankind, I have always found those who would thrust theory into practical matters to be, at bottom, men of no judgment and pure quacks."

– John Smeaton, British Father of Civil Engineering

When speaking to a group of engineers, I often ask for a show of hands from those who have completed a website lead form for a company they have not done business with before. Usually only a few hands go up. The reason may seem obvious: as mentioned in the previous chapter, engineers are skeptical people who loathe marketers and spam email. To a much greater extent than the average person, engineers need to trust that when they complete a lead form, the company will communicate with them respectfully, provide useful information, and not waste their time and stalk them. So when engineers complete lead forms on your site, you have a responsibility to communicate with them in a way that continues to build their trust and not tear it down.

In marketing terms, this is called lead nurturing: the process of educating, building relationships, and growing trust to move leads further down the marketing funnel and closer to becoming a sales opportunity. Just because a person completes a lead form for a white paper or other premium content on your website doesn't mean he is ready to talk with your salesperson or make a purchase decision. It just means he wants to read your white paper. Consider a dating analogy. You wouldn't take a girl to meet your parents on the first date. Instead, you would ask for a second, third, and even a fourth date to get to know her over time and, when ready, make the introduction to your family. By the time you know she is ready to meet your parents, you've built a relationship and trust that she and your parents will get along well.

➔ **To watch a hilarious three-minute video about engineers and dating, visit trewmarketing.com/smartmarketingforengineers.**

With lead conversion, study after study has reinforced what global business leadership and operations advisor CEB[1] found: 57 percent of a typical purchase decision is made before a customer even talks to a supplier. B2B[2] Marketing found that nearly 80 percent of the time engineers spend researching is done online, so when your leads convert on your content, it is a first sign of trust and interest in what you have to say and offer. However, keep in mind those leads are likely to be in the early stages of research. Nurturing these leads means you thank them for their trust with reciprocal communications that offer more opportunities to learn through additional content. In return, you keep your company top of mind as leads continue to research and grow their knowledge of your products and services.

Nurturing leads over time has shown to produce mutually beneficial results. A study by DemandGen[3] found that, on average, companies that nurture leads produce 20 percent more sales opportunities than companies that don't. Plus, Forrester Research found that companies that excel at lead nurturing are able to generate 50 percent more sales-ready leads at a 33 percent lower cost per lead.[4] Email marketing, an important aspect of lead nurturing, requires a thoughtful plan based on personas and campaigns with free and gated content offers along the funnel. Email

[1] cebglobal.com/exbd/sales-service/the-end-of-solution-sales/index.page
[2] sales.linkedin.com/blog/sales-strategy-23-facts-about-buyers-and-purchasing
[3] demandgen.com/why-lead-nurturing-matters-6-reasons-2
[4] Forrester Research, 2011

marketing is most effective and affordable when done with marketing automation tools (covered in the next chapter). To start, you should implement your email marketing with three primary nurturing types: lead follow-up, segmented nurturing, and e-newsletters.

Lead Follow-Up

Follow these 10 steps to begin building an email nurturing program that, when combined with the other nurturing types, generates sales-ready leads and lowers costs.

1. **Be timely.**
   When someone becomes a lead, send a follow-up email as soon as possible and no later than 24 hours after the lead is generated. There is a positive correlation between the recency of a lead's activity and click-through rate.

2. **Be patient.**
   Lead nurturing is not a "one and done" activity. It will take several emails and interactions to guide a lead down the funnel to become marketing- or sales-qualified. When determining the length and frequency of your lead-nurturing campaign, consider your typical sales cycle by looking at past data and talking to your sales team. Monitor your email performance metrics to find the right number of emails that will not overwhelm or alternatively turn your lead cold. Follow this starting formula:

   First-Touch Email

   - Send a thank-you follow-up email within 24 hours of conversion
   - Offer free content, such as blog posts and additional product or service documentation on the specific topic of initial conversion

- Offer at least one new gated piece of content, such as a webcast or evaluation request

Second-Touch Email

- If no response, send a second email within five days of conversion
- Offer more free and gated resources, such as technical flyers, consultation services, and deeper technical content
- Use a different subject line from the first-touch email so readers won't mistake it as the same email

Third-Touch Email

- If no response, send a third email within 15 days of conversion
- Offer a mix of previous content offers
- Use a different subject line from the first and second emails so readers won't mistake it with the previous emails

At any point in this email nurture plan, if leads click on a CTA, you should remove them from this nurture path and communicate with them differently to acknowledge their interest. From there, depending on what they clicked on, you can continue to nurture them to further qualify them. Or, if they are deemed lower in the funnel (again, depending on which actions they took), you may decide they qualify to be passed to sales for follow-up.

3. Focus on the subject line.

When your leads receive the email, they decide within seconds to open it based on a few words in the subject line. In the Smart Marketing for Engineers 2015 study by TREW Marketing and ENGINEERING.com, the majority, or 37 percent, of engineers chose this answer to describe how they interact with e-newsletters: "I scan for subject lines that intrigue me and delete the rest." The subject line is your ocean-front property. It drives your open rate more than any other factor. To get the highest open rates, keep subject lines short and to the point. Specifically, stay under 50 characters for best results and avoid using aggressive sales and promotional terms, all caps, acronyms, or exclamation points. Think of newspaper headlines that grab you in three to five words, and make sure your subject lines match the offer in the email. If your open rates are high but clickthrough rates are low, you have a disconnect and need to modify the offer to more accurately match the subject or vice versa. In step 8, I discuss how you can use A/B testing to generate higher-performing email elements.

4. **Fuel engagement with relevant content.**
In follow-up emails, highlight relevant content to provide clear next-step options for the lead. For example, when leads download a white paper from embedded networking provider Silex Technology, they immediately receive a follow-up email that includes a direct link to the white paper they downloaded as well as links to other relevant information such as an application note and data sheets for similar products. Also included is an email address to contact sales directly. These resources provide the contacts not only an easy way to access the white paper since it now lives in their inboxes but also additional related information on the Silex website to increase their interest in the product Silex offers. This creates the opportunity for the leads to further qualify by reading more free information, downloading another gated piece, or contacting sales directly. The latter two actions make them sales-qualified leads and trigger a sales team member to reach out directly.

White Paper Email Follow-Up

(note: all underlined text is hyperlinked)

Hi CONTACT FIRST NAME,

Thank you for downloading our white paper, Wireless Connectivity for the Freescale i.MX 6 Platform. We hope this guide helps you get started with the evaluation and implementation process.

Have some specific questions? Silex Technology has decades of experience delivering embedded networking solutions, and we would be happy to provide assistance during the evaluation, implementation, or post-launch phases.

Email your Silex sales representative today at (sales email address).

Looking for more resources? Check out the Silex Technology application note titled SX-SDCAN Support on the Freescale i. MX 6 Evaluation Platform and these additional product briefs:

- SX-SDCAN Product Brief
- SX-SDMAN Product Brief
- SX-SDPAN Product Brief

Sincerely,

SALES MANAGER FIRST, LAST NAME/
TITLE

5. **Map offers to the buying cycle.**
As discussed in chapter 6, the type of content you offer is just as important as the timing and relevancy. When leads are in the research stage, they are looking for educational materials such as blog posts and white papers. When a prospect reaches the evaluation stage near the bottom of the funnel, case studies of past work, a free trial, or a request for a technical consultation is most effective. Refer back to the explanation of content along the funnel in chapter 10 for content types recommended for the different stages of the funnel.

6. **Keep it short and simple.**
If you stay focused on one topic, it should not be difficult to keep your email brief. Leads should be able to glance at your email and within a few seconds know the value it provides and the next actions they can take. You accomplish this using a clear opening and a combination of two or three short paragraphs with no more than three bullets listing the content offers. Keep it simple. Now is not the time to use HTML or cool fonts, colors, or styles.

7. **Measure progress.**
Tracking key metrics for your follow-up emails shows you how well your lead-nurturing tactics are performing. The five primary email marketing metrics you should measure are listed in the following table. For reference, the table includes industry average email performance benchmarks from Silverpop's 2014 Email Marketing Metrics Benchmark Study,[5] which uses averages from two specific technology industry groups, Computer Hardware/Telecom/Electronics and Computer Software.

---

[5] silverpop.com/marketing-resources/white-papers/all/2014/email-metrics-benchmark-study-2014

Five Key Email Metrics

Email metric	Average metric
Hard bound rate	1.09%
Unsubscribe	0.16%
Unique open rate	22.6%
Unique clickthrough rate	3.3%
Click-to-open rate	11.6%

Focus on five key metrics and reference these industry averages to gauge the success of your email activities.

If your metrics are getting worse, you need to reevaluate them and try testing stronger subject lines, adjusting the timing of your send, changing CTAs or email body content, or reordering or trying new content offers. The next chapter shows how you can use a marketing automation tool's email metrics dashboard to identify low-performing emails that need attention and, with the same tool, edit, push live, and continue to monitor emails.

8. Test for improvement.

As you implement new or improve existing emails, use A/B testing to experiment with different email aspects. For instance, set up two emails with different subject lines. In email A, use a subject line that focuses on a limited-time offer. In email B, focus on a key feature in a new product. Split your distribution list randomly and send one group email A and one group email B. Make sure you're using a list large enough to demonstrate results with statistical significance. Ideally, you'll have at least 100 contacts in each list, but work with what you have. Monitor the open rates of both emails to find the most effective approach. Do the same for body content and content offers, but remember to test only one variable at a time. This ensures that you can attribute metrics to one specific element. Through testing, you can develop a final email that combines the highest-performing aspects for best results.

9. **Prepare to segment.**
   Based on leads' responses to emails and content offers, you learn a great deal about where they are in the buying cycle and how interested they are in your content. If they engage, you know they are still interested. Using modern email or marketing automation software, you can track what readers click on and begin to segment them with more specific communication (covered later in this chapter).

10. **Have an exit strategy.**
   If leads ignore all of your emails, it's probably time to remove them from any further follow-up emails. You've given them multiple chances, and they're not engaging. If you continue to send emails, they may unsubscribe from all future emails. However, do not delete them from your database, and keep them on your e-newsletter list if they're already on it. You never know when leads will change jobs or become reengaged, so it's important to stay top of mind. Alternatively, once leads become sales qualified (covered in chapter 12), remove them from your marketing follow-up email list; let the salesperson take over with specific, one-on-one communication; and ensure the leads get added to your customer communication workflows.

Segmented Nurturing

To complement your follow-up emails, you should next implement a segmented email marketing program to specific, small groups of leads to move them down the funnel with micro-targeted communication.

It has been proven time and time again that targeted email marketing performs higher than batch-and-blast emails going to a large group. By narrowing the focus and sending segments of your list specific messages, you increase relevance and, in turn, improve results. The "2010 Lyris Email Optimizer Report[6]" found that 39 percent of marketers who segmented their email lists experienced higher open rates, 28 percent experienced lower unsubscribe rates, and 24 percent experienced greater revenue. A 2015 study by MailChimp[7] found further proof of the positive impact segmentation can have on your results:

- Unique opens: 9.68 percent higher than non-segmented campaigns
- Clicks: 51.92 percent higher than non-segmented campaigns
- Unsubscribes: 8.28 percent lower than non-segmented campaigns

The MailChimp study concluded, "…segmenting your email marketing lists has an overwhelmingly positive impact on the engagement of your subscribers. Open and click rates were up across the board in all segmentation scenarios that we've investigated."

You can segment leads into small groups based on a number of criteria, such as interest in a particular product or service, registration or attendance at an event, an abandoned shopping cart, or a buyer persona. If you haven't segmented lists before, start with one group first, such as leads from a specific event or gated piece of content. For a simple example, follow these four steps to execute segmented email communication to all inactive leads in the last 12 months from a webcast:

1. Make sure all leads have a lead source field or separate open-text field with the webcast name and specific descriptor for this segmented effort, such as "Top 5 Test System Fails—Inactive."

[6] fulcrumtech.net/wp-content/uploads/2012/10/Lyris-Annual-Email-Optimizer-Report.pdf
[7] mailchimp.com/resources/research/effects-of-list-segmentation-on-email-marketing-stats

2. Using this name as your criteria, create a unique list for leads from the webcast for the last 12 months who have been inactive (have not opened your emails, visited your website, etc.).

3. Create an email that specifically calls out the name of the webcast in the subject line with an action or offer, such as "How to Avoid the Top 5 Test Fails" or "Offer for Test Fails Webcast Attendees." In the body of the email, acknowledge that in the last year they attended the webcast, and offer the most relevant content to the webcast topic including content and demos, a specific webcast landing page on your website, a deeper dive into specific product features or demonstrations mentioned in the webcast, or pricing and comparison information for those ready to buy.

4. Establish a process to follow up with leads depending on what action they take. For example, for those who click on the bottom-of-the-funnel pricing and comparison content, the next step may be for sales to call those leads. For others who click on free top-of-the-funnel information, such as blog posts, you may set up a second-touch email related to the webcast a few days later to give them another chance to engage further down the funnel. If they don't show interest by opening or clicking, you can remove them from the segmentation plan and continue sending them your e-newsletter.

You can use this process for a wide variety of segments, from service or product interest to specific content offers. For instance, if one of your gated offers is to sign up for an online software evaluation, you may immediately email your leads with more information about how to get the most out of the evaluation, contact information for your product support team, and case studies describing how others are using the software.

Try a few segmented emails using this process and measure their performance. Based on open and clickthrough rates, make tweaks to increase performance over time, such as trying different subject lines or offers along the funnel. Once you have mastered the basic approach to creating, executing, and measuring segmented emails, you can create a more comprehensive email marketing plan for key segments by product, service, persona, event, or the specific activity they originally converted on. Your plan should include a prioritized list of top segmentation opportunities representing the most important areas of your business with a specific, relevant message.

Email Newsletters

Email newsletters (also called e-newsletters) are the third leg of your email marketing stool. They serve many purposes, including keeping your company top of mind with your leads database, promoting new content, nurturing leads to move qualified prospects down the funnel, and increasing customer loyalty by keeping contacts informed about new products, services, trends, and more.

Email newsletters are such an important part of a nurturing program that this was a focus area of the Marketing to Engineers 2014 study. One of the most encouraging data points from the e-newsletter portion of the study was that respondents subscribe to an average of nine email newsletters from a variety of sources, including industry associations, trade publications, and suppliers/vendors. Looking at specific company email newsletter data (i.e., "supplier/vendor"), over 40 percent of respondents subscribe to up to two email newsletters, and over 40 percent subscribe to three or more. Moreover, in the Smart Marketing for Engineers 2015 study, engineers selected "email subscriptions they have set up" as the second common source for finding high-quality work-related content, showing the high value they place on channels like email newsletters.

This data shows that engineers consider email newsletters a valuable source of information from their preferred vendors. But how do you get them to open your email newsletter and click on a story? When respondents were asked what they liked in the email newsletters they read most, the top three content types were new technical content, application stories, and new products/services available.

The study also asked what advice respondents had to improve email newsletters. The top three suggestions were to:

1. Focus on fewer topics and go deeper

2. Be less promotional and more objective

3. Offer more content

Though it's tempting to focus your e-newsletter content on sales-driven topics such as new promotions, this feedback makes it clear that you will have more success attracting and retaining readers if you minimize the sales pitch and focus on creating and offering content that helps them do their jobs better.

This comment is from one respondent about email newsletter frequency: "Only write and send them when there is something that needs to be said. Having to invent content just because a publication is due is a waste of everyone's time." No matter the frequency, your content has to be high quality and relevant and your email newsletter must have a clean and well-branded design with an effective structure. With this in mind, a quarterly email newsletter is the minimum sending frequency you should consider or prospects will likely forget about your company, disengage, and, over time, even become annoyed and unsubscribe. The decision to send email newsletters more frequently should be based on the quality and quantity of new content. If you can sustain a high level of quality at a monthly cadence, do it. If your open and clickthrough rates sustain or increase, continue. If you increase frequency and find the performance decreases, pull back and refocus on subject line and content quality. Avoid too much frequency fluctuation because you want your prospects and customers to perceive you are consistent and reliable and not sporadic and unpredictable.

The top 10 email clients.

A critical aspect of e-newsletter performance is design, including programming and structure. The design should be consistent from issue to issue with strong usability that makes it easy to open, quickly skim, and find compelling articles and links. Ensuring the design is correctly programmed in email engine software is equally critical for display in numerous email clients. Unfortunately, each popular[8] email client on the market today—Outlook, Gmail, Yahoo, etc.—displays images, columns, and other design elements a little differently. Outlook, which has almost half of the email client market, is especially picky and requires specific programming techniques for your e-newsletter to display correctly to your recipients.

With poor design and/or programming, what was once a beautiful e-newsletter in the conceptual planning stage may turn into a mess of misaligned columns, images, and text when your readers open it.

Test your design at emailonacid.com, a web service that (for a small fee) will run the design code through a tool that mimics all popular

[8] Litmus Email Analytics, May 2015: emailclientmarketshare.com

email clients. This allows you to discover and correct layout issues before distribution. As for email newsletter structure, the over 1,000 respondents in the Marketing to Engineers 2014 study indicated they clearly want short paragraphs and bulleted lists. The best practice is to have short headlines followed by one or two sentences to explain the topic further and direct URLs to web pages or articles. The same rules apply for subject lines as covered in the previous email section.

This same research showed that engineers are drawn to content that includes the use of photos, diagrams, and charts. The saying "a picture is worth 1000 words" is true, and a well-placed graphic can slow skimming readers enough to entice them to increase the amount of information they read and retain. In the study, 77 percent and 75 percent, respectively, responded that application photos as well as charts, graphs, and tables are highly or moderately valuable aspects of email newsletters.

For each story, writing the headline and a one- or two-sentence blurb is not enough; you also need to consider a relevant, compelling image.

Most Valued Features of E-Newsletters

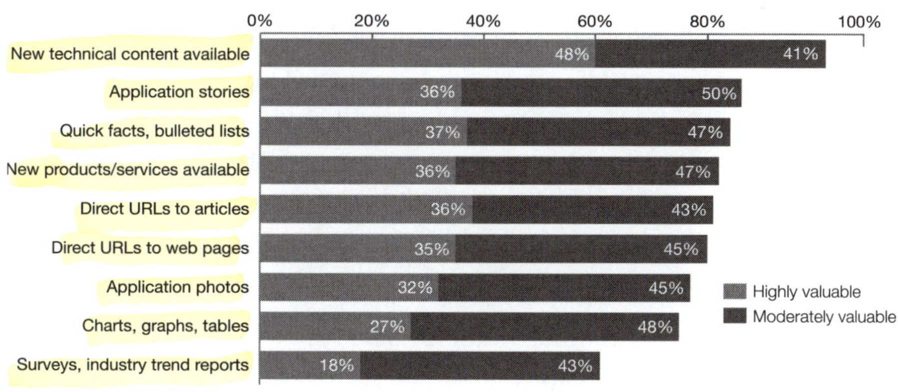

Engineers prefer to see new technical content and application stories above other content types in email newsletters.

The ideal approach to sending your email newsletters is to use an opt-in model for which someone subscribes by filling out a short form, or even a one-field email address form, on your website or from a CTA in your emails, at events, etc. If you are just starting to build your database or implement an email newsletter, then this opt-in approach may not be feasible. You may consider sending it to your database of active leads, customers, partners, and subscribers using an opt-out model. With an opt-out approach, you remove only those who unsubscribe to your email newsletter (or other emails), but otherwise you send it to those audiences listed above. You can then move from opt-out to opt-in over time as your subscriber list grows.

I mentioned the word "active" to describe the leads you should send your email newsletter to (and this applies to all email marketing). You usually know when to add a lead or name to your email newsletter list, but when should you stop sending it to someone? This is a judgment call that can rely heavily on metrics. A good rule of thumb is if recipients have not taken any action with your company (i.e., visited your website or blog, opened an email, downloaded content, talked with sales, etc.) within 12 to 24 months, depending on company size and email frequency, you need to classify them as inactive. By inactive, I do NOT mean delete them from your database. With the exception of a contact whose email address results in a hard bounce (i.e., is permanently invalid because the address or domain name no longer exists or the email server has completely blocked delivery), you should never delete a name with a valid email address from your database, even if that person has unsubscribed to your emails. You don't want to lose the historical information you have about those people if they come back one day. Changes in jobs, employers, or some other career aspect may bring someone back to your company. Rather than delete them, I recommend you archive or make them inactive. This way, you still have their information, but you are not communicating with those who clearly are not currently interested.

Consider these email marketing and legal tips:

1. Purchase lists as a last resort. Emails you send to purchased lists are considered unsolicited email, and they by and large perform poorly given that the contacts do not know your company and have never engaged with you in the past. To be done well, the list must be very, very clean and targeted and the offer must be uniquely compelling and time-bound. The long-term goal should be to grow your database organically through inbound marketing with great content at the heart, but as you are getting started, you may consider this to boost your audience.

2. Only send emails to individuals and not a group inbox used by multiple people. For example, an email address such as info@msn.com or sales@ibm.com should be removed from your list of contacts.

3. Always offer an unsubscribe link at the bottom of your emails and be sure that clicking on it results in the person either immediately being removed from your recipient list or landing on a page where contacts can manage their subscription preferences.

4. Don't forget to offer a prominent "subscribe to our e-news" CTA on your website, in your emails, and in other communication. People who have willingly subscribed have expressed a strong motivation to receive your email newsletter and are therefore some of your most valuable readers.

5. If you have readers outside the United States, remember the opt-in rules are much more stringent than in America. In countries like Germany, where the laws are some of the toughest, a double opt-in is required: the contact must first sign up and then click on a link in an email to confirm subscription. Many US companies are

going this way as well since it results in the highest response rates, albeit at the risk of reducing your database of recipients.

6. Include a link at the top of the newsletter to a web-based version. Often, email clients can distort HTML and mess up your carefully designed content, so it's a best practice to include a version of the newsletter that opens in a web browser. This way, if the email arrives in contacts' inboxes distorted, they can still see your content and design as they are meant to be seen.

7. Consider creating a text-only, HTML-free version for subscribers whose companies block HTML emails. Many large mil/aero companies, for example, do not allow HTML emails because of the slight security risk they present. Some marketing automation platforms include an auto-generated text version of any email you create that can be sent to contacts whose email clients block HTML. If you don't use a platform that auto-generates this version, you can include a "text or HTML?" checkbox on your e-newsletter sign-up page, and use this preference to determine which version to send to your contacts.

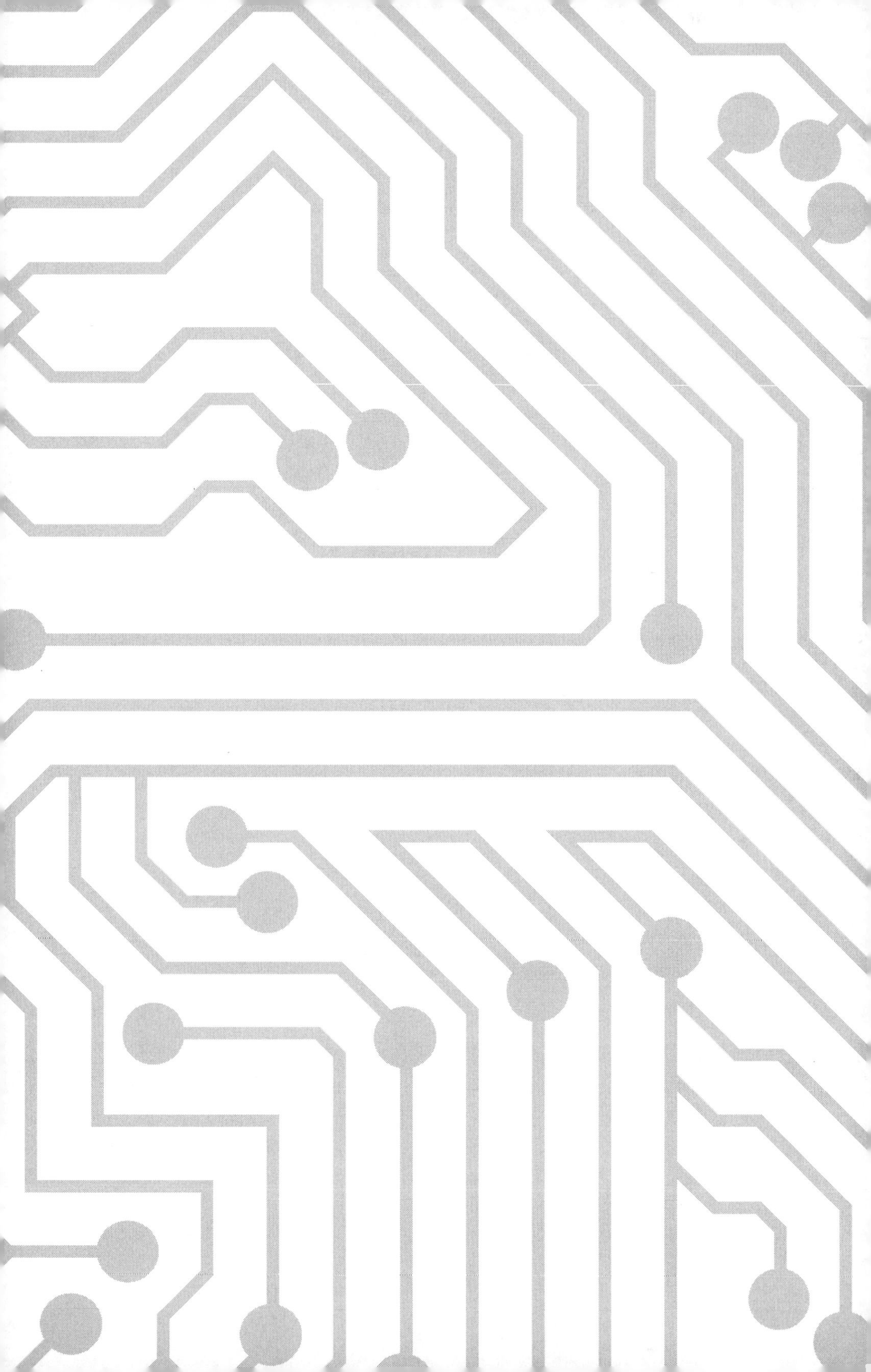

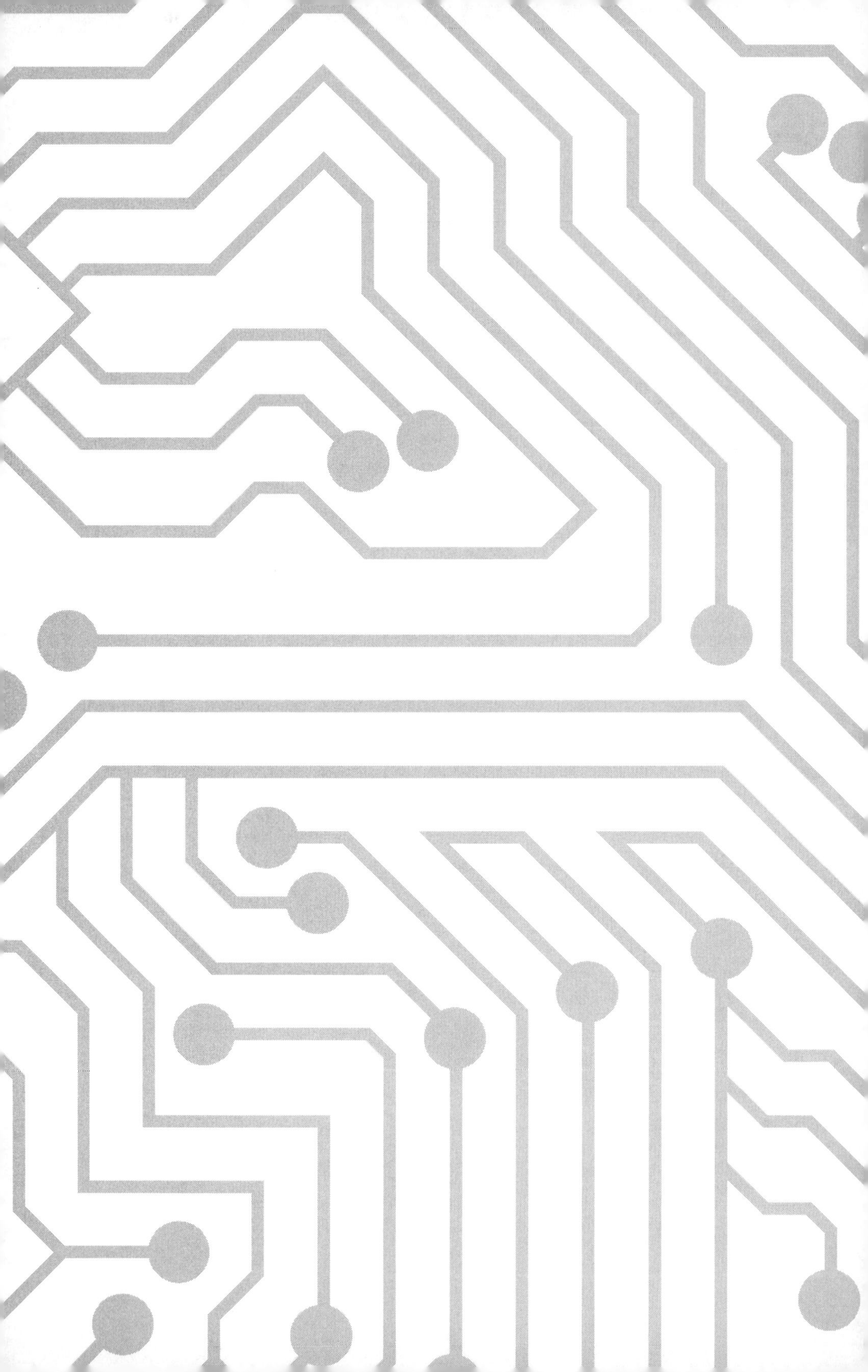

Chapter 11

AUTOMATE TO EFFICIENTLY SCALE

Marketing Automation and Integration with Sales

"It is not the strongest of the species that survive, nor the most intelligent, but the one most responsive to change."

– Charles Darwin, Naturalist and Geologist

As the fruits of your marketing labors grow, you need to think about how you'll scale your team, your processes, and your integration with sales. This requires evaluating the tools you are using and the processes that are in place, with the goal of moving from isolated handoffs to accountability handshakes. You can't keep doing things the same way, but knowing where to start is a challenge, especially with software tools.

I participated in a webcast panel with an audience of about 150 marketers in the manufacturing sector, and an attendee asked, "What kind of marketing automation tools are other companies that market to engineers using?" I was glad someone asked this because everyone these days seems to be talking about marketing automation as they move more of their marketing dollars toward an inbound approach. Marketing automation software is one of the best investments you can make to improve the efficiency of your marketing and stretch limited dollars and resources as your company grows. Equally as valuable if not more is the affordable, highly effective means it offers to gain deeper insight into your prospects and customers. However, technical business leaders possess little true understanding about what this software is and how exactly it can help.

Your company may have an established salesperson or sales team and a customer relationship management (CRM) system such as Salesforce.com or Microsoft Dynamics that it uses to perform customer engagement and opportunity management. If you have an email newsletter, or frequently email customers or prospects, you may use an email tool like MailChimp or Constant Contact to augment your CRM's capabilities. In this scenario, you may not be clear on why you need marketing automation. Your CRM and email tools may meet your needs (although you have very limited prospect intelligence in this scenario). But this system starts to break when the volume of your content publishing, web traffic, and leads grows to the point where it becomes overwhelming for sales to respond to all the leads, and the sales team has no process, or mechanism, to prioritize leads. Having too many leads is a good problem, but it does mean the tools you use, and processes that are in place, need to evolve. This is where marketing automation, and creating a marketing and sales service level agreement (SLA), comes in. Let me first introduce and explain marketing automation and how it complements your CRM. Then I'll explain the SLA.

Marketing Automation 101

Marketing automation software is a web-hosted platform that integrates and automates online marketing programs to nurture online leads through the marketing and sales funnel. These include email marketing, search engine optimization, content publishing and amplification, contacts database hosting, and CRM integration.

The first incarnation of marketing automation focused on email marketing through tools such as Constant Contact. Later, tools like Eloqua began combining email marketing with other parts of the marketing automation process, such as lead scoring and database marketing (i.e., integration of lead forms with contact fields and automated segmentation based on data such as product interest, industry, or application). It makes sense that it all started here. As you read in chapter 10, email marketing takes an enormous amount of time to implement effectively, and it involves a lot of repetition. You have to follow up with all leads quickly and further communicate with them based on their actions. You need to segment your leads, build plans to target subgroups, and further communicate based on their actions. With the first email marketing tools, you could import lists, program your emails or create them from templates, execute your send, and measure your results. You could even do A/B testing as the tools progressed by sending part of your list one version of an email and another part a second version, and compare results.

However, when these tools got their start, leads were still mostly being generated offline or through outbound channels such as seminars, trade shows, advertising, telemarketing, and direct mail. Once leads were captured and entered into the database, lists could then be exported into email marketing tools, but the two environments lived separately.

Today, the majority of the buying process now occurs online, and companies, in turn, are transitioning their marketing efforts online. This has been a key driver of the massive growth in marketing automation software from leading companies such as Eloqua, Marketo, HubSpot, Act-On, Infusionsoft, and many others. Let's take a look at six of the most compelling features of today's marketing automation software:

1. Marketing Contact Database—Gather and Maintain Intelligence

At its most fundamental level, marketing automation software contains your database of marketable contacts. The software holds information on each contact such as name, company, title, etc., as well as custom fields such as product interest or industry. However, in today's leading marketing automation environments, one of the most beneficial features is the record of a contact's online activity with your company. Marketo calls this intelligence the "system of record" and HubSpot calls it the "timeline," but it's essentially a record of your leads' online activities from the forms they complete and videos they watch to the emails they open and blog posts they read. Imagine how this additional information about a contact could help sales customize its first interaction!

Leads Database and Online Activity Record Example

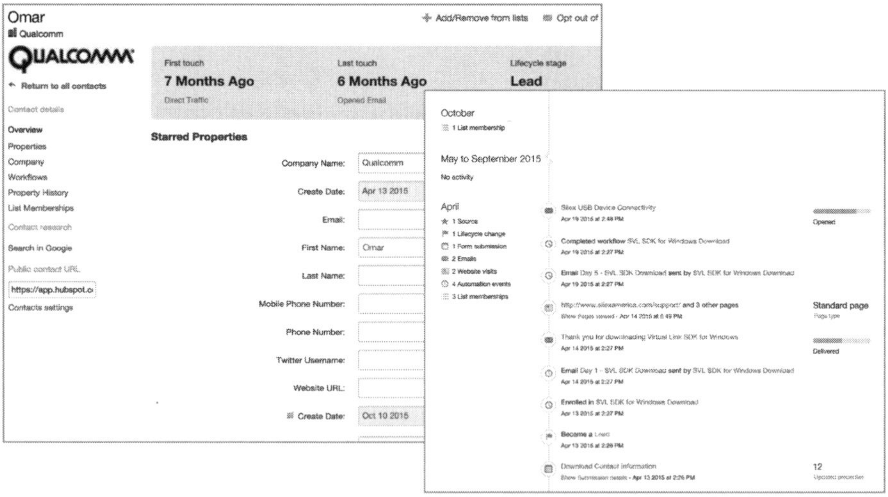

Marketing automation software houses your leads database and records the online activity each lead has, from web and blog pages visited to emails opened and forms completed.

2. Lead Forms—Increase Conversion Rates

Creating lead forms on your website manually can be time-intensive, especially when you consider that you need the data from completed fields on your website forms to automatically populate into your database. This often requires both IT and web resources from internal teams or outsourced contractors. Because of the number of people involved, this process can be fraught with error and involve high ongoing maintenance costs. This is not the case with marketing automation software. In most environments, as part of your landing page creation, you follow a few simple steps to add a lead form, including selecting the fields you want to incorporate in your form. The tool instantaneously adds the form to your landing page and automatically connects to your database since they're all in the same environment.

Moreover, many marketing automation companies have features that not only remember contacts when they return to your website in the future but also help you gather lead information over time. HubSpot calls this Smart Fields, and Eloqua calls it progressive profiling. For your lead form, you may initially require the completion of three to five fields such as name, email, and maybe title or company name the first time a visitor completes it. If you turn on the Smart Fields feature for any of these original fields, when those visitors return to any landing page with a form, the Smart Fields they've already completed appear pre-populated or are replaced by a new field visitors haven't yet completed that gathers information you'd like to know about them, such as product or service interest or telephone number. Then visitors need to complete only that new field to access the next piece of gated information they're wanting. By using these Smart Field features, you can gather more information from your visitors one field at a time after the first form completion.

For large enterprise marketing, web and IT teams used to spend thousands of dollars to implement highly sophisticated back-end features. But today, with most marketing automation software, they're built in. This is a great boon for marketers at companies large and small. These are powerful features that create great user experiences for your customers and web visitors, and they offer significant value to marketers who need to efficiently, elegantly, and affordably gather more intelligence.

3. Automated and Batch Email Marketing—Efficiently Nurture to Qualify Contacts

I've already talked about the importance of lead nurturing, including immediately thanking new leads for their interest in your content, protecting the contact information they've entrusted you with, and offering them additional free and gated content CTAs. Studies I cited earlier have shown that lead nurturing results in much greater conversion than doing no lead nurturing. But email marketing can be time-consuming, and, as your leads grow, responding in a timely and customized manner to each new lead generated becomes significantly more challenging and inefficient. By using marketing automation software, you can greatly reduce the time required to send automated emails when leads convert through an online form. And you no longer need to use your separate email marketing software tool. Take, for example, a new white paper. You set up a landing page that houses a lead form created in your marketing automation software to promote the white paper. When a contact fills out that form to download the white paper, that action triggers a scheduled set of nurturing emails. These emails are part of workflows that begin when the contact performs an action, such as a form fill. As the contact takes (or doesn't take) actions with your content, the workflow pushes the contact down varying paths until the point you choose. Workflows, which require a one-time setup, can run forever or for a certain amount of time. With this type of automated emailing, you are free to focus on other projects while leads continually and automatically enter, become nurtured, and, ideally, improve in quality as they move down the funnel.

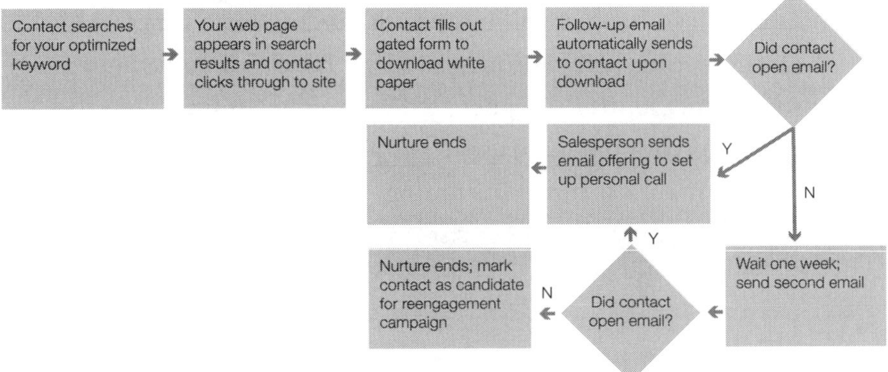

This sample nurturing workflow shows different communication paths based on the contact's activity or lack thereof.

Similarly, you can create batch emails, or one-time emails sent to a group of contacts for a specific reason such as email newsletter subscribers or contacts interested in a new version of a product you're preparing to launch. Like you create your automated lead follow-up emails, with batch emails, you use a WYSIWIG editor to develop your email newsletter or segmented emails without having to involve any IT, design, or programming resources.

In addition to using workflows and sending batch emails, marketing automation tools offer more advanced email marketing functions, such as the ability to easily perform A/B testing on subject lines or email formats, score leads, or send contacts into different workflows based on actions recipients take from an email.

4. Landing Pages—Create in Minutes to Generate More Leads Faster

In chapter 9, I talked extensively about landing pages and how critical they are to successfully generate leads on your website. The design of the page, imagery, page title, and number and type of fields in your lead form are all important landing page components. Without marketing automation, you likely have to involve your web programmer and/or designer to develop the landing page and tie the fields to your database as well as your CRM. This can be pricey, not to mention time-consuming. If you're creating only a few landing pages a year and not consistently publishing lead-generating content, this may be just fine. However, as you adopt an inbound approach with content marketing as the heart of your web traffic and lead-generation efforts, you're going to be creating a lot of landing pages. With marketing automation, you don't have to rely on your IT or web programming teams. Instead, you use a WYSIWYG editor with a graphical interface to create the elements of your page. Many marketing automation tools feature callouts based on best practices to guide you through creating the various elements of your page. As a marketer, you can quickly develop your landing pages in literally minutes and start generating leads instead of waiting on the IT or web teams or paying external web resources to get your page programmed, designed, and pushed live.

5. Lead Scoring—Automatically Calculate Lead Quality and Sales Readiness

You can use lead scoring to prioritize the contacts in your database based on their levels of engagement with your online content and learned information such as how well they align with your personas or actions they take on the site. The more actions they take related to your highest-priority products or services and the better they match your persona characteristics such as job title, department, application focus, or industry, the higher they score. Each time they complete a new field in a form, respond to your email communication, or visit your website, you gain intelligence about their lead quality. If they are a strong match, you want to make sure that lead gets flagged for sales to reach out to immediately. If they don't match as well, for instance, they have viewed only top-level web pages or content such as a few blog posts or a data sheet, their score stays low, and the lead remains in a nurturing stage instead of being passed to sales too early in the buying cycle, which is a distraction for both the sales and the prospect. In fact, some leads may not even be prospective customers. They may be casual browsers, students, readers of your content, etc., and should not be prioritized for attention.

To implement scoring, you establish criteria, assign relative values to define lead quality, and enter that data in your marketing automation tool. Criteria can be explicit profile data, such as industry, job title, company size, etc., or implicit data related to a lead's engagement with your company online. For instance, in a lead-scoring model, you may assign a score of 5 if a lead is from a company with less than 100 employees or under $10 million in annual revenue while a lead at a company larger than 100 employees or greater than $10 million is assigned a score of 10. Similarly, for implicit data, you may give a score of 5 for a web page visit, 10 for an email open, 20 for a completed lead form, and 30 for a consultation request. Relative scores are assigned to these activities and are then added to the explicit scores to provide a combined overall lead score. A combined total score determines the relative quality and priority of a lead as well as your next interaction with the lead.

Lead Scoring Example

Criteria		Score
Company size	<100 employees	5
	>100 employees	10
Annual revenue	<$10 million	5
	>$10 million	10
Web page visit		5
Email open		10
Form submit		20
Request for consultation		30

A lead score model includes explicit and implicit criteria, relative values, and next interactions with the lead based on the score.

Using this model, you may decide that contacts with a score of 30 or more, or contacts who submit a request for information form at any time, become sales-qualified leads and are sent directly to sales. Leads with a score of 20 or above may be marketing qualified and get targeted middle- to bottom-of-the-funnel communication. Leads with a score below 20 qualify as simply those moderately interested in your product or service and go into an email nurturing stream at the top and middle of the funnel. Contacts with a score of 5 or below are considered insufficiently interested in your product or service and are withheld from nurturing or sales communications until they demonstrate sufficient interest. Remember, you don't want to overcommunicate with contacts, especially if they don't seem all that interested in what you're offering. By setting up your system to be automated this way, it analyzes and updates lead scores regularly and places leads in appropriate workflows based on scoring data.

Lead scoring is a win-win. Engineers don't want to be bothered while doing research in the early stages of the buying cycle. Through content marketing and your three-legged stool of lead nurturing—lead follow-up, segmentation, and email newsletters—you can continue to provide valuable content to contacts, in an automated fashion, and wait for them to raise their hands when they're interested (i.e., when they reach a certain score you define as interested or qualified). With this automated approach, you efficiently build trust by continuing to offer information without disruption, and they are free to choose when and how they engage with your company. Although this is the ideal approach, it's nearly impossible to pull off without automation, especially as your lead volume grows.

By setting up lead scoring, you save time by not manually prioritizing your leads for sales or, worse, passing all the leads to sales for them to respond to or cherry-pick through and ignore the rest. Instead, leads are assigned scores as they engage and you learn more about them. The highest-priority leads automatically rise to the top as a marketing- or sales-qualified lead ready for further contact, or to be passed to sales to call.

6. Integrated Analytics—Measure Marketing ROI

Most marketing automation software platforms provide powerful measurement tools, from dashboards with well-designed graphical user interfaces to metrics across channels such as traffic sources, keyword performance, and email engagement by individual contact. With HubSpot's dashboard, for example, you can quickly see a mash-up of the data most important to you, such as total database contacts, the number of marketing-qualified leads (MQLs), leads generated by month compared with the same time last month, blog traffic, and top sources of website visits. You can customize the metrics widgets you select to appear in your dashboard as well as the timeframe you want to view and compare. You can also customize reports that can be turned into a PowerPoint slide deck or PDF image to add to a report or that can be fashioned into a custom report emailed at a set frequency to designated recipients.

As you go deeper, you can see specific data, such as the gated content that's driving the highest conversion. You also can see the lead sources and the different conversion rates across content as well as the trends across different timeframes.

A CRM helps you track opportunities and manage the sales pipeline, and marketing automation helps you to gather lead intelligence, move prospects toward opportunity, and deliver funnel metrics.

These are six of the most significant, time-saving features of leading marketing automation software environments. With these, you see that marketing automation is different and complementary to CRM. A CRM helps you track opportunities and manage the sales pipeline, and marketing automation helps you to gather lead intelligence, move prospects toward opportunity, and deliver funnel metrics. Additionally, you gain intelligence to further nurture and qualify leads, and sales has a holistic view of the life of the lead when it becomes a qualified opportunity in their queue. By integrating your

Marketing Automation Dashboard Example

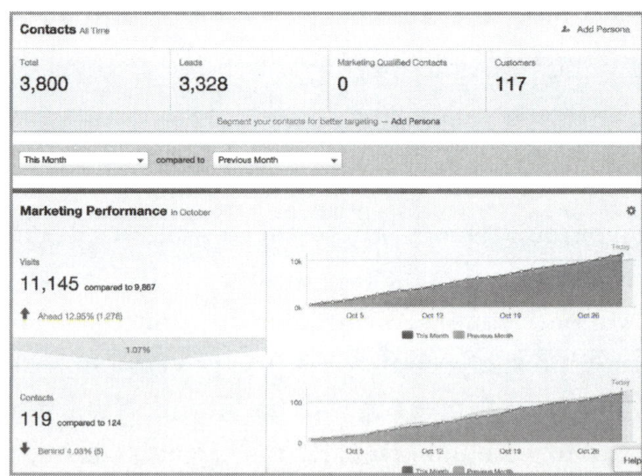

With marketing automation, you can customize your dashboard and set up automated distribution for scheduled reports to be sent to specific team members.

CRM and marketing automation systems, they become a critical, integrated tool for growing inbound marketing and selling programs that can scale. The time you save using these tools will more than pay for the cost of the software on the order of one full-time entry-level marketing person. The ROI will continue to grow as your use of the software scales and you take advantage of more features such as:

- **Social media management**—schedule posts; set up listening, tracking, and custom reports
- **Dynamic content**—customize the content, such as text, images, and CTAs, users receive based on their actions, locations, titles, etc.
- **Leads segmentation**—create micro lists of leads in your database based on demographic information, online actions, and CRM information (e.g., company or account information)
- **Multi-touch lead nurturing**—add leads to specific communication channels, such as your email newsletter, or to targeted multi-touch lead-nurturing campaigns based on demographics, application areas, or related information
- **SEO performance and tips**—track the performance of your keywords, execute suggested actions on web and blog pages to improve keyword performance, and see which backlinks are driving traffic
- **Sales alerts and notifications**—communicate with sales in real time as leads return to the website or reach certain milestones such as a specific lead score level
- **Templates**—browse built-in templates for emails, email newsletters, landing pages, and web pages to streamline content creation
- **Personas**—build your personas inside your marketing automation software environment to tailor communication and customize reports (e.g., tabulate web traffic or leads by persona to know more specifically which personas you're attracting and engaging)

- **Prospect intelligence**—discover information about companies visiting your site before a lead form has been completed, such as pages visited and number/duration of web session

Choosing the Best Marketing Automation Platform for Your Company

Marketing automation tools offer no silver bullets. To be successful, you first need a marketing strategy and execution plan that I described earlier defined and in place, from marketing goals and KPIs to keywords and personas to a well-designed website. You also need a content marketing plan that includes online conversion and lead nurturing. If you don't have these elements well defined and implemented, you will struggle with marketing automation.

A study[1] by Ascend2 shows that 45 percent of marketers agree that the lack of an effective strategy hinders the success of marketing automation, and 40 percent agree that the lack of skilled end users is another challenge. Though automation programs can make life easier for marketers, this is true only if they invest the time to train key users and have a well-defined and documented strategy that guides their use.

[1] marketingprofs.com/charts/2014/25658/2014-marketing-automation-benchmarks-and-trends

Most Challenging Obstacles to Marketing Automation Success

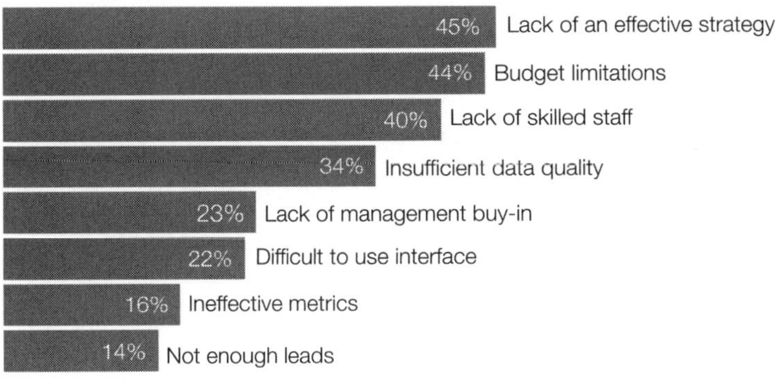

Marketing Automation Benchmark Survey
Ascend2 and Research Partners, July 2014

The lack of an effective marketing strategy is the top obstacle to success with marketing automation. If you don't have a strategy, no software tool is going to fill the gap.

When you are ready to invest in marketing automation, you need to research and vet the different offerings and select one right match for your company and marketing strategy. Start by prioritizing the elements that are most important not only for your strategy but also for supporting your team and other tools. Is your goal to save time in leads management and nurturing? To improve web and content marketing? To better optimize for SEO via keywords? To simplify social media management? Automated lead follow-up? Lead scoring and alignment with sales? Would you prefer a tool that is easier to use or one that has more robust features? Prioritize your top five to 10 requirements and then, for each one, document your ROI and timeframe expectations. ROI can include benefits such as time-savings, increased traffic, higher lead conversion rates, improved email marketing performance, higher rankings for keywords, and more.

In the same study by Ascend2, the top two most important objectives for marketing automation respondents noted were to improve

Most Important Objectives to Marketing Automation

Ascend2/Research Partners
July 2014

Evaluate marketing automation software based on the objectives most important to you, from improving productivity to increasing sales revenue and lead generation.

marketing productivity and increase sales revenue. The next two most important objectives were to increase lead generation and improve lead nurturing.

With your requirements prioritized and ROI defined, you need to start your research. Most marketing automation companies feature robust websites and blogs, with deep content across media types to match your learning style, from video to in-depth e-books. Study their features, compare them with your requirements, and create a list of questions for your top picks. Most also have pricing plans based on criteria such as number of user seats or number of database contacts. You can find a plethora of marketing automation software reviews and comparisons[2] online, and new ones pop up daily. In fact, just as I was completing this book, Gartner released their "Magic Quadrant for CRM Lead Management[3]" that analyzed data from 126 companies and categorized them into niche players, challengers,

[2] marketingautomationsoftware.com/reviews
[3] gartner.com/technology/reprints.do?id=1-2KNMOUI&ct=150804&st=sb

leaders, and visionaries. Study these available resources as part of your research and use the data to form the questions you ask during your demo meetings. Set up demos with the companies you're most interested in and ask them to address your list of questions on features, pricing, etc., to help you decide. Use your prioritized features list as a rubric to score each company with a scoring system such as 3, 2, and 1 for how well each company meets your requirements. By the end, you will have a quantitative score and a qualitative feel for which marketing automation company and specific package are best for you.

Aligning Sales and Marketing

I mentioned earlier that a catalyst for companies deciding to invest in marketing automation is when the volume of web traffic and leads grows to the point where it becomes too overwhelming for sales to respond to all the leads. When this happens, the process in place no longer works, and a huge gap is created with no mechanism to prioritize leads. This is a critical point for both marketing and sales. Though sales can no longer complain that marketing isn't giving them enough leads, the feedback may instead be that the leads are not qualified, or there's too many so they don't know which ones to chase. Or, you may even be asked to stop delivering leads completely because sales has enough. This is the time to introduce a marketing and sales service level agreement (SLA). The purpose of the SLA is to ensure the two teams are acting as one to influence, educate, and support both prospects and customers. This boosts team morale and effectiveness and impacts revenue. In a sales and marketing alignment study conducted by the Aberdeen Group[4] and sponsored by Dunn and Bradstreet as well as marketing software companies Pardot, Silverpop, and Sitecore, well-aligned marketing and sales teams achieved 20 percent annual revenue growth compared with a decline of 4 percent by companies with poor alignment.

[4] dnb.com/content/dam/english/dnb-solutions/sales-and-marketing/aberdeen_report_sales_and_marketing_alignment_2010_09.pdf

The marketing and sales functions of a company are both critical to generating revenue, so obviously when they're aligned, more revenue is generated than when they're not. The Aberdeen study found poor alignment was caused by four main reasons:

1. The sales and marketing functions report to different senior executives

2. Teams fail to deploy common agreed-upon definitions

3. The processes and workflows between sales and marketing are not established or are inadequate

4. Common goals to measure success do not exist

Not surprisingly, sales and marketing teams today often are not aligned because of the immense changes over just the last 10 years in how engineers and scientists are searching for, developing preferences for, and selecting vendors. Most of the buyer's journey is now happening online before a prospect ever engages the company in conversation. Forrester[5] research shows that B2B buyers are finding content in an ever-expanding number and variety of channels and concludes that marketing executives have some catching up to do. With the buyer in control, and meandering through his journey from awareness to consideration to purchase, the sales process has been turned upside down and, in turn, so has marketing.

The processes, tools, and measurement for both functions must change to ensure that every opportunity marketing creates, and sales pursues, is maximized. Use an SLA to define these changes, including handshakes between teams, tools used and for what purposes, and metrics in place to create alignment to drive efficiency between teams.

5 blogs.forrester.com/lori_wizdo/12-10-04-buyer_behavior_helps_b2b_marketers_guide_the_buyers_journey

The steps to creating a marketing and sales SLA are the following:

1. **Establish a sales and marketing collaboration team.** The team's charter is to own shared goals for lead conversion to sales, create a model for lead self-qualification, and establish processes to ensure that each communication touchpoint with prospects takes them a step further in their journey.

2. **Define lead stages, criteria, and response.** Sales and marketing need to agree on the definitions of a lead, a marketing-qualified lead, a sales-qualified lead, and an opportunity. With definitions in place, both teams can then agree on which criteria a lead needs to meet before it passes from one stage to the next, which score to assign each action, and the response time for marketing to nurture and sales to conduct direct follow-up.

3. **Agree on the numbers.** With definitions in place for lead stages, marketing and sales need to sign up for their numbers along the funnel. Marketing needs to set goals for web visits, leads, and marketing-qualified leads, and sales should set a goal for sales-qualified leads, opportunities, and closed sales. An example of how to calculate these numbers is detailed in the next chapter. Sales and marketing use additional metrics to measure their performance in their functional areas, but for the marketing and sales SLA, focus on these key dashboard metrics.

4. **Integrate your CRM and marketing automation tools.** By integrating your CRM and marketing automation tools, sales representatives can access a qualified lead's record in their own CRM views, see the lead's marketing history, and thoroughly prepare for a prospect call with specific information about that lead's interests. On the flip side, when sales representatives enter

new information about the lead, such as if they closed-won the opportunity, the stage of the lead in the marketing automation view is changed to "customer." This in turn can then trigger workflows already set up for customer communication so the customer is no longer treated like a prospective lead but a new customer. You do this by creating a flow of data between these two systems to get a 360-degree view of your qualified leads, opportunities, and customers. Through the integration of marketing automation and CRM software, leads can be added to specific sales queues and alerts can be sent to notify sales representatives of new sales-qualified leads. You can also set up alerts for specific scenarios, such as previously qualified leads who did not close and are now revisiting the website or are converting again on new content. B2B technical companies use many popular CRM systems, from Salesforce and Microsoft Dynamics to industry-specific programs like Deltek CRM for professional services firms. The power generated by integrating these two tools is so apparent, and growing, that marketing automation companies like HubSpot are adding CRM and other inbound selling tools to their platforms to expand a data-driven approach to selling.

5. **Create and map content to the buyer's journey.** Marketing should review the content marketing plan with sales and get feedback. With sales representatives on the front lines working with customers and learning about their applications, pain points, and needs, they are a great resource for marketing to fill content gaps, generate new ideas, and critique what's written.

6. **Close the loop.** The sales and marketing collaboration team should report at least monthly and meet quarterly, if not more often, to review the SLA and metrics performance. Many factors

may cause metrics or processes in the SLA to change. Each team should be prepared to share its metrics, challenges, successes, and feedback on the SLA and suggested tweaks. This is also a great time to discuss plans for the following month/quarter.

With marketing and sales working as one collaborative team, and with an SLA and time-saving CRM and marketing automation systems in place, you will be set up to continually measure and improve ROI as you scale. Marketing, sales, and company leaders must commit to creating a culture of handshakes instead of handoffs. Internally, you'll reap the benefits of more effective campaigns and lead nurturing, reach sales goals, and improve team morale. But, more importantly, your customers and prospects will experience unified and customized communications from anyone they interact with, which shows them you are a well-aligned company they can trust to do business with.

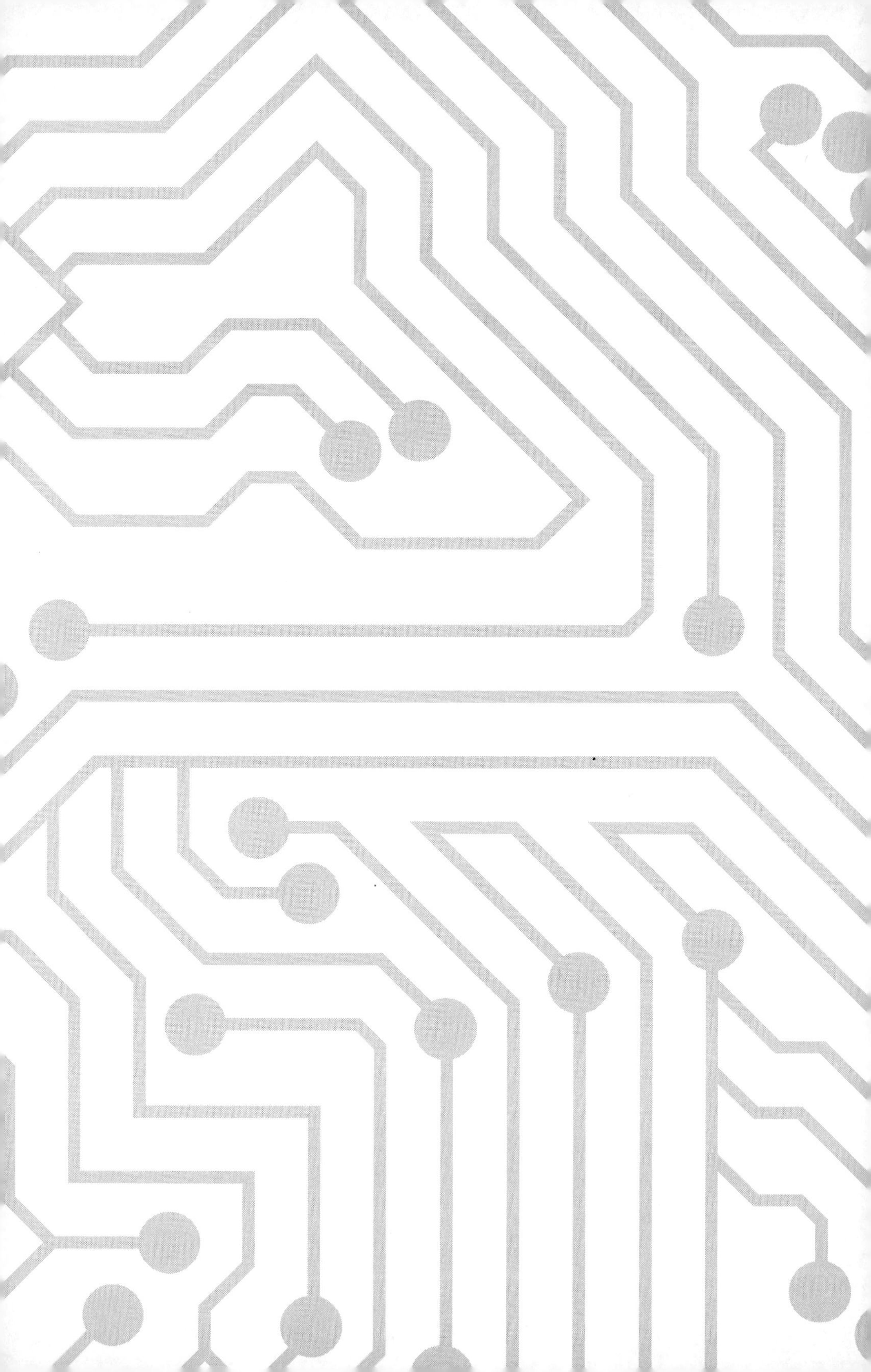

Chapter 12

ORGANIZE AND MEASURE

Define Your Team and Expected Outcomes

"Many of life's failures are people who had not realized how close they were to success when they gave up."

– Thomas Edison, Inventor

You are nearing the end of the process of building your inbound marketing plan to target technical audiences. As a last step, you need to define marketing team roles, determine the timeframe in which you want to achieve results, and document the expected return of time and dollars invested. The organizational structure, pace, and outcomes should be part of your marketing plan, and you should review this plan quarterly and annually to ensure optimal use of limited resources for maximum output.

Several factors influence these three aspects of your marketing, including company culture, budget, and urgency. The most effective marketing program starts with company leaders who are committed to investing in marketing for the long term with a dedicated budget, and who hold marketing accountable to the stated outcomes while providing support and patience as the plan ramps up. A rule of thumb for spending on marketing is 4 percent to 12 percent of gross revenue with higher spending in the early phases as you establish your marketing foundation. You should stabilize at a lower rate of spending as you build momentum but account for spikes in spending as you execute major initiatives such as product launches or a website redesign.

With a budget in place, you need a team with clearly defined roles so you can be as efficient as possible in planning, executing, and measuring your marketing program. You should define and assign responsibilities such as:

- Setting the marketing goals and budget, and reporting to the business on marketing ROI
- Monitoring and analyzing metrics and holding the marketing team accountable for stated goals
- Managing marketing automation components, such as developing and maintaining contact fields, landing pages, lead forms, workflows, and lead scoring
- Executing the content plan, including writing, editing, and publishing to the web
- Making web updates related to content, design, SEO performance, and CMS administration and new functionality
- Owning media channels such as PR or trade shows or serving as the lead on major projects such as product launches or partner co-marketing

Though each company organizes its marketing team based on its unique culture, budget, and expected outcomes, you can choose from three general approaches to take: do-it-yourself (DIY), in-house, or outsourced. Each one has pros, cons, and cost variations to consider and thoroughly evaluate before making the best choice for your company.

1. DIY

In small engineering companies, a few technical staff members often share marketing responsibilities. For instance, an R&D engineer may also fix the website and/or write code and content to update pages. A technical salesperson may be responsible for creating materials for a trade show in between customer visits and writing proposals.

Advantages

- No one knows your products and services better than you. By creating content yourself, you don't have to waste time conveying that information to an outsider who may not be as familiar with your technology.
- With the technical competence of the engineering staff, it's easy to perform tasks such as updating website code.

Disadvantages

- Any time spent marketing takes a technical salesperson away from closing new business or takes a high-value engineering staff member, such as an R&D engineer, away from working on product development or billable client service delivery.
- A marketing professional can execute marketing activities faster, smarter, and more cost-effectively than an untrained, highly compensated technical staff member.

Cost

A bare minimum inbound marketing program requires 15 to 20 hours per week to create one content piece per month, blog once a week, manage leads, support sales needs, improve SEO, update the website, and assess metrics.

You can roughly estimate your annual cost based on the income of the engineer or salesperson who executes the marketing activities.

Using a salary of $90,000, that calculates to $33,750 to $45,000, not including the opportunity cost of that person's time spent on closing business, developing products, or delivering to clients. For this reason, the DIY approach can be quite expensive given an engineer's salary and lost high-value productivity and revenue.

2. Hire an In-House Marketing Specialist

If your company doesn't have the bandwidth or expertise to carry out these marketing tasks in a consistent and timely fashion, you may need to bring on a marketing specialist.

Advantages

- Having a dedicated marketing resource at your company means that person will live and breathe your brand and have the bandwidth to execute the marketing plan.
- It's easier for a dedicated, on-site marketing person to chase people down to get the materials, reviews, and approvals needed to complete activities.
- If your messaging, marketing strategy, or campaign plans are not well defined, you will save money with a fixed-salary in-house marketing person versus an outsourced resource because of the extensive time you'll likely need for numerous reviews and back-and-forth iteration of activity execution.

Disadvantages

- B2B technical marketing is a unique niche that requires people with an aptitude and interest in topics that are considered boring or confusing (or both) to the average marketer. Be prepared to spend a lot of time and effort in the hiring and onboarding process to select and train your marketing specialists for success. If this process is rushed, they will quickly become demotivated and disengaged and leave six months later, sending you back to square one.

- One person will not have enough experience across all marketing disciplines to be able to take advantage of all the best marketing methods. Just as a mechanical engineer has limited electrical engineering knowledge, a marketer who has deep experience in SEO and web marketing may not be comfortable with company positioning or marketing strategy.
- Sometimes the marketing specialist can get commandeered by the sales department to help with its needs and start serving as a part-time sales coordinator, which compromises marketing goals and results.

Cost

The approximate salary of a marketing specialist ranges from $50,000 to $65,000, not including other benefits and taxes. That means this person is now on your payroll, rain or shine, so even if times are lean, be prepared to cover the costs of this overhead expense.

Word of Warning

You may be tempted to hire a "free" marketing intern, but remember, interns are looking for learning experiences and chances to grow their marketing skills. As students, they are much less experienced and require a marketing mentor to spend time guiding them. Be careful whom you choose as a mentor. Bad marketing not only delivers poor results but also damages your company's reputation (think emails with spelling errors or inaccurate images). Engineers have little patience with poor quality.

3. Outsource Marketing

The third option is to outsource marketing to a team of experts with a special focus on targeting technical audiences. Marketing firms come in many flavors. Some focus on only one specialty (e.g., SEO, web design, PR, strategy, or brand), while others are full-service and cover all or most areas of inbound and/or outbound marketing. Some focus primarily on project execution while others tackle marketing from the top down: strategy first and then activities and tactics to follow. Because individual activities may need to change to support the overall strategy, a full-service firm with all the marketing tools at its fingertips can more easily take advantage of opportunities to best accomplish your business goals.

Advantages

- You have a team with years of marketing experience, so you can keep your engineering and sales staff focused on critical R&D, client delivery, and new business projects.
- Acting as one marketing team across all activities helps marketing team members become more efficient, consistent, and self-sufficient with time as they leverage what they've learned from each new project.
- By going with a team of marketing experts instead of a single marketing specialist, you get access to their breadth and depth of marketing and industry knowledge, but you pay for only the fraction of their time you need.

Outsourced marketing features a variable cost: you pay for it only when you need it.

Disadvantages

- The outsourced marketing team members will need a ramp-up period as they learn about your company, so make sure to hire a firm that is comfortable working with engineers and is experienced with technology marketing.
- If you work at a large company or have established in-house marketing functions, you may want a specialized team with deep expertise in one channel or one that focuses on a specific initiative like a product launch.

Cost

Monthly costs for marketing services at SMB technical companies can range from $3,500 to over $20,000+ per month and are driven by the results you are seeking and how quickly you are seeking them. You can turn them off or down as lean times come and go. However, be aware that marketing is a long-term investment and not a one-time expense. To keep visitors coming in and leads converting, you must consistently build awareness, create and promote new content, and execute lead nurturing.

The Best of Both Worlds: A Hybrid Approach

Often, the ideal approach is a hybrid one that optimizes existing resources and areas of expertise (such as technical content development) and focuses outsourced efforts on marketing gaps. For example:

- The outsourced marketing team manages the defined plan and objectives and helps with content plan development, while the internal marketing specialist executes marketing tasks such as emails, web changes, blog articles, and internal reviews and coordinates content development from internal engineers.
- The sales engineer makes first contact with the customer to request approval to write a case study or shoot a video testimonial, and then the outsourced marketing team takes the lead on writing or production.

In terms of internal team structure, as you grow beyond the DIY approach and become ready to hire your first internal marketing resource, I recommend your first hire be a marketing specialist (described in No. 2 of this list). I have seen growing technical businesses hire a senior-level marketing manager only to find they're paying a high salary for the strategy and foundational work but still have to outsource all the execution. Or they hire a narrowly skilled role, such as a graphic designer, who is low in salary and high in management overhead.

Instead, hire a marketing generalist with three to four years of experience and preferably a communications, advertising, or journalism degree. The specialist should oversee the time-intensive day-to-day management and coordination of content generation, reviews, and promotion; website updates and maintenance; SEO implementation on the blog and website and in new content; blog publishing; technical writing (e.g., case studies, top-level web pages, etc.); and your leads database, marketing automation, and lead nurturing. You can stretch your dollars far with highly motivated marketers who are interested in technology and are looking for autonomous roles that allow them to manage their workloads, be held accountable to expected outcomes, and be able to lean on an outsourced, experienced marketing team for strategy, specialized execution support, and mentorship.

From there, the next hires to consider for your marketing team may include a product, service, or segment marketing engineer to help with demos, technical content development, events, and sales support; a part- or full-time writer to develop all content using a journalistic approach to interview subject-matter experts for more technical pieces; and a marketing coordinator to help offload your growing marketing specialist, who may eventually be promotable to marketing manager.

Expensive Sprint versus Affordable Marathon

I often am asked by clients new to modern, inbound marketing, "When will I start seeing results like traffic, leads, and improved search rankings?" The answer is not immediately. This is tough news for anyone to hear, especially those who have relied on traditional marketing channels such as trade shows, advertising, or telemarketing for past marketing efforts. These activities fall in the category I call "expensive, short-term sprints."

With trade shows, for instance, you pay big bucks but get immediate results with leads you can cherry-pick out of the stack of business cards and go after the next day. The pace is fits and starts, with spikes of activity and results. As soon as you turn the money off and stop the activity—not exhibiting at the trade show, turning off outbound telemarketing, or ending the ads—the results stop.

Modern inbound marketing, in contrast, is what I call an "affordable, long-term marathon." With this approach, the cost is spread out over the long term, and is an investment that continues to grow in impact. Your website engine is an annuity that increases in strength and impact as you fuel it with more content, and search engines give you more popularity points as your traffic and links from other sites increase. Unlike the on or off mode of traditional marketing, with an inbound approach, the cadence is a consistent drumbeat that, within a few months, begins to show results and grows from there.

In one survey from marketing automation company HubSpot, about 68 percent of respondents first reported seeing an increase in traffic within two to seven months. HubSpot also asked about leads, and, similarly, it took two to seven months for 64 percent of businesses to see a real increase in leads. This is not a coincidence because, for most websites, traffic and leads go hand in hand. So, if you or leaders at your company are expecting to increase web traffic or leads by 100 percent in the first month, you likely want to consider stats like these to reset expectations.

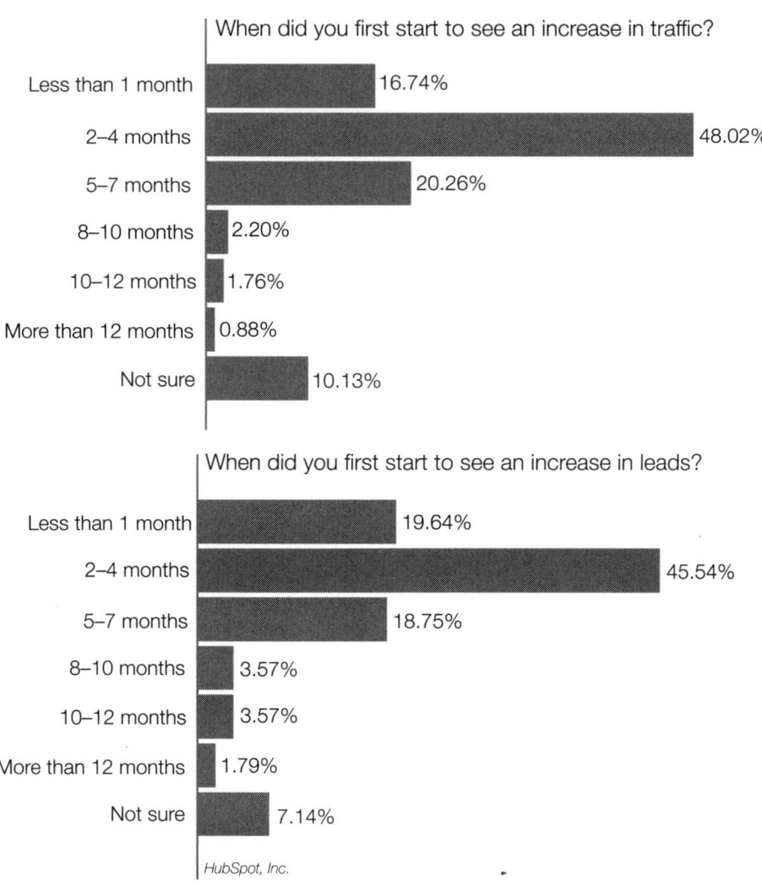

Of the respondents, 68 and 64 percent reported seeing initial traffic and lead results, respectively, in two to seven months following their adoption of marketing automation and inbound marketing.

Defining ROI along the Funnel

Engineers often approach expectations for marketing ROI with a simple formula where x (dollars) + y (time) = z (sales). They want to know if they invest x dollars and y time in marketing, what can they expect for z revenue and when can they expect it. Before search engines came along, when marketing was only outbound, calculating ROI in this way was nearly impossible. With the transformation of marketing to the digital world, however, you can gather much more insight into inputs along the funnel such as website visitors, the rate at which those visitors convert to leads, and how often leads become sales opportunities. And yet most marketers still have difficulty determining ROI and defining expected outcomes from marketing because they don't feel they have the data they need to make these decisions. According to survey results from the May 2014 MIT Sloan Management Review published by MarketingCharts[1], most professionals are being pressured to become more data driven and analytical. However, only a minority of respondents felt they had the data they needed to make decisions.

This is yet another illustration of the importance of having marketing automation tools in place. By leveraging these tools and following the steps below, you can calculate estimates for six simple equations to develop an inbound lead conversion model that turns your sales revenue goals at the bottom of the funnel into definitive sales and marketing objectives upward (and it's a great tool to use when you are preparing for next year's budget discussion).

1. **How many customers do you need to hit your revenue goal?**
   Formula: Revenue Goal ÷ Average Selling Price per New Customer
   First, you should agree on your revenue goal from new customers. In this example, let's assume you want to generate $1,000,000 in new revenue. Next, determine how much an average customer spends with you, also known as your "average sales selling price" (ASP). Let's assume your ASP is $40,000.

[1] marketingcharts.com/online/global-execs-senior-management-wants-more-use-of-analytics-42722

To determine the number of new customers you need to hit your revenue goal, divide your revenue objective of $1,000,000 by your ASP of $40,000. By doing this, you now know you need 25 new customers to reach your revenue goal.

2. **How many opportunities do you need to create one new customer?**

Formula: New Customers ÷ Opportunity-to-Close Rate

Now, taking one step up the funnel, figure out how many opportunities it takes to create one new customer. For this example, let's use an opportunity-to-close conversion rate of 35 percent. Divide the number of new customers (25) by the opportunity-to-close conversion rate (35 percent). This shows that you need about 71 opportunities to create 25 new customers.

3. **How many sales-qualified leads do you need to create one new opportunity?**

Formula: Opportunities Goal ÷ Sales-Qualified Lead-to-Opportunity Conversion Rate

Taking the next step up the funnel, figure out how many sales-qualified leads (SQLs) it takes to create one new opportunity. For this example, let's use an SQL-to-opportunity conversion rate of 15 percent. Divide the number of new opportunities (71) by the SQL-to-opportunity conversion rate (15 percent). This shows that you need approximately 473 SQLs to create 71 opportunities.

4. **How many marketing-qualified leads do you need to create one new SQL?**

Formula: SQL Goal ÷ Marketing-Qualified Lead to Sales-Qualified Lead Conversion Rate

Taking another step up the funnel, figure out how many marketing-qualified leads (MQLs) it takes to create one new SQL.

For this example, let's use an MQL-to-SQL conversion rate of 20 percent. Divide the number of new SQLs (473) by the MQL-to-SQL conversion rate (20 percent). This shows that you need 2,365 MQLs to create 473 SQLs.

5. How many leads do you need to create one new MQL?

Formula: MQL Goal ÷ Lead-to-MQL Conversion Rate

Continuing up the funnel, next calculate how many leads you need to create one new MQL. For this example, let's use a lead-to-MQL conversion rate of 20 percent. Divide the number of new MQLs (2,365) by the lead-to-MQL conversion rate (20 percent). This shows that you need 11,825 leads to create 2,365 MQLs.

6. How many visitors do you need to create one lead?

Formula: Lead Goal ÷ Visitor-to-Lead Conversion Rate

Finally, at the top of the funnel, you determine your last number, which is how many visits you need to achieve your lead goal.

Inbound Lead Conversion Model

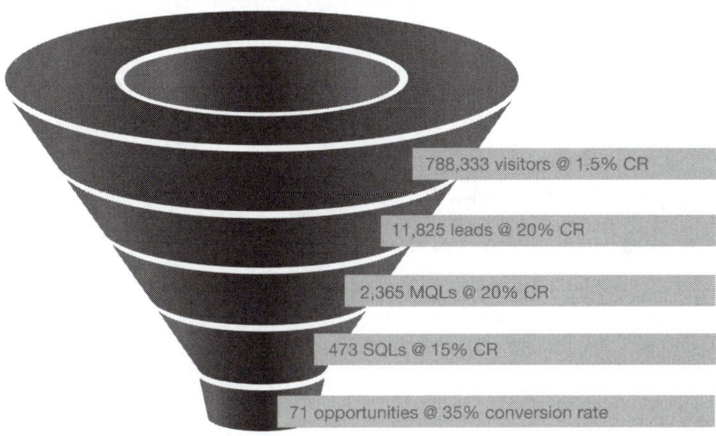

Develop an inbound lead conversion model that turns revenue goals at the bottom into definitive sales and marketing objectives upward.

> To do this, let's assume that 1.5 percent of visitors to your site become leads to calculate the amount of web traffic you will need to create 11,825 leads. To do this, divide the number of desired leads (11,825) by the 1.5 percent visitor-to-lead conversion rate (.015). With this, you now know you need 788,333 visitors to the website. Spread over a year, that's approximately 65,694 web visits per month.

To create this funnel calculation, you have some homework to do. You first need to define each stage of a lead, including MQL, SQL, and opportunity. Next, you need to determine your conversion rates along the funnel. By using an inbound approach and tools such as marketing automation, you have more data than ever about the health of your marketing activities and overall funnel. However, even then, you still need to make assumptions to start building this funnel ROI model. Don't let that stop you. Make educated guesses and then refine it over time as you gather more data and close the loop on your calculations. In the previous chapter, I detailed the steps to create your marketing and sales SLA. This definition and calculation work is part of that process. As you work with sales to create your SLA, execute this calculation exercise together, starting from the bottom with the revenue goal and going up the funnel to calculate each step. As you refine these calculations, you can build a more granular view of metrics along the funnel and ensure processes are in place to hold marketing and sales accountable for their parts.

Parting Measurement Advice: Details and Dashboards

Marketing today involves more measurements than ever before. The data can become mind-boggling, so you need to settle on the key baseline metrics that are most important to your program and then measure them over time. Though the metrics along the funnel are important for monitoring the health of your pipeline and keeping both teams on track to agreed-upon results, you'll want your own baseline inbound marketing metrics to track the results of your activities, including:

- **Web traffic**—year-over-year comparison by quarter
- **Web traffic quality**—average time on site and number of pages seen per visit
- **Leads**—lead conversion rate on landing pages with forms
- **Sources**—breakdown of traffic and leads by source: direct, referral, organic, social media, and email
- **Referral traffic**—list of sites referring traffic to your site; volume and quality of each
- **Organic traffic**—volume of organic visits
- **Conversion rate by source**—rate of leads received from direct, paid search, organic search, referral, social media, and email traffic
- **Email performance**—open rates, click-through rates, bounces, and opt-outs
- **Social media impact**—number of followers, posts viewed, shares, and links clicked on
- **Cost per lead**—costs for manpower, technology/software, and overhead divided by total leads

Finally, I recommend a marketing dashboard featuring the most important metrics that define marketing success for you. These metrics will likely come from multiple areas, including your funnel metrics and your campaigns (discussed in chapter 2), and they will indicate whether you are on track to achieve the marketing goals and objectives you defined in your strategy. Just as a car dashboard has indicator lights for low fuel or high speed, the metrics you include in your marketing dashboard should serve as these indicator lights, or warning signals, for marketing success. For your marketing dashboard, select these key metrics and add the monthly objective for each. Then, each month, add the actual results for each metric and consider an easy "indicator light" system such as highlighting each metric result red, yellow, or green based on whether they are below target, on target, or above target. As you begin to execute and track your progress, you and your team can discuss each metric and determine how to remedy low-performing areas while continuing what's working. You should meet at least quarterly, and ideally monthly, to review the dashboard and discuss new marketing opportunities and changing business needs. This is also a good time to identify the internal staff and external resources you need to execute the activity plan and fill gaps to achieve more greens and fewer reds.

Conclusion:
5 Things to STOP Now and 6 Engineering Statistics for Your Marketing Journey

With your team, timeframe, and ROI defined and measurement tools in place to track the most important metrics for your marketing program, you have completed the final step in creating inbound marketing to effectively and efficiently target your technical audiences and achieve your marketing and business goals. It's a journey that takes time to generate results. You need to set your own and others' expectations for the investment needed and the mental commitment required.

As you begin to build or expand your existing inbound marketing program, you should immediately stop doing these five things:

1. Do NOT keep positioning your company as if it can do anything; it can't, and you will lose the battle on Google and with your competition if you do this. Position for growth by differentiating and say NO to GROW.

2. Do NOT invest in any new marketing activities until your website is fully inbound functioning (designed for modern, responsive usage with a user-friendly content management system that makes uploading new content easy).

3. Do NOT create any new content until you have a plan along the funnel that includes optimizing, amplifying, and repurposing it.

4. Do NOT keep spinning your wheels on repetitive tasks and missing the intelligence gathering and efficiency that come with automation. As your traffic and leads grow, so should your tools and processes. Implement a marketing-to-sales SLA and marketing automation to scale.

5. Do NOT invest in marketing without a clear picture of your expected ROI, timeframe, and process and tools to measure, tweak, and improve.

And remember, engineers have specific preferences for how they find and consume content during their buying process. Below are the six most important statistics about engineers and inbound marketing:

1. The No. 1 place engineers go to find work-related information is Google.

2. Over 80 percent of engineers say they will complete first name and last name lead form fields, and over 70 percent will complete lead form fields for work email address, company name, and job title.

3. Engineers rank trust in content written by engineering experts at vendor companies higher than any other content.

4. Nearly 75 percent of engineers said they are more likely to do business with a company that regularly produces new and current content.

5. 94 percent and over 80 percent of engineers, respectively, said detailed diagrams and images as well as technical accuracy are important to content.

6. Over 40 percent of engineers said they are willing to go four pages or deeper in search before they find what they need or start their search over.

As I continue my research and work with companies targeting technical audiences, I'll add to this list of statistics and offer new best practices, recommendations, and examples. The examples, data, and further reading I reference throughout the book will naturally become dated, and newer references and even smarter tools and best practices will no doubt become available. Visit the book web page, **trewmarketing.com/smartmarketingforengineers**, to see the latest examples, new data, relevant blog posts, and links to informative studies and recommendations to help you with each step.

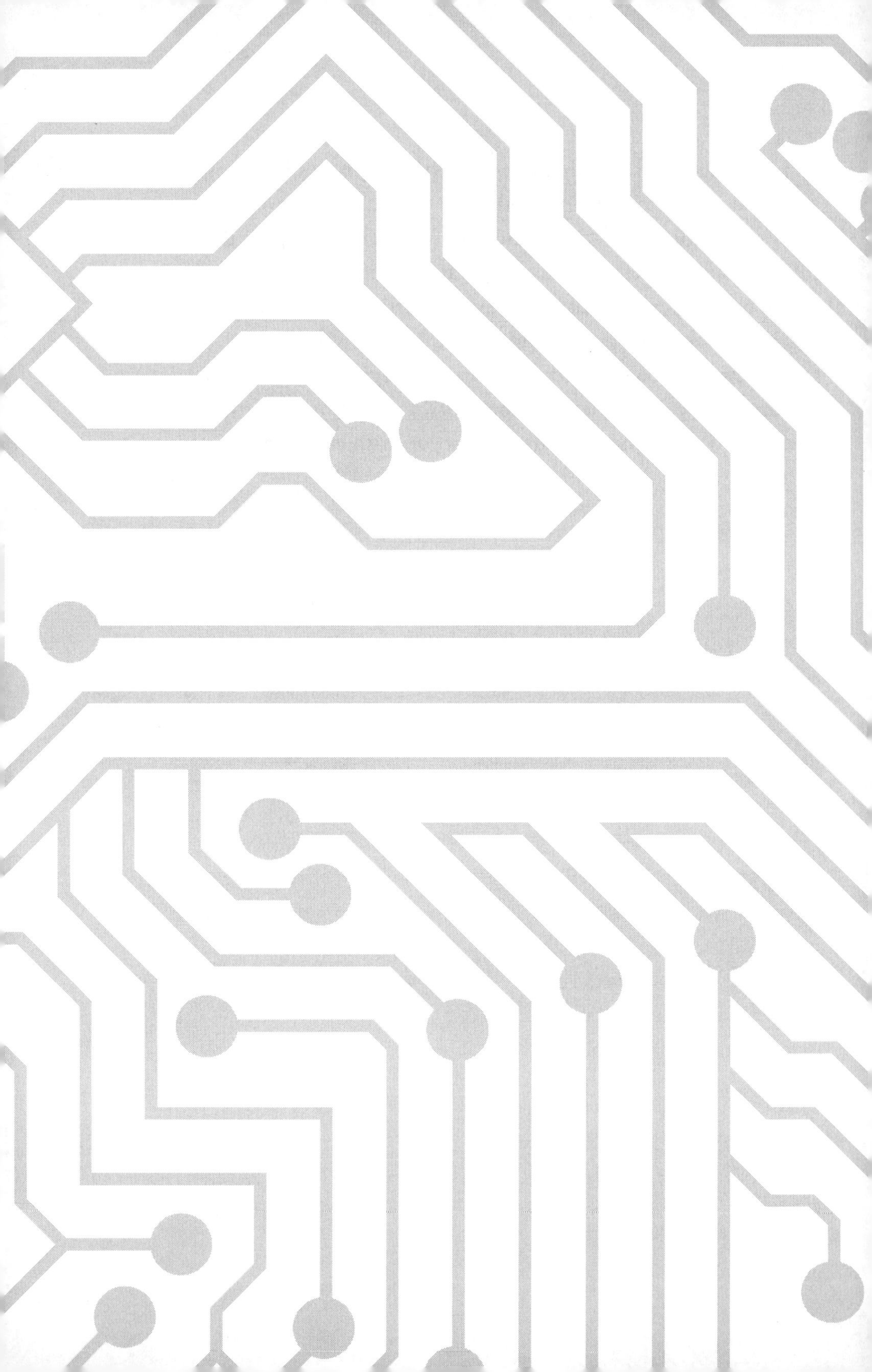

Acknowledgments

As I approached the end of this book project, I was talking to my neighbor, Stephanie, about how ready I was for it to be done, and she asked me, "You've heard of book pregnancy, right?" Whoever invented that term is a genius because, as a mother of two and now an author of one, I can say writing a book does have many similarities to real pregnancy. After nine months, you don't care about the labor anymore—you just want that kid out!

It feels great to have this book done. I've been thinking about doing it for many years. And just like having a child, writing a book takes a lot of people helping and supporting you along the way. I'd like to acknowledge them here, starting with my fifth and sixth grade teacher, Mrs. Stephenson. When I was 10, I landed in her class thanks to impressive efforts by my mom, Mary Cudd, who knew Mrs. S was the smartest teacher in the entire school. After being her student for two years, my life was never the same. To some kids, Mrs. S was kind of scary. Her southern, no-excuses demeanor and obvious intelligence created a high bar of excellence for all her students to strive for. To me, she was smart, confident, and funny, and I wanted to impress her and make her proud of me. To this day, nearly 35 years later, I admire and love her more than ever. Thank you, Mrs. Stephenson, for showing me my bar for excellence. I've strived for it all these years and hope I've made you, and Mr. S, proud.

I first mentioned to my business partner, Wendy Covey, that I wanted to write a book shortly after we started TREW. She was a little dumbfounded at the idea—like I could write a book on the side while starting a business. Duh. Seven years later, the timing felt much better, but I, of course, wanted her support because it meant I would be less available to her and the company. She was 100 percent behind me, and this project, and supported me throughout. She is my greatest critic, biggest supporter, and true friend, and hardly a week goes by that I don't thank God for bringing us together. Only divine spirit could have intervened in my sit-in-the-front-of-the-classroom, turn-my-homework-in-early, steady-paced, risk-averse life and match me up with sprint-to-the-finish, risk-taking, don't-look-back Wendy. And boy am I glad He did. As we have both said many times since starting TREW, it's the best thing we've ever done in our careers, and we've never been happier. And I got a great friend out of it. Thank you, Wendy, for taking a chance with me, with TREW, with the book, and with all my crazy ideas. And thank you for being a final reviewer of the entire manuscript. Your feedback made it better.

The next group to thank is my team. Many on the TREW Crew, as we fondly call our team, helped with content coordination and chapter reviews and provided invaluable critical feedback and expert advice. They are Lee Chapman, Erin Kell, Denise Goluboff, Morgan Norris, Beth Henderson, Emily Thornhill, and Stephanie Logerot. Thank you for your countless reviews, re-reviews, and marketing expertise. I want to say a special thanks to Hollyanne Norrid who helped me project manage the book from start to finish. From gathering and organizing source content to ensuring proper source citation to juggling all the details through design, printing, and e-reader compatibility, Hollyanne was a great partner and did not miss a detail. Thank you. I am so blessed to have such smart, supportive colleagues like these awesome women to work with. I could not have done this book without your expertise. You made me, and the book, better in the process. Thank you.

I also offer a special thanks to a few people who played important roles in the formation of different parts of the book. First, thank you,

Jodi Schrobilgen, for offering to read the book in full (I promise, you really did offer on one of our walks). You were afraid to be critical of me since we're friends, but you overcame your fears and let me have it. Good for you. Your feedback was not scary; it was smart and helpful. You may want to be careful what you offer on our walks, though. I may take you up on it. Thank you, Jason Meeker, for reading the book in spite of a difficult time personally with your father's illness. You went above and beyond, and I was thrilled to hear your positive feedback. Thanks to Senior Airman Sean Heckman (aka Military Technician Tom), the son of our dear friends who is currently serving as an aircraft armament systems technician in the US Air Force. Surprise! We are proud of you, Sean; please stay safe. Thank you to Dr. T for offering to contribute the foreword for the book. As I have told you, I could not have started TREW without the 14-year career I had at NI. It is a special place, and I am so grateful to you and all the intelligent, wonderful people who taught me about marketing to engineers and modeled smart, honest business leadership. Thank you also to Jennifer Dawkins for working with me and Dr. T on his foreword. There are only a few people in this world who can serve in that role, and you are one of them. You agreed to help me without hesitation. I hope to have an equal willingness to help others as much as you have me. Thank you.

Anyone who knows Johanna Gilmore will agree she is the best editor in Austin and, I dare say, in the state of Texas. I was so fortunate she was available and willing to be my editor for this book, given her more than full-time job. Johanna didn't just edit, she gave me explanations, websites to read on grammar rules and links to editing sites, and fantastic alternatives to my many lengthy and confusing passages. Johanna, you took my manuscript from good to great.

Thank you.

We are blessed with wonderful customers at TREW. Some have been with us for many years, such as Wineman Technology and Silex Technology, and I have cited their successful marketing programs throughout the book as best practice examples. Thank you to the teams at Silex and Wineman and thank you to all the other customers mentioned in this book who have supported TREW and made us the trusted, smart agency we strive to be. We would not be here without you, and we are grateful and honored to be your marketing partner.

I had never designed a book before, nor had Laura Lee Daigle, but that didn't stop her from diving in and agreeing to design this book. The creative, cool cover is all her magic as is the circuitry design throughout the interior. With some outside help, Laura Lee took on this project and, in her usual way, was kind, upbeat, responsive, and unshaken by the curve balls. Laura Lee, you have been a wonderful partner to TREW and to me personally. Thank you for your imagination, positive attitude, and collaboration. Put this book design at the top of your portfolio.

You've already heard about my dad, Joe Bob Cudd, to whom this book is dedicated. My dad has traveled the world, first in the Air Force flying KC-135 refueling jets and then for the next 35 years as a pilot for United Airlines, from which he retired as a 767 captain. And yet, as his name indicates, he is never more at home than in his native Texas. He is a proud Baylor Bear. He played offensive tackle for them in the '50s, and loves them almost as much as he loves his kids. My sister, Karen, and my brother, Robert (aka Vice President Victor in chapter 4), lost our mother too soon. But dad made up for it and more. He has taught me so much about values, faith, family, honesty, and the importance of hard work and doing the right thing. I could go on and on. I have the greatest dad in the world. Period.

The one person most impacted by this book was my husband, Tim Geier (aka Oil/Gas Engineer Ed). Many nights and weekends, when it was time to go to Scouts or a school meeting or some other obligation, he and my son, Cooper, would find me in my office, headphones on, typing away, and kiss me goodbye with a smile of encouragement. Tim never wavered or questioned. In fact, toward the end, he encouraged me to slow down, pay attention to the details, and not get impatient. Many of our friends know I chased Tim for many years before he finally took me seriously as his girlfriend. Now as his wife of 23 years, I can tell you it's the best chase I ever won, and I'd do it again in a heartbeat. You are my soul mate and best friend, Tim Geier. Thank you for being the most wonderful husband a girl could have and the best dad to Cooper and Mollie. We love you more.

To everyone mentioned here, thank you.

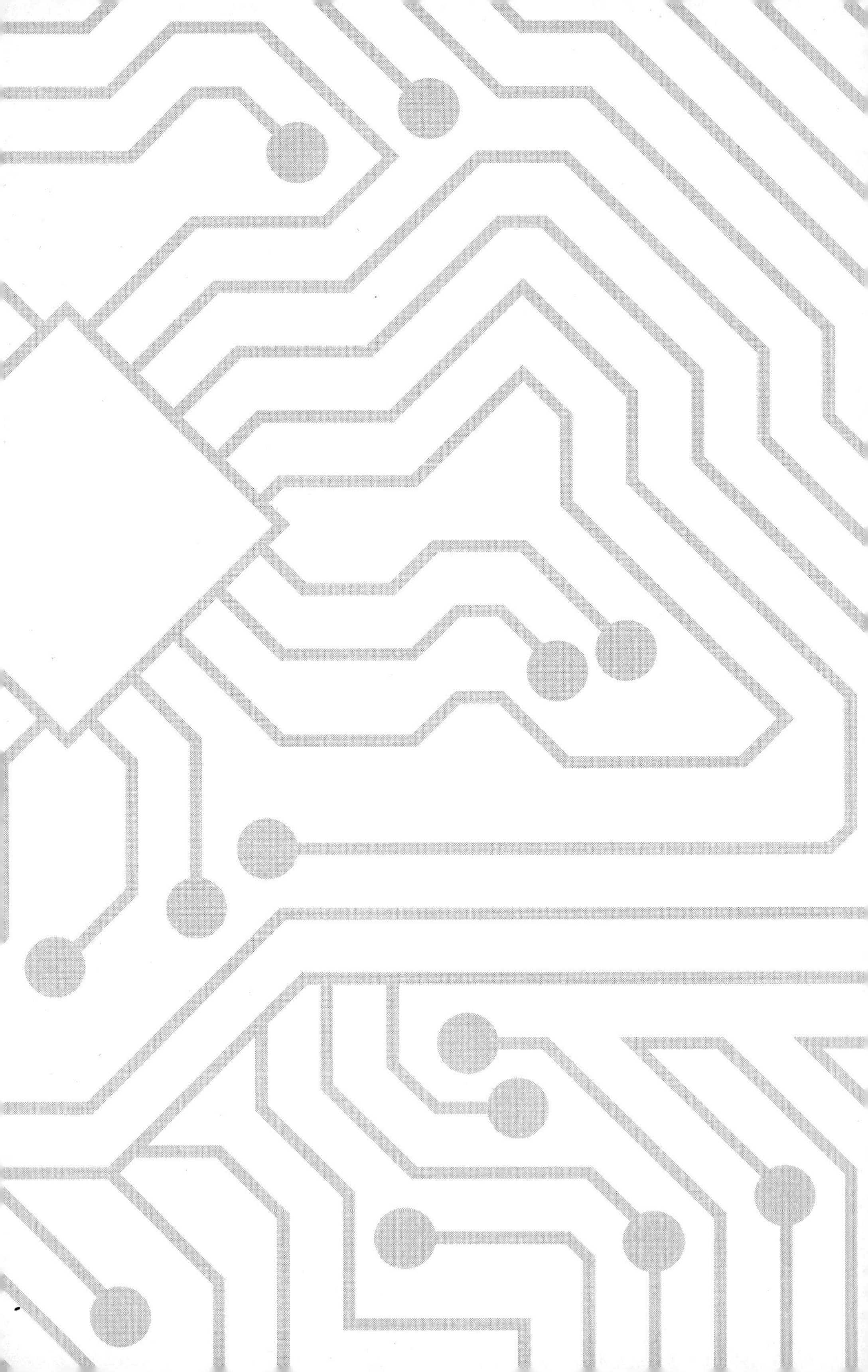